PRAISE FOR *The Nightingale's Song* BY ROBERT TIMBERG

"[A] significant contribution to our understanding of recent political and military history. More than that, it is a fascinating chronicle of the human element behind all history, a story of ambition and sacrifice and how good men can go bad and not-so-good men can skate away. . . . Mr. Timberg writes like the former Marine he is. That's not to say he doesn't write well; only that he can be brutally frank, wielding his pen like a K-bar combat knife."

—Nicholas Proffitt, *The New York Times Book Review*

"A tough and fascinating study of war, heroism, politics, and the American psyche at a profound cultural divide. . . . *The Nightingale's Song* cannily differentiates its five main characters, whose portraits have a novelistic fascination."

—Lance Morrow, *Time*

"This is an amazing piece of work that could make you cry over descriptions of bravery so bold and so big that you wonder how our country deserves such men who step up to the plate in time of trouble. . . . It is about the war in Vietnam. It is about politics. It is about character. It is about the soul of a nation. . . . This is a stunning book."

—Mike Barnicle, *The Boston Globe*

"If you want to read a terrific book about courage and cowardice, honor and betrayal, suffering and death, and the indomitability of the human spirit, get *The Nightingale's Song* by Robert Timberg, a Naval Academy graduate and Marine veteran of Vietnam as well as a superb reporter. It will help you understand why the unhealed wounds of the Vietnam War still pain and divide this American nation and shadow American politics. . . . Robert Timberg explains brilliantly the price paid by those who went, by those who didn't, and by the nation's leadership that failed them."

—Mark Shields, *The Washington Post*

"Historians eager to explain Iran-Contra in terms of hubris and secrecy of the Reagan White House will be startled by this dramatic volume by a former Marine, Annapolis graduate, and current *Baltimore Sun* reporter. . . . With novelistic skillfulness, Timberg weaves the lives of these men from their days at the Academy, through the Vietnam War, and into the tapestry of the eighties. . . . One need not agree with all of Timberg's judgments to find *The Nightingale's Song* both a gripping story and an important contribution to the literature on the Iran-Contra affair. More important, it is an absorbing meditation on the America of the past three decades. When these five men graduated from Annapolis, the last thing anyone would have imagined is that their lives would follow the tortuous paths that Timberg traces. Just as tales at the company level often show more about a battle than the grand, official versions, this book might well be assigned by college teachers as a poignant complement to the history of the era."

—Michael Beschloss, *The Washington Monthly*

"[A] thunderclap of a book. . . . Feel the need to at least get a grip on what went so terribly wrong and how? Then head off to the bookstore and lay your money down. By the time you finish this broadside across America's last forty years, you will understand. Oh, brother, will you understand. . . . [D]eserves to become an instant classic."

—Harry Crumpacker, *The Tampa Tribune and Times*

"Timberg gives the reader remarkable insights into the Navy, Iran-Contra, the Reagan White House, and those of Timberg's generation who served in Vietnam in what Reagan called a 'noble cause.'"

—Peter Braestrup, *Nieman Reports*

"The five lives that form the narrative of Robert Timberg's *The Nightingale's Song* would be interesting and well worth reading about individually. Collectively, however, they become something greater than the sum of their parts. They take the reader on an odyssey across some of the hardest terrain of recent American history. . . . The stories of these five men are the story of the great cultural and political fault line of the last three decades, of wounds that will not heal. The stories have been woven into a single narrative that is as seductive and compelling as the best epic novel. This is a book that will last, one that people will be turning to a century from now when they try to make sense of these times."

—Geoffrey Norman, *American Way*

"A sprawling, passionate account of the Vietnam and postwar journeys of Annapolis graduates John Poindexter, Robert McFarlane, Oliver North, John McCain, and James Webb. . . . Timberg uses the stories of five men and the transformation of the Naval Academy to chronicle America's loss of innocent faith in itself and the consequences of that loss for a generation."

—*Kirkus Reviews*

"In the growing library of Vietnam literature, much has been written about disillusioned infantrymen, arrogant policymakers, isolated generals, civilian war victims, and the resulting loss of American innocence and national confidence. Missing from that library has been an unheralded cohort—those dedicated, maybe even naive, men who grew up in a muscular postwar America, made careers in uniform fighting for it, and begged and connived to go fight, and unlike brother warriors over two centuries, returned to a society that reviled their sacrifice. . . . Timberg has filled that void with graceful prose and exhaustive reporting. His compelling account of five fellow Annapolis grads . . . is a perceptive, passionate, and more readable companion to Halberstam's much-heralded *The Best and the Brightest.*"

—John Kolbe, *The Phoenix Gazette*

"Timberg devises an original theme: The nation's best warriors, stung by the lessons of Vietnam in the 1960s and 1970s, excessively applied their new resolve about American leadership to the 1980s. He uses revealing anecdotes and access to the principals and their peers to weave a mesmerizing tale. . . . He is a seamless storyteller. The fractious potential of describing thirty years in the lives of five men already fully scrutinized by media and prosecutors is avoided with a revealing, conversational account of their experiences and thinking. As a former Marine and now an honored journalist, he has the credibility needed to make his points and criticisms thud with truth."

—Stephen Bell, *The Buffalo News*

"Timberg has done a masterful job by connecting the experiences of these individuals in a way that reflects, as Timberg puts it, the walking wounded of the Vietnam generation. . . . His abiding anger and frustration animate this provocative book."

—Alan Miller, *The San Diego Union-Tribune*

"Some years ago pollster and social philosopher Daniel Yankelovich described American attitudes toward Vietnam as an 'undigested lump.' If you think it's since been digested, read Robert Timberg's truly wonderful new book, *The Nightingale's Song.* When you're finished you won't doubt that there is still smoldering anger among many of the nine million Americans who served in the military during Vietnam."

—Ben Wattenberg, author of *Values Matter Most*

"Curiously absent from the painful media rehashing of Vietnam occasioned by Robert McNamara's recent memoir was one significant viewpoint: that of the members of the sixties generation who believed in America, who sought careers in fighting its wars, and who believed then and now that support for South Vietnam was right morally and geopolitically. Timberg has written a remarkable book about five such men. . . . They all strove to get into the war, and were all deeply frustrated by the paralyzing restrictions placed on them by the McNamara Pentagon, by the command bureaucracy, and by the military leaders that Mr. Timberg calls 'terminally inept.' . . . Timberg has done a remarkable job of biography. His research is thorough and his approach sympathetic (although not always sympathetic to his subjects). . . . What emerges is an engaging drama of five very different men, complex and talented, whose personal lives intertwine. Each has been enormously shaped by great events, and each has in turn helped to shape the history of our time."

—John Lehman, *The Wall Street Journal*

"*The Nightingale's Song* is a rich collection of gripping and insightful stories."

—Myron A. Marty, *St. Louis Post-Dispatch*

"The product—part biography, part combat leadership instructional, part history, part political science primer—is a captivating work, which I could not put down. Timberg has written a subtle masterpiece."

—Maj. Michael E. McBride, *Marine Corps Gazette*

"Combat changes men. Vietnam was no exception, but its effects on those of us who were there have been puzzling. Robert Timberg does a masterful job of deciphering the consequences of the war on the lives of five key figures of this decade."

—Walter E. Boomer (General, USMC, Ret.)

"Robert Timberg's *The Nightingale's Song* belongs high on the list of memorable literature of the Vietnam War—a book riveting, provocative, and pungent. It is not, nor is it intended to be, a history of the Vietnam War and postwar era, but it polishes facets of that hard stone to brilliance. . . . This is a book of power and dignity, perceptive and painful."

—Woody West, *The Washington Times*

*f*P

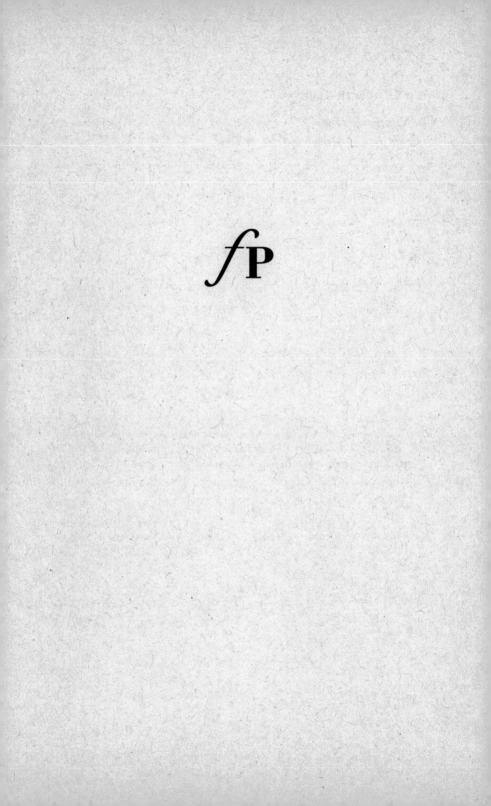

ALSO BY ROBERT TIMBERG

The Nightingale's Song
State of Grace: A Memoir of Twilight Time

John McCain

AN AMERICAN ODYSSEY

Robert Timberg

FREE PRESS
New York London
Toronto Sydney

FREE PRESS
A Division of Simon & Schuster
1230 Avenue of the Americas
New York, NY 10020

First Free Press trade paperback edition September 2007

Free Press and colophon are registered trademarks of Simon & Schuster, Inc.

For information about special discounts for bulk purchases, please contact Simon & Schuster Special Sales at 1-800-456-6798 or business@simonandschuster.com

Designed by Jenny Dossin

Manufactured in the United States of America

10 9 8 7 6 5

Library of Congress Control Number: 99036447

ISBN-13: 978-1-4165-5985-6
ISBN-10: 1-4165-5985-X

To my children,

Scott, Craig, Amanda, and Sam,

the only grand slam I ever hit

Contents

John McCain

AN AMERICAN ODYSSEY

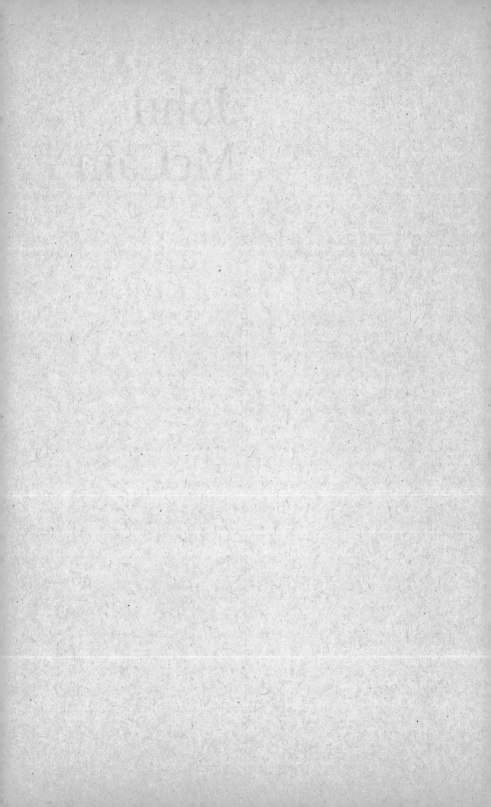

Foreword to the 2007 Edition

As I write this, in the early summer of the non–election year of 2007, John McCain has just been pronounced a "dead man walking." ABC's George Stephanopoulos says that was the collective judgment of his political sources when he polled them on the prospects of the Arizona senator's campaign for the 2008 Republican presidential nomination. Stephanopoulos delivers this news to McCain as he conducts a televised interview on his Sunday morning talk show *This Week*. If McCain is shocked, stunned, or otherwise distressed by the message, he doesn't show it. Instead, he smiles and replies that he's quite happy with how his campaign is positioned. Whistling past the graveyard? Maybe. Or else he has taken to heart the truth that my old *Baltimore Sun* colleague, the distinguished political reporter Jules Witcover, brought to light thirty years earlier: a modern presidential campaign is a marathon, not a sprint. But I doubt Jules ever envisioned this.

As we approach the midpoint of the year prior to the 2008 presidential election, there already have been three full-scale televised debates by candidates from each of the parties. So far there are ten Republicans, with an eleventh, ex-senator and veteran character actor Fred Thompson, about to make his entrance. And Newt Gingrich, the polarizing former House Speaker, is dancin' in the moonlight, observing the others, probing for a soft spot. The eight Democrats cannot be sure their field is complete, either, as they watch for telling shrinkage in the currently ample waistline of former vice president Al Gore—Oscar at the ready, Nobel Prize possibly in the offing come October.

Oh, this just in: the Republican mayor of New York, former Democrat Michael Bloomberg, has announced that he is changing his spots still again, or perhaps completely bleaching them out this time, and reregistering as an Independent. Bloomberg told the press he has no intention of running for President, but aides to the man of many political faces let it be known that he plans to see how the early primaries play out before deciding if there is room in the race for a man without a party, but with a personal fortune in the billions available to make his case.

If McCain is, as Stephanopoulos suggests, a dead man walking, it won't be the first time, which may account for the senator's unflappability in the face of the chilling prognosis. Considering the perils he has encountered, he has at seventy had a surprisingly long life, and he has dodged death many times:

- at Navy flight school in 1959 when the engine of his trainer quit and plunged into Corpus Christi Bay;
- when he crashed his plane in Tidewater, Virginia, in 1965;
- on the flaming deck of the USS *Forrestal* in a fire that took the lives of 134 men;
- in his A-4E Skyhawk over Hanoi during the course of tweny-three bombing missions;
- on the shore of a lake in Hanoi as North Vietnamese captors bayoneted him repeatedly after shooting him down with a surface-to-air missile in 1967;

- in prison a number of times between 1967 and his release in 1973, including an attempt to take his own life after he broke under torture and wrote a bogus confession.

A great deal has happened to John McCain since this book was first published in 1999, just as much has happened to America in those intervening years. That volume concluded with McCain's announcement that he would seek the Republican nomination for President in 2000. But the odyssey of John McCain had, and I believe still has, a long way to go.

I could, of course, be wrong, and at the moment there are reasons falling just short of compelling that suggest McCain has played out his hand, run out his string, stumbled out of the starting gate. Essentially he has managed to satisfy every cliché that translates into, uh, dead man walking. His fund-raising at midyear has been, if not puny, well below expectations, expectations that assumed he could bring in $100 million in 2007. At the moment he has a paltry $2 million in the bank and has had to lay off a host of campaign staffers and slash the salaries of many others. His campaign manager and chief strategist have just quit. It doesn't help that he has taken positions, championed legislation, and advocated policies that have turned one bloc of supporters or another against him, or reinforced the doubts of those who already distrust him. In truth, he has been an equal-opportunity antagonist. And the fact that he has taken tough stands, sponsored reform measures, spoken out on nearly every issue, and made himself more available to the press than any of the other candidates of note has gained him no obvious traction. But he's still in the race. These days he reminds me of fabled Marine Chesty Puller, who told his freezing troops at the Chosin Reservoir, "They've got us surrounded. The bastards won't get away this time."

They got away in 2000. A dark horse from the beginning in the race against Texas governor George W. Bush, the choice of the party's power brokers and moneymen, McCain raised his national profile enormously in mid-1999 with the publication of his autobiography,

Faith of My Fathers, coauthored by his longtime chief of staff, Mark Salter, a gifted writer who channels his boss's voice. The book told a stirring, dramatic, and heroic tale, but in a manner so lacking in bravado that few read any self-serving elements into it. It was, without question, a campaign biography, something of a de rigueur item in modern presidential races, but unlike most, it was so well written and the story so compelling that it quickly became a national bestseller.

Faith of My Fathers went a long way toward leveling the playing field for McCain, though he remained a decided underdog against Bush. A few months later, though, he rode his electric-blue campaign bus, the Straight Talk Express, to a stunning 19 percentage-point victory in the first-in-the-nation New Hampshire primary. Central to his success was that he had developed a national reputation as a different kind of politician, one who did not trim his sails whenever the political winds shifted, could not be programmed by his handlers, said what he thought, and was unafraid to take on the tough issues. Only three of his fellow senators (one of them Fred Thompson) were supporting his candidacy, but so what? He had trounced the well-financed Bush in New Hampshire, a stunning upset, and now it was on to South Carolina, a state where Bush had a strong organization, but which had a high percentage of veterans likely to be open to the message of one of their own.

South Carolina was a disaster from which McCain never recovered. Two weeks after the rousing victory in New Hampshire, he was beaten badly by Bush, losing the primary by 9 percentage points and his hard-earned momentum as well. The campaign also lost its cool, though one could hardly fault McCain and his team for their anger. A whispering campaign had swept the state in the days leading up to the primary: it claimed McCain had fathered a biracial child with a black woman and pointed to his dark-skinned Bangladeshi adopted daughter, Bridget, as proof. Bush supporters reportedly employed a tactic called "push polling" to circulate the lie, asking GOP voters by phone under the guise of a public opinion survey if they would support McCain if they knew that he had a black daughter. That wasn't all. His wife, Cindy, was portrayed as a drug addict on flyers distributed at McCain political events. At one, Mark Salter was seen charging off in pursuit of a man who had been passing them out.

The campaign never regained its footing even though it scored one final major primary victory, in Michigan. Any chance of capitalizing on that triumph went by the board shortly thereafter when McCain, campaigning in Virginia, denounced conservative Christian leaders Pat Robertson and Jerry Falwell in their front yard as "agents of intolerance." McCain lost the Virginia primary and Bush effectively cleared the field a week later in the Super Tuesday primaries, besting McCain in nine of thirteen races, including the all-important California contest.

Bush, with help from McCain on the campaign trail and the U.S. Supreme Court after Election Day, took the White House, besting Al Gore in the electoral college but losing the popular vote to the Vice President. In the months that followed, Bush and McCain engaged in some well-choreographed Kabuki to show there were no hard feelings despite their bruising primary clash. McCain may have been able to tamp down his anger—at least he made a good show of it—but for his campaign and senatorial staff, as well as many of the better-informed voters who had rallied to his standard, emotions ranged from hatred of the Bush team to blind hatred. John Weaver, the campaign's chief strategist, was so alienated he reregistered as a Democrat.

That anger was not solely an outgrowth of the push polling. Dirty tricks, detestable but legal, had emerged in late 1999, well before the New Hampshire primary. The tale this time was that McCain's five and a half years in prison had so unhinged him that he would endanger the nation if elected President. The source of the allegation was never fully exposed, but it was widely believed to have originated with a group of pro-Bush Republican members of Congress whose service to the country during the Vietnam War—which most of them supported—did not require the wearing of a flak jacket.

During the years leading up to Bush's 2004 race for reelection, McCain became one of the most influential and popular members of the Senate. The GOP's right wing, a not inconsiderable force in any Republican primary, seemed the major holdout. But that distaste for McCain only served to enhance his popularity among the liberals and moderates of both parties, along with Independents, who had been steadily gravitating to him from 2000 on. And he remained a thorn in the side to the Bush administration, initially opposing the President's tax cuts, denouncing the humiliation of prisoners at Abu Ghraib, leading the fight to forbid torture of detainees, and questioning the conduct of the war in Iraq.

He added to his luster with many Americans by joining with liberal Democrat Russell Feingold of Wisconsin to sponsor major changes in the nation's campaign finance laws, a body of statutes so riddled with loopholes that it seemed a generation of lawyers had grown rich piloting Mack trucks through it.

McCain and Feingold first introduced the measure in 1995. Both men were unrelenting in their efforts to gain its passage, crisscrossing the country more than once to build grassroots support for the bill. They finally succeeded in 2002. Not everyone was pleased, least of all many of McCain's fellow Republicans who saw their great advantage in campaign fund-raising being severely curtailed by the measure. Essentially, this related to large contributions given to political parties for "party-building" activities, but which candidates for federal office were forbidden from accepting. Invariably, these funds, overwhelmingly from pro-Republican business interests, would find their way into political campaigns in the form of so-called soft money, meaning money not controlled by the contribution limits that applied to federal elections. Bush had been lukewarm to the McCain-Feingold bill, but eventually signed it into law, saying, "I believe that this legislation, although far from perfect, will improve the current financing system for federal campaigns." But other Republicans never forgave McCain, even after they found fresh loopholes to exploit.

As President Bush's first term moved toward its conclusion and he began gearing up for a tough reelection battle, McCain had become perhaps the most popular politician in America. In the eyes of some, he was seen as the inevitable Republican standard-bearer in 2008 despite the continued resistance of the party's powerful, religiously tinged conservative base. The conventional wisdom was that McCain could handily win a general election if he could get the GOP nomination, which was more problematic. Even many liberals and moderates who opposed the March 2003 invasion of Iraq, which McCain strongly supported, seemed to feel the war would be going better if the Arizona senator were running it and not George W. Bush, the "Bush with Brains" argument.

In a telling, if bizarre, concession to McCain's standing, Massachusetts senator John Kerry, after wrapping up the Democratic presidential nomination but before his party's national convention, asked his fellow Vietnam veteran to consider joining him as his vice presidential running mate. Sources say Kerry sweetened the pot with the mind-boggling suggestion that McCain serve as Secretary of Defense as well as Vice President. The political illuminati were aghast when the story broke that Kerry had, at the very least, asked McCain to think about running with him. McCain, questioned about his talks with Kerry on ABC's *Good Morning America*, said, "Obviously I would entertain it." Then, seemingly dismissing the idea, he added: "It's impossible to imagine the Democratic Party seeking a pro-life, free-trading, nonprotectionist, deficit hawk. They'd have to be taking some steroids, I think, in order to let that happen."

It didn't happen, though the *Los Angeles Times* later reported that the two men had discussed the matter on seven different occasions. Curiously, that summer of 2004 may well have been McCain's high-water mark in terms of popularity. By the end of the year, two issues had begun to take their toll—The Embrace, aka The Hug, and The War.

Rather than running with Kerry, McCain became George Bush's most ardent champion, campaigning with the President whenever asked, which was often, as Bush, fighting for his political life, sought the halo effect he believed McCain conferred on him. Jeff Zeleny of the *Chicago Tribune* put it this way:

> Few leading Republicans have aggravated the Bush administration more in the past few years than McCain. But through his wide appeal to independent voters and his indisputable military credential, few Republicans can be more of a symbolic help than McCain.

His efforts on Bush's behalf set off criticism—which has extended to this day—that he was making a clumsy and pathetic attempt to curry favor with the party establishment in an effort to position himself for the nomination in 2008. To many of his most devoted backers, he had thrown in with essentially the same forces that he had challenged so forcefully—and forthrightly—four years earlier. He was not, they seemed to feel, the man they thought he was. Others saw his pro-Bush activities cynically, but perhaps more realistically, viewing them as an unpleasant burden he had to shoulder if he hoped to win the nomination of a party that had long been wary of him. This group was able to make the telling distinction between 2000, when his freewheeling, antiestablishment campaign never truly had a prayer, and 2008, when he might actually have *a chance to win.*

McCain's perfidy, as many of his supporters considered his stumping for and often with Bush, was made flesh in August when at a campaign event in Florida Bush turned to McCain, threw his arms around him, and clasped him in a warm embrace that observers described as a bear hug. Overnight, The Hug became proof positive of the gnawing suspicion among McCainiacs that the revered captain of the Straight Talk Express had made a Faustian bargain. In the months and years that followed, it came to symbolize for many McCain's betrayal of himself, of his message, and of the men and women whom he had wooed and won and had now cast into existential despair. I saw less symbolism in The Hug. As I recall, Bush was the aggressor, or the initiator, stepping toward McCain and throwing his arms around him. It seems to me McCain was in a most awkward situation: he could either just let it happen and try to enjoy it, or, to maintain his purity, punch the President of the United States in the mouth.

Not everything was wine and roses between Bush and McCain.

Pretty much lost in the ambient noise of the 2004 campaign was an incident that belied the belief that McCain had become an American breed of "Bush's poodle," a homegrown version of the label British critics had slapped on their Prime Minister, Tony Blair. In August, McCain called on the President to disavow the televised antics of a group of Vietnam veterans calling themselves Swift Boat Veterans for Truth who had mounted a campaign questioning Kerry's wartime heroism. They promoted their views through at least four TV ads, interviews, and a book trashing Kerry, *Unfit for Command*. Kerry's initial reaction was to ignore them. By the time he challenged them it was too late; they had already drawn blood.

"I think the ad is dishonest and dishonorable," McCain told Associated Press political correspondent Ron Fournier. "As it is none of these individuals served on the boat [Kerry] commanded. Many of his crewmates have testified to his courage under fire. I think John Kerry served honorably in Vietnam." Bush never disavowed the Swifties.

Over the next few years McCain disappointed his early and still most fervent supporters by a number of actions that collectively became known as "pandering to the Right." Declaring peace with the Reverend Jerry Falwell, one of the conservative Christian leaders he had denounced as one of the "agents of intolerance" during the 2000 campaign, became the most grievous and symbolic gesture. Not only did McCain meet with Falwell, he gave the 2006 commencement address at Falwell's Liberty University. As ABC News put it on its Web site, "Since McCain denounced him in 2000, Falwell has said that Jews can't go to heaven unless they accept Christ, that the Prophet Mohammed was a terrorist, and that gays and feminists bore responsibility for 9/11."

That pretty much nailed it.

The problems McCain faces within his own party mirror broader difficulties resulting from widespread opposition to The War, meaning the war in Iraq. McCain has supported it from the beginning, right up through this writing. On this issue, he has been Bush's most dependable foxhole buddy even as the country has soured on a conflict that has ground up a new generation of Americans, killing more than 3,500 and leaving thousands more bearing grievous scars of battle. Today, national polls show McCain's support draining away because of Iraq, but he has resisted turning against the war, vowing to be the "last man standing" if necessary, and so be it if that means the end of his quest for the presidency. Whatever grudging respect his consistency has earned him has not been reflected in poll numbers, but in the early days of summer 2007 there was a sense that the question he has asked repeatedly was gaining purchase in the minds of a growing number of Americans:

What happens if we pull out?

He has not been a passive supporter of the President's policy. Since the end of the war's first phase, the conventional combat portion, he has time and again questioned the manner in which the conflict has been waged. His has been a constant refrain: not enough troops; not the right mix of troops; torture is un-American and counterproductive. The Bush administration, he has said and continues to say, has badly mismanaged the war. Not exactly the words of a poodle. And, while he supports the so-called surge of 28,000 troops Bush ordered to Iraq in early 2007, McCain said at the time that he preferred a substantially larger contingent.

There is a personal element to his support as well, one that echoes the McCain family heritage of service to the nation. His son Jack is a midshipman at the U.S. Naval Academy, and Jimmy, Jack's younger brother, enlisted in the marines in 2006.

On issue after issue McCain is accused of pandering either to the Right or the Left. On the Right, Falwell and The War. On the Left, Abu Ghraib, torture, and immigration, the issue that galvanized Washington and much of the nation into the summer. Hard to figure why every position he takes falls into the category of pandering to the [your call]. Maybe, just maybe, he believes in the positions he embraces. Kind of reminds me of *Breakfast at Tiffany's* and what O. J. Berman, Holly Golightly's fast-talking agent, says about her: "She believes all this crap she believes. You can't talk her out of it."

I don't know how long McCain's run for the presidency is going to last or how it's going to turn out. I love reporters, having been one myself for the better part of my adult life, and admire their hard work and professionalism, often under stressful and perilous circumstances. But they are perhaps the world's worst prognosticators. They can tell you what's happening and what it means. But, though few will admit it, the future is a black hole to them. I remember back in 1983 when I was covering the Reagan White House for the *Baltimore Sun*. One of my colleagues, an exceptional reporter, looked at the severe economic problems the nation was experiencing and said Ronald Reagan's chances for reelection were nonexistent. The next year Reagan carried every state but Minnesota, the home state of his Democratic rival Walter Mondale. He even carried what then White House chief of staff James A. Baker III called "the People's Republic of Massachusetts." So here's what I think: Only a fool underestimates John McCain.

In the acknowledgments to his memoir, *Faith of My Fathers*, McCain says of me: "Bob Timberg . . . often gives me the unsettling feeling that he knows more about me than I do." That comment relates to my first book, *The Nightingale's Song*, which chronicled the intertwined lives of McCain and four other Naval Academy graduates against the backdrop of the Vietnam War and its aftermath. Much of this book is distilled from that one, though there is an abundance of fresh material as well.

Of course, McCain's comment is not true; I don't know him better than he knows himself. But, as you will see as you read through this book, I know a lot and it's a helluva tale.

ROBERT TIMBERG

Annapolis, Maryland
July 2007

AUTHOR'S NOTE

In July 1995, when my book *The Nightingale's Song* was published, John McCain was in recovery; that is, he was still working his way through the aftermath of his involvement, such as it was, in the Keating Five scandal. That he had been effectively cleared of any wrongdoing mattered to him, but not as much as one might have thought. Although I don't recall him using the words, his feelings seemed to mirror those of Ray Donovan, Ronald Reagan's first Labor Secretary, who, on being acquitted of the criminal charges that had forced him to resign, angrily turned to the prosecutor and said, "Which office do I go to to get my reputation back?" In McCain's case, he had paid a fearsome price for his good name, and he wondered if he would ever be able to retrieve it.

Today, though it hasn't been easy, he has done so. He is now a candidate for the Republican presidential nomination in the year 2000.

John McCain was one of five U.S. Naval Academy graduates whose lives were chronicled in *The Nightingale's Song*. Taken together, their stories were meant to dramatize the tortured legacy of the Vietnam War and how it continues to haunt the nation more than three decades later. The other Annapolis men were Oliver North, Robert McFarlane, and John Poindexter, all of whom had been caught up in the Iran-Contra scandal, and James Webb, author, highly decorated combat Marine, and later Secretary of the Navy. Each played a part.

McCain was the one who, despite having the worst war of any of them—nearly six years as a prisoner of war—had moved the furthest beyond it. Or so he would have us believe.

This is John McCain's story. Much of it has been distilled from *The Nightingale's Song*, but there is a considerable amount of fresh material. There are new chapters on his boyhood and youth, on the Keating Five scandal, and on the years since that ordeal ended. The Prologue has been recast and the Epilogue is new. As with *The Nightingale's Song*, McCain neither sought nor was given any control over the content of this book.

A small book, but a big story. John McCain, warts and all, soldier, ladies' man, maverick, hero. He may become president, he may not. But it has been more fun than should be legal to get to know him and a privilege to tell his remarkable tale.

ROBERT TIMBERG

Bethesda, Maryland
April 1999

PROLOGUE

Last year at the dedication of the National Prisoner of War Museum in Andersonville, Georgia, former Attorney General Griffin Bell, a Democrat, introduced Senator John McCain, the featured speaker, with these words: "We often hear people now say, where are our heroes, where have all our heroes gone? Well, Senator McCain is an authentic, living American hero."

Over the years, the Arizona senator with the hard-won head of white hair has survived three plane crashes, a firestorm at sea, North Vietnamese prison camps, a national scandal, as well as his own mercurial and lusty temperament, to emerge as a major player on the national political stage.

During four years in the House and twelve in the Senate, he has defined himself as a mainstream conservative, though neither a dogmatic nor a predictable one. He has earned a reputation for independence that some say borders on stubbornness while displaying a willingness to take on tough, often thankless issues. He is called a maverick, which in some ways is accurate and may appeal to voters. But the term can be a two-edged sword in that it may trivialize the decade and a half he has spent in Congress as a hardworking, effective legislator.

Today, having just won reelection to a third six-year term, he is running for the Republican presidential nomination. He faces formidable obstacles—modest name identification, no national political or financial base, and the hostility of many fellow Republicans because of his efforts to pass campaign finance and antitobacco legislation. But, as with Ronald Reagan, one of his enduring political heroes, only a fool underestimates John McCain.

Nor should anyone underestimate the impact on McCain of a long-ago war, a war that fractured a generation of young Americans and created a divide that may never be bridged. McCain spent five and a half years in North Vietnamese prisons, thirty-one months in solitary. Brutally tortured, he left prison crippled. And yet, almost immediately upon his release in 1973, he began putting Vietnam behind him. He told himself that whatever destiny had in store for him, good or bad—and it had both—he was going to fulfill it, prison or no prison. And somehow he has. But this sunniest, most life-affirming of men rarely loses sight of what he has called "the shadow of Vietnam."

To understand McCain and how he arrived at where he is today, one must first recognize the role played by Ronald Reagan in bringing Vietnam veterans—and with them the rest of the armed forces—back into the mainstream of American life. Absent Ronald Reagan, there certainly would have been a John McCain. But there may never have been a Senator John McCain, let alone the prospect of a President John McCain.

In the fall of 1980, a few weeks before Election Day, my newspaper job took me to Carter campaign headquarters in Austin, where I hoped to get a sense of how the presidential race was taking shape in Texas, a crucial battleground state. Talking with Carter political aides, still a cocky bunch at that point, I noticed some news clippings tacked to the wall, an irreverent mishmash, like "Far Side" cartoons slapped on the refrigerator door.

The articles on display related to the Reagan campaign, selected to demonstrate the essential looniness of the GOP standard-bearer. The one I remember was about a speech he had given a few days earlier. The headline, as I recall, was "Reagan Calls Vietnam 'Noble Cause.'" One of the Carter guys smirked as he gestured toward it, as if to say, Can you believe this antediluvian horseshit?

Though I had served in the war, I had long since moved beyond thinking of Vietnam as a noble cause, or so I thought. "Nobility" was not the word that sprang to mind in light of the costly misjudgments and tawdry machinations of the men who got us into the war, then found themselves stumped for a way to get us out.

I was thus surprised to find myself seeing red when Reagan's remark met with such ridicule, not just by the Carter aides in Austin but by press colleagues who dismissed it with superior grins and smug putdowns, the newsroom equivalent of boos and hisses.

Years later, as three of John McCain's fellow U.S. Naval Academy graduates—Oliver North, John Poindexter, and Robert McFarlane—were being swept up in the Iran-Contra scandal, that scene in Austin came back to me, made me wonder whether the attitude I encountered there had played any role in driving them to do the things they supposedly had done. I had a strong but vague sense that it had, but I was having trouble putting it together.

Barbara Feldon did it for me. One day in 1987, as Iran-Contra was at its height, old Agent 99, Maxwell Smart's trusty sidekick, spoke at a Labor Department symposium in Washington. Appearing in her capacity as president of the Screen Actors Guild, she told a little story.

"Did you know," she asked, "that a nightingale will never sing its song if it doesn't hear it first?" If it hears robins or wrens, she said, it will never croak a note. "But the moment it hears any part of a nightingale's song, it bursts into this extraordinary music, sophisticated, elaborate music, as though it had known it all the time.

"And, of course, it had."

She explained that scientists had learned that the nightingale has a template in its brain that contains all the notes for the music, but that the bird cannot sing unless its song is first triggered by the song of another nightingale.

Feldon's speech had nothing to do with Iran-Contra or John McCain. However, the tale of the nightingale, it seemed to me, harmonized perfectly with the burgeoning scandal. I began to think of McFarlane, North, and Poindexter in their pre–White House years as akin to young nightingales, voices caught in their throats, awaiting the song of another nightingale. And, on finally hearing the melody, responding with a vigor and enthusiasm that resulted in several notable achievements, but perhaps Iran-Contra as well.

The "noble cause" speech was part of the song that attracted McFarlane, North, and Poindexter to Ronald Reagan. It did the same for John McCain and millions of other Vietnam veterans. Not that Reagan or McCain did not know by then that incompetence, cynicism, and double-dealing had gone into America's failed commitment to South Vietnam. What Reagan was saying, and more important, what John McCain and men like him were hearing was that when they or their fellow soldiers headed off to war, they did so believing that the cause was just—indeed, in its way, noble.

They were also hearing Reagan say that even if the mission was later tarnished beyond redemption, in a distant land under the most brutal of circumstances their friends and comrades, in some cases they themselves, often acted with a raw courage that by any measure qualified as noble.

Reagan was not a newcomer to the issue. In his unsuccessful 1976 presidential campaign, he had repeatedly declared, to what Reagan biographer Lou Cannon remembers as rafter-shaking applause, "Let us tell those who fought in that war that we will never again ask young men to fight and possibly die in a war our government is afraid to win." By 1980 he had distilled it to its essence: "No more Vietnams."

The Nightingale's Song, as rendered by Ronald Reagan, did more than attempt to recast Vietnam as a noble cause. Throughout that 1980 campaign and well into his presidency Reagan regularly portrayed servicemen not as persons to be feared and reviled—ticking time bombs, baby-killers, and the like—but as men to whom the nation should be grateful, worthy of respect and admiration. To the men of the armed forces, he had a single, unvarying theme: I appreciate what you have done. The whole nation does. Wear your uniforms with pride.

Vietnam veterans, of course, were not nightingales waiting to sing for the first time. Before the war, their voices had been lusty and full-throated, their pride a seemingly immutable part of them. But the vocal cords of many had been stunned into silence during the Vietnam era by the hostility and ridicule heaped on them by their own countrymen.

John McCain had been silent by choice. Vietnam, he knew, could kill dreams as surely as it had once killed men. Best not to monkey with it. Use it when you can, learn from it, but don't get too close to it.

For him, the Nightingale's Song performed different roles. At first it served as his overture, priming the audience for his entrance onto the national political stage. After that it became his theme, a tune that greeted his every appearance without his ever having to hum a note, though occasionally, when it suited his purposes, he did.

CHAPTER ONE

The Punk

As a teenager, John McCain didn't talk much about the Navy, but when he did it was evident that he understood he was the inheritor of an uncommon seafaring legacy.

"That's my grandfather, right there," he would tell friends, pointing excitedly to a framed photograph of the historic Japanese surrender ceremony aboard the battleship *Missouri* in 1945.

On such occasions, he abandoned his studied nonchalance toward things military. With good reason. The solemn, somewhat cadaverous figure in the picture had evoked both cheers and howls in his lifetime, but never indifference.

John Sidney McCain defied the image of the senior naval officer. Bony, wizened, with a hooked nose and sunken cheeks, he turned sixty during World War II and looked at least ten years older, according to naval historian E. B. Potter.

Poorly fitting false teeth, which caused his speech to be plagued by whistles, compounded the problem, as did a herky-jerky gait and a high-strung, fidgety nature, characteristics he passed on to his son and grandson.

"There were few wiser or more competent officers in the Navy than Slew McCain, but whenever his name came up, somebody had a ridiculous story to tell about him—and many of the stories were true," said Potter.

One tale unearthed by Potter goes back to January 1943 when

McCain, Pacific Fleet commander Chester Nimitz, South Pacific commander William F. "Bull" Halsey, and Navy secretary Frank Knox were making an inspection tour of Guadalcanal. The island was secured by then, but Japanese aircraft still bombed regularly. That night, as the visiting dignitaries slept in a hut, they launched a vicious bombing attack. Nimitz, exhausted and afraid of mosquitoes, stayed inside, but the others, half-naked, raced from the shelter and dove for the nearest trench. McCain landed in a warm, soupy hole that until a few hours earlier had served as the receptacle under a portable latrine.

True or not, the story was consistent with McCain's performance at the Naval Academy, where he stood a lackluster 79 out of 116. "The skeleton in the family closet of 1906," or so his yearbook described him.

Like his son and grandson, both of whom ranked even lower, Slew McCain would prove that a second-rate record at Annapolis did not foreclose success in the Navy. Over the next two decades he outpaced most of his classmates to fashion a remarkably eventful if occasionally turbulent career. He became a pioneer in the development of naval aviation, notably in the strategy and tactics for employing attack carriers. In the early days of World War II he served as chief of the Navy's Bureau of Aeronautics. *Collier's* magazine was so taken by his crusty demeanor that it featured him in an admiring cover story entitled "Navy Air Boss." In the final months of the Pacific war, commanding Bull Halsey's fast carrier task force, he rained destruction on the crumbling Japanese fleet.

Aboard the *Missouri* in Tokyo Bay on September 2, 1945, as MacArthur, Nimitz, and Halsey stood behind the surrendering Japanese envoys, Vice Admiral McCain took his place in the front rank of senior American officers. The ceremony recorded for posterity, he lunched with his son, Jack, a decorated submarine skipper, then left for his San Diego home. He was dead of a heart attack four days later. *The New York Times* reported his death on its front page. Congress, citing his war record, promoted him posthumously to the rank of full admiral.

Halsey's chief of staff, Rear Admiral Robert Carney, later insisted that McCain had suffered an earlier heart attack while at sea but had somehow managed to hide it so he wouldn't be forced to relinquish command. "He knew his number was up," said Carney, "but he wouldn't lie down and die until he got home."

Two decades later, in another war and vastly different circumstances, his grandson would find himself facing a similar challenge. Again, the temptation was to lie down and die. But the old man had set the McCain family standard for grit and courage, and John McCain, sometimes clumsily, often grudgingly, always did his best to live up to family standards.

Princeton did not meet those standards. On a prep school athletic trip, he had fallen in love with the campus, been intrigued by the possibilities. He could study things he cared about there, history and literature, might even fool everybody and turn out to be a decent student. There were other attractions. A hot-blooded romantic, he could easily imagine himself pointing out Fitzgerald's old room to some visiting coed from Vassar, then casually guiding her down a shaded gravel path to a secluded trysting spot.

But Princeton was a pipe dream. As far back as he could remember, Johnny McCain knew he was going to Annapolis, knew it with such unshakable finality that he never really thought twice about it, at least not seriously. It was part of the air he breathed, the ether through which he moved, the single immutable element in his life. He also knew that if he said what he thought—hold it, screw Annapolis, the place sucks—shock waves would reverberate through countless generations of McCains, shaking a military tradition that could both inspire and bully.

That tradition stretched back to Colonial times. In 1764, Johnny's ancestors, Captain John Young and his brother Thomas, clashed with an Indian force at the Battle of Back Creek in Virginia. John survived, but Thomas was killed and scalped. John pursued the Indians for three days, resumed the fight, and reclaimed Thomas's scalp so it could be buried with him. Johnny's later forebears would go to West Point, among them a distant uncle, Major General Henry Pinckney McCain, who set up the World War I draft and became known as the father of Selective Service.

The Annapolis tradition was more recent, but by the time Johnny arrived on the scene, it was even more compelling. He was the grandson of Admiral Slew McCain, Annapolis '06, the legendary geezer who fought the Japanese from Guadalcanal to Tokyo Bay, watched them surrender, then, as if on cue, dropped dead. He was the oldest son of John Sidney McCain, Jr., '31, a World War II submarine skipper climbing steadily toward flag rank himself. So everyone, including Johnny himself, took it for granted that the Naval Academy alumni register would one day contain another entry: John Sidney McCain III.

And so it does, but it was a close call. Although resigned to Annapolis, Johnny was fully capable of sabotaging his chances, both for admission and graduation. Rebellious by nature, he viewed rules and regulations through a highly personal prism, as challenges to his wit and ingenuity. And as a succession of individuals and institutions would learn to their chagrin—among them his parents, teachers, Annapolis officialdom, and his jailers in Hanoi—all bets were off when Johnny McCain thought the rules were unfair, stupid, or, as most were in his estimation, made to be broken.

The U.S. Navy into which John McCain was born in 1936 was a sleepy service. Promotions were slow, the pay a joke, and congressional appropriations meager, befitting the isolationist sentiment that gripped the nation between world wars. The officer corps was small but tightly knit, its code of conduct both uplifting and stultifying. Assumed to be a man of honor, a naval officer could stroll into an officers club anywhere in the world and sign a chit for his food and liquor. But divorce was taboo, a career-ending event, and there were few secrets within the fraternity. Roberta McCain, Johnny's mother, said she knew when an officer was cheating on his wife even if he was an ocean away.

For those willing to play by the rules, the pre–World War II Navy had its compensations, and more than a whiff of romance. In the early 1930s, when Jack and Roberta McCain were stationed in Honolulu, officers in starched whites would join their ladies for afternoon cocktails on the manicured grounds of the elegant Royal Hawaiian Hotel. In the evenings, usually after a bracing game of tennis, the McCains would dress for dinner—Jack in black tie, Roberta in a long dress. A Japanese maid served the meal by candlelight.

Whatever the realities, naval officers and their wives encouraged the perception that the Navy was the most aristocratic of services. You borrowed the silver for a big dinner party, shortened an old dress for a special occasion, did whatever was needed so that guests recognized you as a person of taste and breeding when they entered your home, as perfection when you entered theirs. Navy families of that era adopted an old southern expression as their credo: Too poor to paint and too proud to whitewash. "In other words, we in the Navy never really had anything," said Roberta, "but we never took second best."

Roberta gave birth to Johnny at Coco Solo Naval Air Station in the Panama Canal Zone on August 29, 1936. The timing was auspicious. The base commander was his grandfather, who earlier that month, at the advanced age of fifty-two, had earned his wings as a naval aviator. Johnny's father was stationed nearby, at a small submarine facility. Jack McCain was transferred to New London a few months later, but for that brief period Panama became the epicenter of three generations of a family whose distinguished naval service would eventually span the great national upheavals of the twentieth century, from World War I through Vietnam and its still murky aftermath.

Johnny's father and grandfather may have made history, but nobody ignored his mother, the spunky, occasionally ditzy Auntie Mame of Navy wives. Though the family lived on Jack's salary, Roberta Wright McCain was born to wealth. Her father struck oil in the Southwest as a young man, made his fortune, and retired at forty, soon after Roberta and her identical twin, Rowena, were born. "I've accomplished more than most men ever accomplish," he told his wife. "I've just had twin daughters, and I'm going to stay home and enjoy my family." He never worked another day in his life. Instead, as his daughters were growing up, he took them to school, escorted them to the theater, delivered them to dancing class.

Roberta and Rowena had another advantage: They were gorgeous. Years later, when the McCains were stationed in Norfolk, Annapolis midshipmen on summer training there would talk about "getting lucky." That meant catching a glimpse of the admiral's wife on the base tennis court during their daily run. By then Roberta was in her fifties. Over the years, Roberta's and Rowena's spectacular good looks set up Jack McCain's most memorable wisecrack. Asked how he managed to tell his wife and her sister apart, he'd puff on his trademark cigar, flash a devilish grin, then harrumph, "That's their problem."

Her charm and beauty notwithstanding, Roberta's defining quality, as it was to be her son's, was an unquenchable spirit. Along with a religiously grounded fatalism, that spirit carried the family through difficult times. If her husband served as the role model for Johnny, his older sister, Sandy, and younger brother, Joe, Roberta made the family work. She dealt with the illnesses, picked out the cars, bought the houses, selected the schools. Once she went out to buy a dress and came home with a Mercedes. That got a minor rise from Jack, not much more. He did not like to shop and he hated paying bills. "What he really wanted to do was work," said Roberta. She didn't even bother to fake his signature on checks, just signed his name in her own handwriting. "If Jack McCain ever paid a bill, they'd send it back as a forgery," she said.

When John McCain was twelve, his father received orders transferring him from Washington to the West Coast. His mother let the three kids finish their term at school, then piled them in the car and began one of those cross-country migrations so familiar to service families. The first night, after getting the children settled, she sat down to write her husband. "Guess what?" she began. "Guess who was a nuisance today? Johnny." She was mystified. Usually he was everything a mother could hope for—quiet, dependable, courteous to a fault. She figured it was a momentary mood swing. She was wrong: "From that time on, he was a pain in the neck."

Others had seen the change coming sooner. At Saint Stephen's, an exclusive private school in the Washington, D.C., area, he had begun to display a defiant, unruly streak. But it was not until a few years later when he entered Episcopal High School, a boys' boarding school in Alexandria, Virginia, that those qualities emerged with a vengeance.

"Unlike those Northern schools that lured students with glitz and glamour, Episcopal found its identity in the proud but threadbare gentility of the Reconstruction South," wrote *Washington Post* reporter Ken Ringle of his old school on its 150th anniversary in 1989. "Tuition was low, living conditions Spartan, most of the staff unaccredited. We lived in curtained alcoves like hyperglandular monks; slept in sagging pipe-frame beds; drank milk drawn from some dairy where, it seemed, the cows grazed on nothing but onions, and amused ourselves at meals by covertly flipping butter pats with knives onto the ceiling, where they would later melt free to drop on other, unsuspecting skulls."

When Johnny arrived at Episcopal in the fall of 1951, the school was still drawing nearly all its students from the better families of the Old South. Like most prep schools of the time, Episcopal was lily white (it has long since integrated), its faculty all male, the students required to wear jackets and ties to class. A sampling of McCain's cohorts gives a flavor of the student body: Percival Cabell Gregory III, Greenville, South Carolina; Angus Murdock McBryde, Jr., Durham, North Carolina; Nathaniel Holmes Morison III, Roanoke, Virginia; Joshua Pretlow Darden, Jr., Norfolk, Virginia. If an impressive name meant you belonged, John Sidney McCain III should have been right at home.

To hear him tell it, he was, at least to the extent he was comfortable anywhere during his nomadic childhood. In recent years he has spoken with great affection of Episcopal, often contrasting it with the Naval Academy, which he found tolerable at best. But old friends and acquaintances from Episcopal days think the passage of time has warmed his memories.

Rives Richey, one of his closest friends back then, remembered McCain as rambunctious and combative, at times "just repelling," the type of kid who had a few good pals within a student body that either actively disliked him or gave him a wide berth. "He was considered kind of a punk," said Richey.

In fact, he was known as Punk, alternatively as Nasty, in another variation, McNasty. He cultivated the image. The Episcopal yearbook pictures him in a trench coat, collar up, cigarette dangling Bogey-style from his lips. That pose, if hardly the impression Episcopal sought to project, at least had a fashionable world-weary style to it. Generally, though, he mocked the school's dress code by wearing blue jeans with his coat and tie and otherwise affecting a screw-you raffishness.

"John used to wear his jeans day in, day out, week in, week out to where they would almost stand up in the corner by themselves," said Richey. "And a lot of people thought he maybe should have washed a little more or something. His blue jeans would be just filthy."

The rest of his outfit was not much better. "His coat would be something the Salvation Army would have rejected," said Riley Deeble, an Episcopal master, as teachers were called. "And his shoes would be held together by tape."

As at Annapolis, Episcopal tradition encouraged the hazing of new students, who were forced to endure the indignities of the school's Rat System even if they entered after their freshman year. McCain, who enrolled as a sophomore, was named Worst Rat after his first year. He wore the title as a badge of honor, which in some ways it was. One of his few friends, Malcolm Matheson, remembered him fondly as "a hard rock kind of guy, a tough, mean little fucker." Not everyone was so charmed by those qualities. Said another schoolmate, "He prided himself on being a tough guy. He was seemingly ready to fight at the drop of a hat. He was easily provoked, ready to be provoked."

Deeble ascribed McCain's behavior to his pre-Episcopal years as a Navy junior, trailing his father around the country and going to many different schools. "Most of these kids have a little bit of a shell," he said. "They have to develop it to survive. So they're skeptical of any new system they come into, and they've got their guard up and they're sort of looking around. And I think the thing that's important to them is not to let anything be imposed on them. . . . McCain has that kind of lopsided grin. He just comes in here and looks around, and he's going to do as he pleases as much as he can. He lets you know that. I think you could call it constructive irreverence."

Rives Richey and John McCain, mainstays of Episcopal's wrestling team, were partners in crime as well, routinely flouting school regulations. "We kind of decided which rules we wanted to keep and which ones we didn't," said Richey. They were motivated by something else as well. "The game of it was appealing to both of us—to outfox the school, the stealth involved, the brazenness. We made our own law a little bit."

McCain and his cronies occasionally snuck off on nocturnal sojourns to downtown Washington, often ending up at the Gayety or some other burlesque house on Ninth Street. McCain ran with a small clique that had a reputation, deserved or not, for doing what one schoolmate, Bentley Orrick, described as "deliciously unimaginable things with women.

"Their sins were more fancy than ours, whatever they were," said Orrick. "If we went over the wall to see a movie, they'd walk over the wall to get laid, or at least that was the projection. Everyone petted like crazy, but hardly anyone had hit the big four-bagger."

As a wrestler, Johnny was good, not great. Competing at 127 pounds, he could be counted on to win when he was supposed to and sometimes spring an upset. In one match he pinned his opponent in thirty-seven seconds, setting a school record. McCain and his teammate, Richey, seemed like peas in a pod, small, tough, cocky. "Maybe Napoleon was like that when he was young," said Riley Deeble. "But a lot of people who are small physically do seem to, certainly in the school atmosphere, become a little extra aggressive to make up for it. They create a little more space around themselves so they don't get stepped on."

Deeble, who coached the wrestling team for a time and remained an avid fan thereafter, discerned an indomitable quality in McCain and Richey. "They might be up against somebody a lot more knowledgeable or stronger or tougher and they might be getting knocked all over the mat," he said, "but they never backed off."

On one occasion having nothing to do with wrestling, McCain failed to display the fortitude others ascribed to him, and his friend paid the price.

During a summer vacation, Richey, who was fifteen, bought a car, a '47 Chevrolet coupe. One night he and McCain, who lived nearby in northern Virginia, and a third teenager decided to try their hand at picking up girls.

With Richey at the wheel and the other two boys jammed into the front seat with him, they cruised a nearby housing development. "We were total novices at this," said Richey, "all of us nervous, trying to be macho." Their pickup lines ranged from the surefire "Hey, you want to go for a ride, honey?" through its equally slick variations, earning amused looks and occasional guffaws from their elusive quarry. Seemingly immune to ridicule, they continued their quest until two girls, older than the others, told them to go to hell.

Their contempt was too much for McCain. Leaning across Richey, he shouted from the driver's window, "Shove it up your ass." Having delivered that show-stopper, the boys sped off. Richey had been driving for all of a week at that point and quickly got lost. Suddenly another car cut them off, forcing them to the side of the road. The car contained the girls who had been the target of McCain's wit and two very unfriendly men, the husband of one, the boyfriend of the other. Police were summoned. Names were taken.

A few days later the three miscreants, accompanied by their red-faced parents, were hauled into juvenile court on charges amounting to verbal assault. At the hearing, said Richey, the girls embellished their story. "They got up there and said that we used foul language, that we insulted them—all total lies," he said. "All we did say was do you want to get picked up. The only person that said anything was John, who told them to shove it."

Both girls mistakenly identified Richey as the boy who had used the profanity, probably because he was the only one they got a good look at. Richey, aghast, waited for McCain to speak up and clear his name. Soon he was fuming at his friend's silence. It was a standoff. McCain wouldn't confess, Richey wouldn't squeal. The judge suspended Richey's license for six months, let McCain and the other boy off with a warning.

A week later Richey's parents made him sell his car. Afterward he confronted McCain, demanded to know why he had let him take the rap alone. "He had sort of a vague, 'Well, I didn't think you were going to get into any trouble anyway and I just thought the less we said the better,'" recalled Richey. "He may have been right." McCain did not dispute Richey's account, but said he didn't remember the incident well, adding, sheepishly, "Probably with good reason."

The episode cooled the friendship between Richey and McCain, but did not shatter it. They had two more years together at Episcopal and, even though the car incident still rankled, Richey eventually regained his high opinion of McCain.

"I would say that John was basically a true friend, and he would have been a guy that I would have liked to have had walking down an alley with me," he said. "You just get the feeling that John would be there. He wouldn't duck out on you."

Near the end of their time at Episcopal, Richey was surprised to learn McCain was going to Annapolis. He had never heard him talk about it. And, as much as he liked him, he had never noticed anything remotely resembling leadership qualities in his friend.

"You know, frankly, honest to goodness, if they'd have rated everybody in the class for likely to succeed, I guarantee you he'd of been in the bottom ten, without any question."

Much the same might have been said about Jack McCain in his youth. At Annapolis he stood 423 out of 441 in the Class of 1931, eighteenth from the bottom, worse than his father, better than his son. His problems were not solely academic ones, either. For most of his senior year he was banished from Bancroft Hall, the midshipmen dormitory, and forced to live in hack on the *Reina Mercedes*, an old rust bucket moored to the Academy seawall.

The seagoing life made him largely an absentee father, though his workaholic temperament no doubt contributed to that. His son recalled that one day in 1941, when the family was living in New London, a fellow officer drove by, hollered out, "Jack, the Japs have attacked Pearl Harbor," and that was the last he saw of his father for more than a year. To John, then only five, it no doubt seemed that way. Actually, his father didn't leave for several months, but he was rarely home, laboring day and night to get his crew and World War I–vintage submarine ready for action.

Jack, or Junior as he was more commonly known in the Fleet, commanded three submarines during the war, winning both the Silver and Bronze Stars for heroism. He was known as an able commander at sea and a wild man ashore. By war's end he was battling a drinking problem, a malady that afflicted many submariners, who relied on alcohol to ease the tension of sixty-day combat patrols. At one point, according to a fellow submarine officer, a senior admiral warned Jack that drinking was jeopardizing his career. He got the message. He did not beat the bottle, but his drinking became more circumspect.

Moving up the Navy ladder, he made a name for himself by putting together a much admired lecture and slide show extolling the importance of seapower to the security of the nation. Small, feisty, his chest overflowing with medals, he plugged the Navy to anyone who would listen, from powerful congressional committees to local service clubs. In the opinion of many, the seapower presentation became the vehicle that McCain rode to four stars.

During this period McCain took on two jobs that some feel jump-started a career on the verge of stalling. As the Navy's first chief of information, a public relations post, he cultivated influential Washington correspondents. A short time later he became the Navy's senior congressional lobbyist. Soon many of the nation's most powerful politicians were streaming to the spacious McCain town house at First and C., S.E., now the Capitol Hill Club, the GOP's official watering hole.

Few men who rise to the Navy's top ranks are universally admired, and Jack McCain was no exception. At times, report some observers, his ambition to emulate his father so gripped him that he seemed possessed. But he had amazing resilience, thanks in part to his wide-ranging political contacts. By the mid-sixties he was considered washed up. Yet in 1967 he was dispatched to London as Commander-in-Chief, U.S. Naval Forces, Europe, his fourth star firmly in place.

With the promotion to full admiral, Slew and Jack McCain became the first father and son to achieve that rank in the history of the

U.S. Navy. Jack's joy was short-lived. A few months after arriving in London, he learned that John had been shot down and taken prisoner in North Vietnam. A year later Jack was handed new orders. He was being transferred to Honolulu as Commander-in-Chief, Pacific, the senior military man in the theater of operations that included North and South Vietnam.

Whatever his own failings, Jack attempted to instill in his son the same code of personal honor by which he tried to live. "My strongest impression of my father is of this sense of integrity and honor, a code of gentlemanly conduct that was a trademark of his behavior until the day he died," said John. But Jack had no avocations, so father and son did not hunt or fish together, go to the movies, museums, or ball-games. Nor was there much give and take to the relationship, though occasionally they would disagree over the length of John's hair or if he should be smoking during wrestling season. Roberta said she doesn't remember Jack ever disciplining John. "Jack was really kind of removed from things in a way," she said.

John spoke of pride, honor, and integrity when discussing his father, but rarely love, as if their relationship was one of respect, but not real affection, at least from John's standpoint. There also seems to have been some resentment, hints of which occasionally peek out from between the hundred-dollar words. "I didn't spend as much time with him as maybe I would have if he'd been more committed to being around me," he said on one occasion.

Jack's drinking, which he never fully conquered until friends helped him battle it late in life, also took its toll on the relationship. "Obviously, it wasn't disabling, but from time to time he would drink way too much," said John. "I didn't like to see him drunk. It changed my image of him." Normally open and gregarious, he grows guarded when asked about his father's drinking. Was it a serious problem? "Yes, it was a problem." For a long time? "Yes."

• • •

Its silly aristocratic pretensions aside, Episcopal High School left a lasting impression on McCain. The academics were challenging, the athletics invigorating, the all-male faculty in the main thoughtful, well educated, and committed to the school and the boys.

In McCain's day, all masters had to live on campus. From the small homes provided for them on the lush, tree-shaded grounds, they and their wives would dispense tea and sympathy and otherwise guide the development of the boys in academic and social areas. Episcopal boys normally gravitated toward one master with whom they had a special rapport. In McCain's case, it was William Bee Ravenel III, football star at Davidson College, holder of a master's degree in English from Duke, and much-decorated veteran of Patton's tank corps. "Every school has its master teachers, and during our time here, he was one of the gods," said Sandy Ainslie, '56, the current headmaster.

Ravenel headed the English Department. After classes he coached the junior varsity football team, on which McCain was a scrappy, underweight linebacker and offensive guard. Short, muscular, and outspoken like McCain, Ravenel seems to have served, if not as a surrogate father to John, then as a combination big brother and Dutch uncle.

"I worshiped him," said McCain. "He saw something in me that others did not. And he took a very personal interest in me and we spent a good deal of time together. He had a very important influence on my life."

The Episcopal class of 1954, McCain's class, dedicated its yearbook to Ravenel. "Teacher, leader, coach—he taught us what we know about writing and about literature; he directed and sustained our best efforts; he inspired us on the athletic field." Said McCain, "He was the one guy I wanted to see when I got out of prison. . . . There wasn't anybody I felt I could talk to about it. I just wanted to see Ravenel. I wanted to tell him that I finally understood there in

Hanoi what he had been trying to tell me all those years about life and what it means. I wanted to thank him and apologize for being so stupid." He never got the chance. Ravenel collapsed and died of a massive heart attack in 1971. He was only fifty-three. McCain didn't find out until he was released from prison two years later.

McCain cannot explain his erratic behavior at Episcopal in any logical way. Usually he describes himself as a rebel without a cause, a James Dean type, though it's just as easy to imagine him as Holden Caulfield, red hunting hat askew, railing about phonies, sneaking cigarettes, driving old Ackley-kid crazy. In part he seemed to fit Riley Deeble's picture of the wary, much-traveled Navy junior. Beyond that, though, he resisted throwing in with any organization capable of imposing on him a conformity that might rob him of those unique qualities that made him who he was. At the time he did not know what they were, only that they were worth defending against all comers.

The specter of Annapolis also influenced his behavior. "All my life I knew I was going to the Naval Academy," he said. "From my earliest age I remember people saying, 'He's going to be at the Naval Academy like his father and grandfather.' It was just something that was going to happen. And perhaps that's why I practiced this rebellion against the system, always walking the edge."

Interestingly enough, he was not turned off by the idea of becoming a naval officer, thought he probably would enjoy it for a few years, if not a full career. The more he thought about it, in fact, the idea of flying jets off a carrier sounded like a hell of a lot of fun.

Annapolis was a different story. He thought he would hate it, as indeed in many respects he did. But he saw no alternative. Like many boys his age, he had no focused career goals, just a fuzzy sense of his own competence and individual worth. At Princeton or some other civilian college he might have used the early undergraduate years to seek his own direction. But Annapolis, with its regimentation and lockstep curriculum, would provide no such opportunity. Annapolis was a commitment, more so for McCain because of the family tradition. Under the law he could get out of the Navy four years after graduation, but would he? Here he was at Episcopal, feeling himself drawn toward a school he despised by forces he felt incapable of challenging. Was there any reason, then, to believe that after four years at Annapolis and a similar period as a naval officer he would be able to defy those same forces—whoever they were, whatever they were—and resign his commission to embark on some new, ill-defined career path?

In some ways McCain at Episcopal was like a man trapped in an unhappy marriage who is unwilling to take the painful actions necessary to terminate it. Rather than tell his wife he wants a divorce, he puts himself in a variety of compromising situations, subconsciously hoping that the word will filter back to her so that she will take the initiative, leaving him guilt-ridden but free. One can almost picture the scene between father and son.

"John, this time you've gone too far," says his father. "You'd better forget about Annapolis."

"What?" says John, seemingly horror-stricken. "No. God, you're kidding."

"No, John. Forget Annapolis. Start thinking of someplace else."

"Omigod," John says to his father; to himself, gleefully, "Holy shit!"

But McCain at Episcopal never went too far. He flouted the rules, sure, but given his pedigree it would have taken the hand of God to transform his childish pranks and boyish transgressions into something serious enough to bar him from Annapolis. And God, it seems, was otherwise occupied or knew something about McCain that McCain didn't. McCain himself seemed unwilling to make the moves that might have kept him out of the Academy. An indifferent student except in English and history, he might have taken a dive on the entrance exams. Instead, he aced them, claiming his birthright. And so, on an early summer's day in 1954, in a car driven by his father, John McCain journeyed to Annapolis, raised his right hand, and marched joylessly into his future.

CHAPTER TWO

IHTFP

> We're a group of people who are being trained to fight. We're not businessmen. We deal in stress. We deal in intense catharsis. We don't deal in sales.
>
> Rear Admiral Howard W. Habermeyer, Jr., Commandant of Midshipmen, 1987–89

One day not long ago James Webb, '68—highly decorated Marine, critically acclaimed author, Secretary of the Navy—and another Annapolis graduate of similar vintage were reminiscing about their Academy days. After several rounds of sea stories, Academy slang for tall tales, Webb said, "You know, I hated that fucking place."

His friend laughed. "Yeah, I hated that fucking place, too." The words affirmed their kinship. As midshipmen they had uttered the same phrase with minor variations many times—at reveille, in the Mess Hall, racing back from a date cut short by the expiration of liberty.

Over the years, the phrase "I hate this fucking place" has become the equivalent of a secret handshake between Annapolis men. It's so common the actual words are superfluous. Usually you just say IHTFP.

Midshipmen mean it when they say it, if only for the moment. Old grads routinely fall back on it when nostalgia threatens to smother the enormous complexity of their feelings for a place where they had once been young and whole.

Midshipmen reach for lofty phrases to describe the Academy to outsiders. Among themselves they rely on the wisdom of inspired forebears. Thus, within the Yard, the Academy has been known at various times as

- the only place in the world where they take away the basic rights of man and give them back to you one by one as privileges;
- an institution where you get a $50,000* education shoved up your ass a nickel at a time;
- a four-year breaststroke through a pool of shit.

Let it also be said that the Academy is a place of tradition, pride, and honor that over the years has turned out many of the nation's finest and most heroic combat leaders, among them Admirals Dewey, Nimitz, Halsey, King, Leahy, Burke, Spruance, and Mitscher.

Since the Academy was established in 1845, seventy-two graduates have been awarded the Congressional Medal of Honor, the nation's highest award for gallantry, eighteen of them posthumously. Members of fifty-four Annapolis classes, all the way back to 1892, served in World War II. Six percent were killed in action. They received

*The figure has escalated over the years. In 1994 it was nearly $200,000.

twenty-seven Medals of Honor, fourteen of them posthumously. Annapolis men won three more Medals of Honor in Korea. During the Vietnam War, 122 Academy graduates were killed in action, and James B. Stockdale, '47, received the Medal of Honor for heroism while a prisoner of war with John McCain.

Though much remains the same, dramatic changes have occurred at the Academy over the past three decades. This is how the molding of future combat leaders worked when McCain was serving his apprenticeship.

Then as now, the process started in early summer with the arrival of the incoming class and the beginning of Plebe Year, a trial by ordeal with roots in the Crusades. Its purpose was to weed out freshmen who were not up to the rigors of military life and the challenges of command. Fred Fagan, '64, a retired Marine colonel, explained how he ran plebes as an upperclassman: "I tried to give 'em more than they could handle and see if they could handle it."

The system was untidy, often sophomoric, always vulnerable to abuse. Some good men quit; nearly everyone considered it at least once. The price was high: your youth, at times it seemed your soul, for a slogan—duty, honor, country. That was hard to remember when you were scrambling around on all fours, a jockstrap over your face, running Greyhound Races.

Then as now, a pocket-sized handbook called *Reef Points* was the plebe's bible. It contained nearly three hundred pages of naval lore that new midshipmen were required to master. When an upperclassman asked a plebe how long he'd been in the Navy, the plebe was expected to fire back the appropriate passage from *Reef Points:*

> All me bloomin' life, sir! Me mother was a mermaid, me father was King Neptune. I was born on the crest of a wave and rocked in the cradle of the deep. Seaweed and barnacles are me clothes. Every tooth in me head is a marlinspike; the hair on me head is hemp. Every bone in me body is a spar, and when I spits, I spits tar! I'se hard, I is, I am, I are!

Reef Points also contained, then and now, a four-page poem called "The Laws of the Navy," by Admiral R. A. Hopwood of the Royal Navy. Plebes had to memorize it. The last stanza, a troubling one in retrospect, goes like this:

Now these are the laws of the Navy
And many and varied are they
But the hull and the deck and the keel
And the truck of the law is—OBEY.

About the time they cut off your hair—in other words an hour or so after reporting to the Academy—you received a small pamphlet entitled "A Message to Garcia," the inspirational retelling of a Spanish-American War tale of dubious authenticity. In 1898, President McKinley ordered a young naval lieutenant named Rowan to deliver a letter to a Cuban general named Garcia. Without further discussion, so the story goes, Rowan set off on his mission. A month later, having journeyed to Cuba, he disappeared into the jungle, traversed the country by foot, and delivered McKinley's missive. If the details of the parable grew hazy in later years, the theme never did. You don't piss and moan and talk the job to death. You just do it and report back when it's done.

For most new midshipmen the transition from civilian to military life was brutally abrupt. They quickly learned that they had ventured into a curious subculture whose inhabitants lived by a rigid set of rules and conversed in a language all their own. Floors were decks; walls, bulkheads; stairs, ladders; bathrooms, heads; beds, racks. That was all standard Navy lingo, but the plebes also had to master Academy slang. Seniors were first classmen, or firsties; juniors were second classmen, or segundos; sophomores were third classmen, or youngsters. Freshmen were fourth classmen, or plebes. An Irish pennant was an unseamanlike, dangling loose end of a line or piece of clothing, usually a thread on your uniform. A sandblower was a short guy, a drag a date, a draghouse a place in town where a drag might stay on an Academy weekend. A brick was a homely drag, to bilge was to flunk a course or make someone else look bad. "Never bilge a classmate" may be the most enduring of the Academy's unwritten rules, though it didn't apply to matters of honor. In other words, you were neither expected nor permitted to affirm a classmate's lie or to cover up his cheating or stealing.

The word "grease" had many variations. As a noun it meant your aptitude for the service, more simply leadership ability. Your grease grade revealed how your superiors and your peers rated you as a leader. You were said to have good grease or bad grease. Grease could be misleading. Often it depended on the degree to which you bought into the system, an attribute that could lead to disaster later in life. John Poindexter, John McCain's classmate, had great grease. McCain himself had terrible grease. Greasy denoted a midshipman overly concerned with his grease, an apple polisher whose ambition was more naked than most. Greasy midshipmen normally did well early on but eventually fell of their own weight. You might fake who you were and what you were outside the Yard, but there were few secrets within its walled confines.

The jargon only added to the new midshipman's confusion. A few weeks earlier he may have been a hotshot member of his high school senior class, possibly a free-spirited college student or footloose enlisted Marine or sailor. Now he was the lowest of the low, and not just because that's how *Reef Points* defined plebe. The system that blotted up his every waking second seemed intent on crushing his last shred of individuality in order to transform him into something else—a name, a number, another hapless face in the crowd.

He learned the first day the six verbal responses acceptable to his seniors: Yes, sir; No, sir; Aye, aye, sir; I'll find out, sir; No excuse, sir; or the right answer to any question put to him. Even more quickly he was introduced to bracing up, the exaggerated position of attention achieved by forcing his chin toward the back of his neck to form double, triple, quadruple chins. He braced up everywhere in Bancroft Hall except in his room, which he typically shared with one, two, or three other frazzled newcomers—even there when an upperclassman or commissioned officer entered. Venturing outside his cubicle, he tucked in his chin and double-timed through the corridors, obsequiously plastering himself to the bulkhead to make way for his betters. In the Mess Hall, braced up on the forward two inches of his chair, he ate a square meal, his fork rising vertically from the plate, horizontally to the mouth, then back to the plate by the same route. If his deportment displeased an upperclassman, he might be told to shove out. That meant to remain braced as if seated, but without even the lip of the chair for support.

At odd hours his seniors dispatched him on whimsical missions to the farthest reaches of Bancroft Hall, the cavernous midshipman dormitory that housed the entire Brigade within its central structure and six (later eight) contiguous wings. That meant some long, wearying jaunts. As every plebe knew, courtesy of *Reef Points*, the Hall in those days contained 3.6 miles of corridor. (The subsequent expansion occasioned a minor variant in the riddle to which Bancroft Hall is the answer: What has eight wings, 360 heads, and sucks?)

Uniform races required changing from one uniform to another in, say, two minutes, then changing back again, and again, sometimes curled up in a wooden footlocker. To add spice, there were other games—Swimming to Baltimore, Carrier Quals, Sweating a Penny to the Bulkhead, Sitting on the Green Bench, and the always popular Greyhound Races.

Plebes enjoyed one advantage during the summer. There were more than a thousand of them compared to the small, elite corps of upperclassmen and junior officers selected to train them. Their numerical edge came to an abrupt end after Labor Day when the rest of the Brigade returned from leave and summer training. Suddenly the plebes were outnumbered nearly three to one and every upperclassman, it seemed, wanted a piece of them.

Once the academic year commenced, the ability to juggle the conflicting demands of upperclassmen and instructors determined who survived and who didn't. It was easy to see that later. Going through it, all you knew was that you were alone, as alone as you'd ever been in your life, and no one seemed to care whether you made it or not. If anything, the upperclass seemed intent on driving you out. Their ridiculous and demeaning demands consumed every free moment. When they weren't hazing you physically, they were ordering you to find the answers to mindless questions that left no time to study for class.

Your instructors, meanwhile, studiously oblivious to the antics in the Hall, were giving written quizzes each day, more challenging exams called P-works every other week. They were no more interested in your excuses than the second classman who turned beet-red and shoved you out when you told him your four classes between breakfast and noon meal left no time to find out the name of the lead elephant in Hannibal's caravan when the Carthaginians crossed the Alps to invade Italy.

Despite your best efforts, life was fast becoming a descent into madness. Nothing pleased the upperclass. Wrong answers incited abuse, right answers more questions. In class you were barely passing. You were angry, scared, confused, lost. No one was looking out for you except perhaps your classmates, and they had big problems of their own. By now the idea of quitting had crossed your mind, but the thought of going home and confessing to family and friends that you couldn't take it kept you stumbling through another day. One day an upperclassman braced you against the bulkhead, tuned his voice so low you could barely hear him, and snarled, Face it, boy, you got no balls, turn in your chit, go home to Mommy. And, Christ, by then you wanted to. No matter what you came from, squalor, familial dysfunction, nothing could be worse than this. You didn't know who you were or why you were at Annapolis. All you knew was that the guy with the stabbing whisper was right, you didn't have it.

By now you wanted out for sure, the only question how to ease the sting of quitting. Lying in your rack after lights out, you tried to concoct a story that your buddies back home would buy. Hey, the place was just infantile bullshit, man, I wasn't learning a goddamn thing. Hell, yes, I could take it, but I didn't need that crap.

Maybe you didn't. As you polished your breakout story, though, you noticed something. You were still there. And as you edged closer and closer to resigning, you began asking yourself some hard questions, harder even than the one about Hannibal's goddamned elephant. This was the hardest: Even if I can explain away quitting to my friends and family, will I ever be able to explain it to myself?

Suspended between quitting and staying, you hung on a few more days, trying to balance the unrelieved craziness in the Hall and the relentless demands in the classroom, realizing you could bring it all to an end with a stroke of the pen. But you also started thinking about the upperclass, the third classman who winked at you when a firstie was shoving you out, as if to say, Hey, I understand, I'm just a few months removed from all this shit myself. We all understand, you know. We've all been through it.

You always knew that, but as you dangled between leaving and staying, it began to mean more. All these guys, so crisp and squared away, so seemingly indifferent to your fate, they had all been through it, braced up, shoved out, sweating pennies, chewed out by assholes.

Your sense of self-preservation now abandoned you. The world outside the Yard lost meaning, the sole reality Bancroft Hall, and making it there. The decision out of the way, you reached deep down and found you had something left. The next time a sneering upperclassman growled, Turn in your chit, maggot, you bellowed back at him, Not a fucking chance, sir!

Eventually, June Week arrived. You joined the throng storming Herndon Monument, a tall, pyramidal granite monument across from the Chapel. The firsties had slathered grease all over it to deny you a handhold. Laughing and cursing, starched white uniforms stained beyond repair, you and your cohorts scrambled onto one another's shoulders, ascending by fits and starts, finally placing a hat atop the pinnacle. Plebe Year was over, you'd made it through, and, wonder of wonders, you were not a different person after all. But you were not the same, either.

Today, plebe indoctrination is kinder and gentler, if still no fun. The old system lasted as long as it did partly because of tradition, but also because generations of Annapolis men looked back on it as a crucial experience in the formation of their characters, a time for discovering that when the stakes were high, they could play over their heads.

During your four years at Annapolis you came to understand that more was expected of you than of other young men. Since the first anguishing days of plebe summer you had been trained to shoulder a daunting responsibility, leading other men in combat, bravely, wisely, and with minimum loss of life.

They told you that in lectures, but you learned it by osmosis. On the way to class you passed an officer, noticed his ribbons, recognized the Purple Heart, Silver Star, perhaps the Navy Cross. The monuments in the Yard usually blended into the landscape, but when you took time to read the inscriptions you experienced a chill and wondered if you would measure up if your time ever came. You felt certain at such moments that it would.

The Academy reinforced your love of country. It was not blind affection, and certainly not an overweening patriotism. You knew the United States had its faults, serious ones, none so serious as the institutional racism that had stained the nation since before its birth. But you also felt an optimism that the country could come to grips with its problems if given a chance. That was your job, to give it a chance. You were to be its protector, and that seemed like a worthwhile way for a man to spend his life.

There was something else, best approached indirectly. Three decades ago a firstie named Ron Benigo, on hearing a friend accuse another midshipman of insufferable grandstanding, laughed and said,

"Come on, we're all applause seekers, you know." It was a curious comment coming from Benigo, the most modest of men despite standing fourteenth in a class of over nine hundred. The friend, suspecting he would not like the answer, did not ask him what he meant.

Some years later, after Benigo had won a Purple Heart and Silver Star as a Marine in Vietnam, then embarked on a successful business career, the same friend recalled the applause-seeker line and asked him to explain it.

"I think I meant to say that our prime motivation for suffering through all that USNA put us through was the prospect of glory," he said in a letter. "I believe most of us felt that we would one day be tested in some form of combat—after all, WWII and Korea were not that long ago and our relations with the Soviets were being severely tested—and if you really looked at what a professional warrior could hope for in his career, it was just that test. After all, one doesn't get one's name in *Reef Points* by being the best darn administrator in the Naval Service. It takes great deeds in the face of overwhelming odds to implant your name indelibly in the minds of all the plebes yet to scale the Herndon.

"Perhaps some of us entered USNA thinking that it would lead to just a job, but after the intensity of the plebe experience, I believe we survivors had more going for us than the prospect of twenty-years-and-out to a nice second career selling life insurance to the next generation of junior officers. I believe we had visions of being someday at that critical moment when what we did would change the course of history."

CHAPTER THREE

Halos and Horns

In June 1954 more than twelve hundred young men in varying states of anxiety assembled in Annapolis, took an oath to support and defend the Constitution of the United States, and transformed themselves into the Naval Academy Class of 1958. Among the uneasy novitiates that day were John Marlan Poindexter and John Sidney McCain III. Four years later, the Class of '58 had been whittled down by 25 percent. Of the 899 survivors, Poindexter, a small-town banker's son from landlocked Indiana, stood number one in the class. As a senior, he wore the six stripes of the brigade commander, the top leadership post at Annapolis. McCain, the scion of one of the most illustrious families in the annals of the Navy, stood 894, fifth from the bottom. He never smelled a stripe.

The two Johns had little in common beyond their first names, McCain rowdy, raunchy, a classic underachiever ambivalent about his presence at Annapolis; Poindexter cool, contained, a young man at the top of his game who knew from the start that he belonged at the Academy. In neighboring Bancroft Hall companies, they were neither friends nor enemies. They moved along paths that rarely intersected, Poindexter walking on water, McCain scraping the ocean floor, a bottom feeder, at least academically.

There was one important similarity. Both McCain and Poindexter were leaders in the class, the former in a manic, intuitive, highly idiosyncratic way, the latter in a cerebral, understated manner that was no less forceful for its subtlety. As the Academy was fully capable of accommodating both leadership styles, they might easily have found themselves competing for top positions within the Brigade. But little else was equal. "John Poindexter was the sort of guy with a halo around his head," said classmate Bill Hemingway. "McCain was the one with the horns." Hemingway was Poindexter's roommate, but not even McCain would contest the point.

To his surprise, McCain enjoyed plebe summer, thriving on the physical activity and drill. To Ron Thunman, the newly commissioned ensign in charge of his summer company, he displayed a dynamic quality, a scrappiness that revealed itself most clearly in the plebe summer boxing smokers. Unschooled as a boxer, McCain would charge to the center of the ring and throw punches until someone went down. That summer it was always the other guy. He won all his fights by knockouts or TKOs.

His fortunes took a downward turn when the upper three classes returned in September. The least docile of plebes, he refused to accept the notion that someone could demean and degrade him simply because he had been at Annapolis two or three years longer. As he saw it, a lot of guys who had never done anything in their lives suddenly had the power to make his life miserable. "It was bullshit, and I resented the hell out of it," he later said.

As at Episcopal, he reacted by challenging the system, quickly piling up demerits. Shoes unshined, late for formation, talking in ranks, room in disorder, gear improperly stowed. Academically, he spent time, not a lot, on the courses he liked—English, history, and government—ignoring the rest, about 75 percent of the curriculum.

He treated the system throughout his four years like a hostile organism, something to beat back, keep at bay, as if any compromise meant surrendering a part of himself that he might never retrieve. John McCain at Annapolis, however, was not the John McCain of

Episcopal days. He shed the punk image and became one of the most popular midshipmen in his class, if one of the least conventional.

He proved to be a natural leader, his magnetic personality making him the unofficial trail boss for a lusty band of carousers and partygoers known as the Bad Bunch. "People kind of gravitated to him," said Chuck Larson. "They would respond to his lead. They pretty much cared about his approval and they cared about what he thought." Larson, an ex-officio member of the Bad Bunch, was McCain's closest friend at the Academy and for some years after. They were known as the Odd Couple: McCain short, scrappy, the consummate screwup, Larson the model midshipman, tall, handsome, smooth, bright. They shared a sense of the absurd and an eye for the ladies. Larson, though, was cautious. Of course, he had more to be cautious about. McCain didn't know what the word meant. As one classmate put it, being on liberty with John McCain was like being in a train wreck.

Even so, his classmates clustered around him, followed his lead, a modern-day Pied Piper decked out in Navy blue. "Whatever John would suggest that we do, whether it was at the Academy or on liberty, I tended to follow," said classmate Jack Dittrick. "And I don't think I was alone in that. I've talked with other classmates and we all marvel at how much control John had over what we did."

He lived on the edge, which only added to his popularity. Even if you held back a bit, followed him so far and no further like Chuck Larson, it was still a hell of a ride.

One night McCain led the Bad Bunch over the wall to a watermen's bar on a small creek outside Annapolis. The place was little more than a screened-in shack with sawdust on the floor and an electric shuffleboard machine in the corner. Its appeal lay in a feature close to the heart of real estate agents and thirsty midshipmen alike: location. The bar was situated about an eighth of a mile beyond the seven-mile limit, within which midshipmen could not be served alcohol. The catch was that midshipmen on liberty were not permitted to wander beyond the seven-mile limit.

Two dozen midshipmen were drinking alongside the bar's usual clientele of fishermen and crabbers when the Shore Patrol burst through the door. "Nobody move," shouted the officer in charge, triggering a mad dash for freedom. Midshipmen crashed through the mesh screens that passed for walls and scurried into the surrounding woods, tearing their clothes, losing their caps. Some reversed field, hid in boats tied to the dock across from the bar. Others huddled in ditches or behind fences. McCain and a couple of buddies were sprinting down a road when a car slowed alongside them. "Get in," said the driver, laughing like crazy. He turned out to be a recent Academy graduate showing his girlfriend one of his old haunts. After dropping McCain and his friends in Annapolis, he returned to the bar and picked up another carload of mids. Everyone made it back one way or another, hitching rides, scooting over the wall, slipping into Bancroft through any open window they could find.

For all his notoriety as the instigator of madcap escapades, John McCain had less flashy qualities that became part of his Annapolis persona. He could not be intimidated, he said what he thought, and he stood his ground. Frank Gamboa, who roomed with him for three years, can tell dozens of stories about McCain, most of them hilarious, but he usually starts with this one:

Early in their sophomore year, McCain and Gamboa were dining in the Mess Hall one Saturday, a day when midshipmen did not have to sit at assigned tables. Barely more than plebes, they were feeling their way, treading lightly, hoping to get through the meal unnoticed. There were also some plebes and juniors at the table, which was presided over by a senior nobody knew. The first classman's mood was dark, his manner unpleasant. During the meal he became angry with the Filipino steward serving the table. The plebes and juniors, sensing trouble, ate quickly and left. In a serious breach of protocol, the firstie began dressing down the steward, as if he were a plebe. The steward, anxious to please, grew flustered under the sustained abuse.

Glancing nervously at McCain, Gamboa saw him grinding his teeth.

"Hey, mister, why don't you pick on someone your own size?" McCain finally blurted out.

"What did you say?" the firstie snapped.

"I don't think it's fair for you to pick on that steward," McCain shot back. "He's doing the best he can. You're picking on him. That's what I said."

"What's your name, mister?" snarled the firstie, the usual preamble for placing a subordinate on report.

"Midshipman McCain, third class," said McCain, eyes blazing. "What's yours?"

Furious, but seemingly aware that he was on shaky ground, the firstie grabbed his cap and retreated from the Mess Hall, never to be heard from again.

Looking back, Gamboa said the incident epitomized McCain's intolerance for anyone lording rank or social position over others. McCain, he said, was probably the only guy in the company who would have reacted as he did, then and there, when it counted. "Give me a couple of weeks to think about it, and I might have been that brave," said Gamboa.

McCain had an advantage shared by few of his classmates. He knew the Academy was not the real Navy. Senators, congressmen, admirals, and generals were frequent visitors to his parents' home in Washington, where his father held several senior Pentagon posts, so the ire of an upperclassman did not buckle his knees. Some felt his family background accorded him special status, that as long as he kept his hijinks within reasonable bounds he could get away with just about anything.

Had McCain relied on that, which he and others said he never did, he might have quickly reverted to civilian life. His grandfather had been dead for nearly ten years when McCain entered the Academy. His father, though a rising star in the Navy, was still a captain at the time. Navy captains command aircraft carriers and battleships, but they do not swing enough weight to finesse their kids through Annapolis. McCain's younger brother, Joe, in fact, bilged out as a plebe in 1961, three years after John graduated. By then Jack McCain was a rear admiral. John McCain, moreover, made every effort to downplay his father's rank. Ron Thunman said he never learned of McCain's lineage till long after plebe summer even though as his company officer he had daily contact with him for two solid months.

Like many Annapolis men, McCain felt ambivalent about the Academy. "I hated the place, but I didn't mind going there," he once said. On the plus side, the uniform helped him get dates, not that he needed much assistance. Most weekends he could be seen escorting beautiful women, each more dazzling than the one who preceded her. Roommate Jack Dittrick used to tag along, hoping for a discard. "Women were just drawn to him," said Dittrick, even today amazed by the response McCain evoked in females. "What is it about him?" he once asked a woman friend. "Jack," she said, "the guy just plain has sex appeal. Don't ask me to explain it." Back then midshipmen had a more ribald way to describe the impact McCain and men like him had on women: When they walked into a room, so it was said, you could hear the skivvies drop.

Despite his woeful class standing, McCain was smart, quick, and thoughtful, if not intellectual. So how did he wind up scraping bottom at the Academy? For one thing, class standing was not solely a function of academic performance. A grease grade, relating to conduct and leadership, was also cranked in, and those factors dealt McCain's standing a severe body blow. He piled up an astonishing number of demerits, though always just below the threshold that meant dismissal. The leadership issue was more complicated. Whatever your talents, you cannot routinely thumb your nose at the Academy and expect the system to reward you. Personal appearance, for example, was an important element in the leadership grade. Outsiders may think that all midshipmen look shipshape in their uniforms, but within Bancroft Hall there are sharp divisions. Do shoes gleam from spit-shining? Has a toothbrush been run around the soles to scrape off the mud? Do brass belt buckles have a mirror finish? Does the collar stay, known as a spiffy, sit out of sight under the collar? Is the dimple in the tie dead center? Do any extraneous creases show up below the knot? Are shirts tucked correctly in back, with equal widths of overlap on each side? Are uniforms free of all lint and Irish pennants? There is more, much, much more, and in that game McCain was a real loser. "I don't want to say seedy, but he was just not your squared-away midshipman," said Frank Gamboa. "He just didn't put any effort into it. I just don't think he gave a shit." Said Jack Dittrick, "Nobody was as sloppy as John."

Academically, he survived because he had a gift for cramming and friends willing to tutor him. He wasn't confused by the course material, he simply didn't want to spend time on subjects that bored him. Many evenings he would drop in on classmate Ron Fisher, seeking enlightenment on such matters as Ohm's Law, inductive impedance, covalent compounds, entropy, Bernoulli's principle, and differential equations. His needs were simple, said Fisher: "He only wanted to know enough to get by." Fisher, who stood twenty-ninth in the class, was amazed that McCain picked up the key points of a lesson in a matter of minutes. Fisher never resented the intrusions; in fact, enjoyed them. After a while, though, he began to think of himself as a drug dealer and McCain as an addict coming around for his daily fix.

In his senior year McCain and a classmate, Ted Smedberg, were waiting outside the Officers Club for their fathers to emerge. Smedberg, the son of Rear Admiral William R. Smedberg III, the Academy superintendent, was in his fifth year at Annapolis, repeating a year because of academic problems. Departing the club, Admiral Smedberg said to Captain McCain, "There stand my two biggest disappointments as superintendent of the Naval Academy."

In June 1957, John McCain sailed off on first-class cruise aboard a destroyer. Late in the month the ship docked in Rio for a nine-day port call. He and a few friends rented an apartment and set up an Annapolis-style snake ranch ashore. The next four days were a blur, involving liquor, women, and nightclubs, everything except sleep, as Rio embraced McCain and his pals in its many charms, X-rated and otherwise.

The four-day spree over, a bone-weary McCain was dragging himself back to the dock when he ran into Chuck Larson, whose cruise ship was berthed nearby. Larson told him that a Brazilian fashion designer had taken a liking to the midshipmen contingent in Rio. He was going to take everyone up to Sugarloaf that afternoon and throw a party for them in the evening. Models were mentioned. "That sounds great, but I'm just too tired," said McCain. "I'm just beat. I couldn't stay awake." McCain hung tough. In other words, it took Larson two or three more minutes to talk him into joining the group.

Before long, the fashion designer's four-car caravan pulled up to the pier. The midshipmen piled in, then headed off for a day of sightseeing in the mountains. Later, the designer took them to his luxury apartment, which was spacious enough for the small band he had hired for the occasion and a makeshift dance floor.

At about eight, the models began to arrive. Bedazzled but hardly becalmed, the midshipmen began pairing off. All but the bedraggled McCain, beyond exhaustion, totally wrung out from his four-day debauch. As his friends swayed to soft Latin rhythms, he chatted with the designer, an engaging but undemanding conversationalist.

At about nine-thirty McCain stuck out his hand and said to his host, "Look, I'm going to go back to the ship. Thanks for the hospitality."

"No, no," the designer said, "there's a very beautiful girl I want you to meet."

McCain agreed to hang around a little longer. Around midnight, his deteriorating condition got the better of his curiosity.

"I have to go," he said.

"No, no," said the designer, "just a few more minutes."

McCain was insistent. "I've got to go."

The door opened and the most beautiful woman McCain had ever seen walked in. Recalling that moment through the mist of three decades, he remembered that the band and everything else seemed to stop as Elena (not her real name), slim and blond, made her entrance. The designer escorted her over.

"How are you?" she said, offering her hand.

"Fine," said McCain, coming alive.

The next five days were a merry-go-round of parties, receptions, and dinners, each more lavish than the last, interspersed with long walks on the beach. Elena, he learned, was one of Brazil's most famous and successful fashion models. She lived with her aunt and a coterie of servants in a penthouse apartment atop one of Rio's tallest buildings. In one direction they could see Sugarloaf, from another, Corcovado, from a third, the sparkling waters of the bay stretched out below them. What they could not see, because of the aunt and the servants, was each other alone.

On the final day in port, five minutes before the ship was to depart, Elena's Mercedes sports car roared up to the pier, butterfly doors popped open, and McCain leaped out to the cheers and catcalls of the midshipmen lining the rail of the destroyer. As the ship got under way, Elena stood on the pier, waving her handkerchief, dabbing her eyes.

McCain dashed home to Washington after cruise, repacked his bags, and caught a military flight back to Rio where he and Elena resumed the gay social whirl. There were more parties and dances, more romantic walks on the beach. Every time McCain looked at a newspaper or magazine, he saw Elena's picture. For all the excitement, though, they were never really by themselves.

Throughout the fall, McCain and Elena corresponded furiously. Sometimes she would send telegrams, at other times a wide-eyed plebe would summon McCain to the phone to take a long-distance call from Brazil. Elena's picture appeared in the Christmas issue of

The Log, the Academy's humor magazine, the knockout among knockouts adorning a page bearing the caption "So Nice to Come Home To . . ."

McCain flew down to Rio during Christmas leave. Because of military aircraft schedules, he had only four days. At first he and Elena picked up where they had left off the previous summer. But on the third day they sat on the beach for hours trying to come to grips with their differing obligations and desires. She was not prepared to move to the States and become an ensign's wife. He was not willing, or even able by law, to abandon his career and move to Brazil.

The following night, McCain's last in Rio, the designer who brought them together had scheduled a farewell party for McCain. He and Elena planned to go to dinner first. He arrived at her apartment about eight, knocked on the door, and readied himself to be greeted by the aunt or one of the servants. No one answered his knock. He tried the door, found it unlocked, and let himself in.

"I'll be right out," Elena called from the bedroom.

McCain wandered onto the terrace. The moon was glinting off the bay. A bottle of champagne was chilling in a bucket of ice. When Elena joined him a few minutes later, she was not, McCain would later say, dressed for dinner.

The next morning McCain raced to the airport to catch his plane. Elena did not go with him. He never saw her again.

Even though he lived it, or something like it, McCain recounts his romance with Elena these days as if it were a dream. In some ways it was. But it wasn't just his dream. With minor variations it was a dream of all but the most inert midshipmen. Duty, honor, country, sure, those things were important, indeed, for most, compelling. For all that, the chance of someday being swept away and ravished by a beautiful woman in some exotic locale has always been an unspoken part of the deal. Annapolis men, at least in the days when they were aspiring to the Academy and during their years there, before they started fretting about career paths, before the Vietnam War bloodied their futures, before they resigned themselves to being cast as warmongers, dullards, or dreary pillars of society, were good at a lot of things, but probably nothing so much as stumbling blissfully, all boyish innocence, as if the devil made them do it, into what Catholics charmingly call the occasion of sin. McCain's fling with Elena, though rare, was not all that rare. Things like that happened often enough to keep that goofy dream alive.

At commencement President Eisenhower personally presented diplomas to the one hundred or so midshipmen graduating with distinction. John Poindexter, the number one man in the class, received his diploma first. "Congratulations. I hope it won't be too much of a burden for you," said Ike as he shook Poindexter's hand. John McCain, lost in the sea of white that was the rest of the class of 1958, looked on impassively, clapped politely.

The *Indianapolis Times*, noting that the Hoosier State had always been well represented at the highest echelons of the Navy, applauded Poindexter's achievement in an editorial headlined "Another Cornfield Admiral?" Graduating at the top of his class did not guarantee Poindexter flag rank, the paper said, "but it is a lustrous honor . . . and something in which his home state can take pride."

McCain hung around Annapolis long enough to usher at several weddings, then dashed off to Europe to meet his newest flame, a tobacco heiress. A few days earlier he had received a short telegram: "Congratulations on your graduation. I'll always love you. Elena."

Three decades later, in 1989, as John Poindexter was preparing for his trial on Iran-Contra charges, John McCain got a letter from Senator Sam Nunn, chairman of the Armed Services Committee. The Georgia Democrat informed McCain that he was naming him to the Naval Academy's Board of Visitors, the elite panel that oversees the operation of the school. Jack Dittrick couldn't contain himself when he heard the news and immediately called his old roommate in Washington.

"Jack," laughed McCain, "it just goes to show that if you live long enough anything is possible."

CHAPTER FOUR

Fields of Fire

Mark went to Canada. Goodrich went to Vietnam. Everybody else went to grad school.

James Webb, *Fields of Fire*

WASHINGTON—President Johnson has nominated Secretary of Defense Robert S. McNamara as the new president of the World Bank.

The New York Times, November 27, 1967

John Kennedy primed the pump. On a bitter cold day in January 1961, he proclaimed the United States and its citizens willing to "pay any price, bear any burden, meet any hardship" to advance the cause of freedom around the world.

Cheers greeted the declaration. For that moment the youthful, vibrant new President embodied the far-flung, seemingly limitless ideals of the nation that had chosen him as its leader.

Kennedy was wrong, of course, assuming as he did that the generation then moving toward its majority would be like those that had preceded it, including his own, men and women who could imagine something to die for.

The Brigade of Midshipmen, toes numb, lips cracked, fingers frozen on the stocks of rifles, marched in the inaugural parade. Approaching the reviewing stand, the midshipmen executed a crisp eyes left, unaware that the pledge spoken minutes earlier by their new Commander-in-Chief had unleashed forces that would soon thin their ranks and reshape their world.

Kennedy was dead less than three years later, but the legacy of that pledge, the Vietnam War, bruised American society like nothing else in this century. The nation split over the war, as did the generation that has now come of age. Those who opposed the war forged a movement that eventually led to the withdrawal of American troops from Vietnam and created a counterculture that dominated much of the life of the nation in the late sixties and early seventies. By the mid-1970s, unscarred by Vietnam combat, these former antiwar activists had moved into the mainstream of American life, assuming positions of stature in politics, government, education, law, finance, and the arts. By then many were serving in Congress. In January 1993 the first of their number moved into the Oval Office.

For those who served in Vietnam, the war and its aftermath ushered in troubled times. Unlike veterans of other wars, many came home to hostility, contempt, ridicule, at best indifference. Their experiences were at first disorienting, then alienating. As they saw it, they had fought bravely against a resilient and implacable foe, innocently trusting the leadership of the nation that had sent them off to war. Many saw comrades killed and wounded. Thousands came home maimed themselves.

They reacted in different ways. The stereotype became the so-called ticking time bomb, the vet who dashes to the roof of a building in some sleepy southwestern town and guns down a dozen people with a sniper rifle. Others, emotionally shattered by the war, found little meaning to their lives in the confusing aftermath of the conflict. Some became derelicts, street people, drains on society. Still others turned against the war, hurling their medals at the steps of the Capitol. For most, anger, bitterness, and distrust of the institutions of the nation for which they had fought became the prevailing emotions.

John McCain belongs to still another group, probably the largest, the one that "went to ground," waiting patiently for America to "come to its senses," as Harold G. Moore and Joseph L. Galloway wrote.

Though many were no less angry, bitter, and confused, these men were, above all, survivors. However painful their individual wartime experiences, they knew they had to put Vietnam in a safe place, let it scab over and get on with their lives. And so they did. Before long they were working side by side with men and women who had opposed the war, with others who avoided military service by jiggering their college schedules, marital status, or health histories.

They were not immune to the occasional dark thought. They noticed, for example, that the antiwar movement lost much of its vigor when draft calls slackened and the white, middle-class kids who had been its center of gravity no longer felt threatened. They noticed as well that the officials who had maneuvered the nation into the war, then managed to lose it through arrogance, deceit, and incompetence, were making a slick escape, like Robert McNamara, exiled to the World Bank. For a time, though, they were able to ship such thoughts off to the same safe place where they kept other, more brutal Vietnam memories.

For some of these men, though, no place was safe enough. You couldn't tell by looking at them, probably not even by talking to many of them, but they were the walking wounded of the Vietnam generation. And down the road, in some cases, there would be hell to pay.

The numbers were always important, especially body counts. Since you controlled only the patch of ground you stood on, and since the ground was probably worthless anyway, the body count became the measure of success on the battlefield. There was no Monte Cassino in Vietnam or Mount Suribachi, either, places you took and held, then jumped off from on the way to some new objective closer to the heart of the enemy, whether it was Rome, Berlin, or Tokyo. In Vietnam the enemy's heart was in Hanoi, and that was off-limits, at least to ground troops, so you settled for any hill or ridgeline or ville or stand of elephant grass where you thought enemy troops might be lurking. Then you attacked. If you were right, they fired back. When it was over, you counted the bodies, theirs and yours, though only theirs went into the body count. The brass cared deeply about the body count. Sometimes they'd send you out to count bodies after a battle even though this meant exposing yourself and your men to further casualties. Such orders led to the coining of the term REMF, an atonal acronym popular with the troops that stood for rear echelon mother fucker.

Other numbers were important, too. Kill ratios, sorties flown, bomb tonnage dropped, all figures regularly trotted out to show we were winning the war. Since the numbers lied, over the years they passed into well-deserved oblivion. When it was all over, though, some numbers surfaced that told a fascinating tale, one that had the added virtue of being true. A sampling of the more important statistics:

- About 27 million men came of draft age between 1964 and 1973, roughly the decade of the Vietnam War. Of that number, 11 million entered the service either as draftees or volunteers. More than 2 million served in the war zone.

- Of those who went to Vietnam, 58,000 died. Another 270,000 were wounded, 21,000 of whom were disabled in some manner. Five thousand lost one or more limbs.

- Sixteen million, or 60 percent, of the 27 million draft-age men escaped military service by a variety of legal and illegal means. *Sixteen million.*

The numbers were compiled by Lawrence M. Baskir and William A. Strauss for their 1978 book, *Chance and Circumstance*, an authoritative account of how millions of able-bodied young Americans outmaneuvered the Selective Service System and left the fighting and dying to others.

"Through an elaborate structure of deferments, exemptions, legal technicalities, and noncombat military alternatives, the draft rewarded those who manipulated the system to their advantage," say Baskir and Strauss. All it took was "background, wit, or money."

For those with such attributes, a network of draft counselors, attorneys, physicians, and other professionals was available to champion their cause. "By the late 1960s, the only real challenge left to the draft was to find the right advice in time," the authors say.

How did they do it? First, there were college deferments, undergraduate and, until 1968, graduate as well. For part of the Vietnam era, married men and, later, married men with children were deferred, giving rise to practices known as "marrying out" and "babying out." You could gain a hardship deferment if you were the sole support of a widowed mother, or younger sisters and brothers. You didn't even have to be poor to qualify. Actor George Hamilton was excused because, Baskir and Strauss say, his mother lived in his Hollywood mansion and relied on his $200,000 annual salary for support.

Preinduction and induction physicals were standard vehicles for avoiding the draft. Young men, often armed with letters from sympathetic doctors, feigned every conceivable malady to win the coveted 4-F deferment. They starved themselves for weeks so they could report for their physicals underweight. Others stuffed themselves and showed up overweight. Some cut off their own fingers (or prevailed upon a friend to do the deed), claimed psychological problems—often severe depression complete with suicidal tendencies—or homosexuality.

Still others introduced alien substances such as amphetamines into their systems, though a common substance often did just as well. Baskir and Strauss quote a Milwaukee draft counselor as saying, apparently without irony, "The long-term casualties are unbelievable. I know someone who ate six dozen eggs and got an exemption for excessive albumin. Now, for as long as he lives, he has to maintain the lie that he is allergic to eggs."

Grad school deferments were terminated in 1968, so many young men flocked to divinity schools. David Stockman survived the war in this manner, later becoming Ronald Reagan's budget director and spearheading an effort to scale back military pensions and other benefits. Some who dodged the draft emerged in the 1980s as champions of the Reagan administration's tough-talking foreign policy, loudly endorsing a confrontational stance with the Soviet Union, aid to the Nicaraguan guerrillas, and military ventures into Lebanon, Grenada, and the Persian Gulf. They came to be known as chicken hawks, men whose testosterone gland abruptly began pumping after age twenty-six, when they were no longer vulnerable to the draft.

The National Guard, traditionally undermanned in peacetime, became the preferred haven for many men who feared both being stigmatized as draft dodgers (an unnecessary concern as it turned out) and a horizontal, flag-bedecked homecoming. Say Baskir and Strauss, "At the end of 1968, with the draft still in full force, the Army National Guard had a waiting list of 100,000. After two years of shrinking draft calls, that waiting list vanished. Six months later, the Guard found itself forty-five thousand men under strength." Dan Quayle is the best-known Vietnam-era militiaman. He supported the war but cushioned himself against its more unpalatable aspects by writing press releases in the Indiana Guard.

Baskir and Strauss handle the 16 million gently, concurring with a *Washington Post* editorial that called the war "a generation-wide catastrophe," a phrase that sticks in the craw, as if the young man doomed to a life of politely declining egg dishes equates to the veteran with an itch where his leg used to be. The authors suggest, moreover, that a great many men who did serve during the Vietnam era would have availed themselves of the smorgasbord of deferments had they only been sophisticated enough or rich enough to take advantage of them. They may be right. A 1971 Harris poll found that most Americans believed those who went to Vietnam were "suckers, having to risk their lives in the wrong war, in the wrong place, at the wrong time."

Interestingly, according to author James Webb, an unpublished 1980 Harris poll determined that veterans in the main were proud of their Vietnam service and would serve again if the occasion arose. This result cut severely against the grain of popular perceptions, as if there might well be a few million men out there who hadn't gotten the word.

Many, it seemed, even wanted to serve, not because they thought it would be a great adventure, though that was certainly the case for some, but because with their nation at war they felt an obligation to do so. Looking back, especially in light of the numbers served up by Baskir and Strauss, it seems a quaint notion.

World War II, the myth as well as the reality, was probably responsible, both for those who went and those who didn't. The Vietnam generation grew up on tales of sacrifice and heroism, of long lines in front of recruiting stations the day after Pearl Harbor, of a terrible burden equally shared. The movies of the day romanticized war, or so it was said. Thus, when Sergeant Stryker, the John Wayne character, is killed in *Sands of Iwo Jima*, he takes a clean shot in the back rather than being graphically shredded à la *Platoon*, *Full Metal Jacket*, or *Saving Private Ryan*. But even back then young men weren't so dumb. They knew dead was dead, and they knew it could happen to them.

That was a sobering thought and provoked different reactions. Author James Fallows quotes a friend, a former Rhodes Scholar who became a corporate lawyer, as saying, "There are certain people who can do more good in a lifetime in politics or academics or medicine than by getting killed in a trench."

Certain other people, some reasonably bright and promising in their own right, could not imagine staying home while members of their generation risked their lives fighting a war. Once their buddies started getting killed and maimed, when they themselves were forced to contemplate a future sightless, with a limb or two missing, or in a wheelchair, feelings such as rage, resentment, and disbelief took root. Try as they might, they could not get it through their heads that those who avoided serving did so because of higher morality, greater love for their fellow man, or a sudden attack of religion on the Stockman model.

The generational schism broadened with the blossoming of the antiwar movement and the counterculture that accompanied it. Ultimately, those who opposed the war prevailed, but along the way they made a strategic error. They did not attempt to make common cause with their peers in uniform. Instead, they treated the men fighting the war with contempt, spitting on them, calling them fascists and babykillers, as if by a simple act of labeling they could transform them into beings different from and less worthy than themselves, with less reason to live.

Paul Goodwin, who commanded a Marine rifle company in Vietnam, experienced a variation on that theme. Goodwin was tough and profane, a tiger in combat. At home he was a soft-spoken if occasionally prickly southern gentleman. On recruiting duty in Kansas City in the early 1970s, he was living among civilians for the first time in a decade. As he and his neighbors grew friendly, Goodwin was confused by the way they related to him, as if they needed to see him as an anomaly, the exception that proved the rule. It drove him crazy. "This is a horrible war and our troops are doing terrible things over there," his neighbors would say, "but we know you're not like that, Paul." Sputtering, Goodwin would reply, "I am them. I am typical. I am what the Marine Corps is all about."

From where men like Goodwin stood, a different picture was taking shape. The protesters and draft dodgers seemed to be of the privileged class, more prosperous, better educated, predominantly white. The press and many politicians appeared to be cheering them on. Was it possible that they really were smarter, more aware, and as courageous in their own way as the men in Vietnam?

Rightly or wrongly, those questions were answered no, no, and no, but it took a while because it wasn't an easy call. Some antiwar activists won grudging respect, the ones willing to go to jail rather than accept induction. A U.S. prison may not have been quite as perilous as the Vietnam outback, but both were Indian country and everyone knew it. For all the chants of "Hell, no, we won't go," however, few were willing to put themselves on the line as had their jailed comrades. They played the deferment game instead, manipulating their college schedules, accelerating their marriage plans, running off to Canada (which was decidedly not Indian country) or Sweden (ditto), and otherwise avoiding and evading.

For many who served in Vietnam, the crucial question became, Could I have done any of those things and still lived with myself? Those who answered in the negative would never see America and many members of their own generation the same way again, especially as they watched their old tormentors and fellow travelers prosper in the aftermath of the war.

"What it does is dislocate loyalty," said Bob Bedingfield, a Navy chaplain with the Marines in Vietnam. "It says that I can never believe the system again. That's now part of the means by which I interpret the world I live in."

Milt Copulos, an Army veteran, spent three and a half years in the hospital and received the last rites seven times as a result of his Vietnam service. He put it this way: "There's a wall ten miles high and fifty miles thick between those of us who went and those who didn't, and that wall is never going to come down."

CHAPTER FIVE

Fire at Sea

After a European fling with the tobacco heiress, John McCain reported to flight school at Pensacola in August 1958. As at Annapolis, he was brash and immature, at times reckless, a man who turned a night on the town into a test of survival skills. His life revolved around the beach, his new Corvette, the coupe du jour for fledgling jet jockeys, and women, the flashier the better. He dated everyone from schoolteachers to the strippers at Trader John's, the fabled airdale raunch bar, often returning to base just in time to change clothes and drag himself out to the flight line.

Graduation transformed neither his style nor his low tolerance for authority. One night he was playing shuffleboard at the Officers Club. His nondescript outfit included cowboy boots and a chewed-up crewneck sweater. A cigarette dangled from his lips as an irate commander stormed over. "Ensign McCain, your appearance is a disgrace," said the officer, four grades his senior. "What do you think your grandfather would say?" Squinting through the smoke, McCain replied, "Frankly, Commander, I don't think he'd give a rat's ass."

He learned to fly at Pensacola, though his performance was below par, at best good enough to get by. He liked flying, but didn't love it. What he loved was the kick-the-tire, start-the-fire, scarf-in-the-wind life of a naval aviator. There was an added attraction. Flying was something his father, a submariner, had never done, and he wanted to be seen, for better or worse and at almost all costs, as his own man, not Jack McCain's kid.

He and Chuck Larson roomed and partied together at a series of flight schools over the next two and a half years, Larson the calm if mischievous eye of the hurricane, McCain the hurricane itself. At advanced flight training at Corpus Christi, they took adjoining rooms in the BOQ, moved the beds into one room, turned the other into an all-purpose party room, stag bar, and penny ante gambling den. The decor was early landfill, artfully set off by empty beer cans, dirty clothes, and cigarette butts.

One Saturday morning, as McCain was practicing landings, his engine quit and his plane plunged into Corpus Christi Bay. Knocked unconscious by the impact, he came to as the plane settled to the bottom. Cracking the canopy against the weight of the water, he squeezed out and fought his way to the surface, where he was raced to the dispensary. His back ached, but X rays showed no serious injuries. Laughing off advice that he spend the night in sick bay, he hurriedly returned to the BOQ, popped some painkillers, and climbed into bed, hoping to recuperate in time to keep a brush with death from ruining an otherwise promising weekend.

Jack McCain, meanwhile, learned of the accident and dispatched an admiral friend stationed nearby to check on his son's condition. Larson was shaving amid the debris of the previous night's poker session when he was startled by a loud knock. Strolling to the door, straight razor in hand, he heard a second knock, more insistent than the first. "Hey, hold your horses, dammit," he said. "There's a guy trying to sleep in here." Nonplussed, he swung the door open, saw the admiral, snapped to attention, nearly sliced off his eyebrow trying to salute. Thanks to grit and codeine, McCain was on his feet for Saturday night. The following weekend, though, the entire BOQ stood a white-glove inspection.

McCain was an adequate pilot, but he had no patience for studying dry aviation manuals. Instead, he would spend two or three hours each afternoon, whatever time he had between the end of the day's classes and the commencement of happy hour, reading history. At Corpus, he worked his way through all three volumes of Gibbon's *Decline and Fall of the Roman Empire.* When Larson asked why, he said his father had urged him to do so, told him it was the kind of thing a naval officer should know about.

A change, subtle at first, came over McCain during a series of deployments to the Mediterranean between 1960 and 1964. To the unpracticed eye it looked suspiciously like maturity. Those who knew him better passed it off as an extended hangover. In time, though, even the cynics had to concede he was taking his job more seriously. He liked flying off a carrier, enjoyed being at sea, and seemed to flourish when assigned additional duties. He volunteered to stand bridge watches, eventually qualifying as officer of the deck underway, which meant he was considered capable of maneuvering the ship at sea. Rather than bridling at the confinement of long cruises, he seemed to be thriving, in part because he liked it but also because he was cut off from the temptations that awaited him on the beach.

To the relief of McCain watchers everywhere, these early glimmers of maturity did not signal a radical transformation. His professional growth, though reasonably steady, had its troubled moments. Flying too low over the Iberian Peninsula, he took out some power lines, which led to a spate of newspaper stories in which he was predictably identified as the son of an admiral. The tale has gotten better with age. These days they talk about the day McCain turned the lights out in Spain.

He continued to play hard on liberty, drinking, gambling, and otherwise availing himself of the charms of the Mediterranean littoral. In 1964 he was back in Pensacola, a short tour notable for the beginning of his romance with Carol Shepp. The two had known each other at Annapolis, where Carol dated a classmate of McCain's, whom she later married. By 1964 she was the divorced mother of two. She and

McCain met again while she was visiting a friend and renewed an old flirtation that quickly became serious.

Carol, a slim five foot eight, had been a model in her hometown of Philadelphia, where she was again living. Warm, vivacious, and fun-loving, she was a more polished, slightly less electrified distaff version of John McCain. By the time he was transferred to Meridian, Mississippi, as a flight instructor a few months later, he was flying up to Philadelphia nearly every weekend to visit her.

Meridian was, to McCain's mind, the "crummiest place in America," but he enjoyed instructing, becoming a better pilot by teaching others to fly. The days were long, usually three training flights a day, not counting preflight briefings and the debriefings once back on the ground. His fitness reports by now were looking very good, and he was named instructor of the month.

Off duty, he and his bachelor cronies brought sleepy Meridian to life. A benighted plan for base beautification became the vehicle for their efforts. The plan called for creating a series of man-made lakes, bulldozers digging the holes, nature providing the water in the form of rainfall. Lake Helen, named for the base commander's wife, was dredged behind the BOQ. More swamp than lake, it soon became a festering depression of standing water, mosquito larvae, and pond scum. Before long Lake Helen was renamed Lake Fester. The tiny island in the middle, a decorator touch about the size of a large room, was dubbed Key Fess.

The Key Fess Yacht Club inevitably followed, complete with membership cards, club officers, and a single vessel, a leaky old rowboat christened *The Fighting Lady*. McCain was named vice commodore. All hands turned out in yachting dress—blue jackets, white trousers, white shoes, white cap—to celebrate the launching of the club. Lights adorned the five hapless trees sprouting against all odds on Key Fess. The commodore, a boozy Marine captain, struck a Washington-crossing-the-Delaware pose aboard *The Fighting Lady* as he and several other tipsy partygoers shoved off on a ceremonial journey to the island. Overbooked, the boat sank a few yards from shore. The scramble to safety resulted in a broken wrist, a few torn ligaments, and some mild trampling of passengers. Evacuation of the wounded barely interrupted the revelry.

Key Fess Yacht Club parties quickly became the focal point of social activities on the base. There was a Roman toga party in which the Officers Club was stripped of furniture and filled with mattresses lugged in from the BOQ. At a Roaring Twenties party, a gilded bathtub was filled with a daunting mixture of French brandy and champagne. Rock bands were brought in from Memphis. The parties became magnets for local women, few of them debutantes. And the word was spreading. When McCain was elected commodore, pilots flew in from as far away as the West Coast for his change-of-command gala. There were flags, banners, side boys, hundreds of people crowding the shore, Richard Rodgers's rousing score for the documentary series "Victory at Sea" blaring from loudspeakers. For the invocation, a Marine serving as chaplain read from *Catch-22*, Joseph Heller's antiwar classic.

By then McCain had become a one-woman man, logging his flying time on weekend trips to Philadelphia to see Carol and inviting her down for the best parties. In July 1965 they were married at the Philadelphia home of Carol's friends Connie and Sam Bookbinder, the reception catered by the family's seafood restaurant, Bookbinder's, a city landmark. The transformation from playboy to family man was a smooth one. He was twenty-eight and ready to settle down. He loved Carol's children, Doug, five, and Andy, three, who were fun and well behaved. A year later he adopted them. Rather than settling into domesticity, he and Carol remained fixtures on the party circuit. In a rare concession to his new status, he resigned as commodore of Key Fess, explaining that only a bachelor could uphold the club's high standard of inspired lunacy.

That fall he flew a trainer solo to Philadelphia for the Army-Navy game. Flying back by way of Norfolk, he had just begun his descent over unpopulated tidal terrain when the engine died. "I've got a flameout," he radioed. He went through the standard relight procedures three times. At one thousand feet he ejected, landing on the deserted beach moments before the plane slammed into a clump of trees. A chopper picked him up fifteen minutes later. His injuries were minor. The Navy classified it as a "routine ejection." McCain figured that was about right. As he later said of the incident, it wasn't as if he had collided with another plane, or been shot down.

In September 1966, Carol gave birth to a daughter, Sidney. Soon after, John was transferred to Jacksonville and assigned to a squadron slated for Vietnam in mid-1967. He had pulled strings in Meridian to get there sooner, but to no avail. He deployed in the spring, aboard the carrier *Forrestal*, expecting to be home in less than a year.

Carol, who had never been to Europe, decided to move there with the children until John returned. She flew to London, where Jack and Roberta McCain were stationed, then set off with her three kids on a driving tour through West Germany, Denmark, Holland, and Belgium. Her destination was Garmisch, which had an American school for the boys.

July 29, 1967. On the flight deck of the *Forrestal*, McCain climbed into the cockpit of his A-4E Skyhawk. Two years into the war, he was finally where he wanted to be, on Yankee Station, about sixty miles from the coast of North Vietnam in the South China Sea. He was there for a number of reasons, including the professional. No naval aviator was going to ascend the career ladder unless he flew combat missions in Vietnam. More compelling, if less discussed, was the excitement, the exhilaration, even the fear. Unlike ground pounders, for whom the shit never ceased, McCain and other carrier-based combat pilots flew missions that rarely lasted more than an hour from takeoff to landing, sixty minutes of gut-wrenching, scrotum-shrinking frenzy. Then they were back in the ready room, cooling out with their buddies, telling war stories, lying about women.

McCain's A-4E and the other Skyhawks, the *Forrestal*'s attack aircraft, were wingtip to wingtip on the port side of the flight deck, angled toward the bow. They were armed with five-hundred- and one-thousand-pound bombs. To extend their flying range, their bellies were fitted with detachable two-hundred-gallon fuel tanks containing highly combustible aviation gas.

On the starboard side, across from the A-4Es, angled forward as well, were the fighters, the F-4 Phantoms that flew cover as the Skyhawks delivered their deadly payloads. The F-4s were armed with air-to-ground Zuni rockets for flak suppression and air-to-air Sparrow rockets should they encounter North Vietnamese MiGs.

In preparation for launching aircraft, the carrier's massive prow swung slowly into the wind. The sea was choppy, but the crew hardly noticed, the carrier slicing through the water like a European touring car gliding along the autobahn.

Strapped into the cockpit, McCain watched a little yellow cart connect up to his A-4E. The cart, which pilots called the Huffer, blew air into his engine, turning the blades. McCain hit the igniter. As his engine roared to life, he went through his preflight checks, then passed his flight helmet down to a crewman so he could wipe the visor. It was a ritual, born of concern. McCain never felt he could see clearly through the thick plastic shield.

Across the way, an F-4 had just hooked up to an external power generator that would jump-start its engine. Unknown to the pilot, a small wire called a pigtail was attached to one of his Zuni rockets. For safety reasons, the pigtails, which carry the electrical charge that fire the rockets, were not supposed to be plugged in until just before launch. His engine started, the pilot pressed the button that switched his aircraft from external to internal power, a routine procedure. This time, though, the switch-over sent a bolt of stray voltage through the errant pigtail, igniting the Zuni.

McCain never saw it coming. He had just snapped the cockpit shut when the Zuni punched through his exterior fuel tank. A tremendous jolt shook his plane, bouncing him around the cockpit as two hundred gallons of highly flammable aviation gas streamed onto the flight deck. Billowing black smoke engulfed him. Below, a lake of burning fuel had formed, its edges lapping eagerly across the flight deck. Shutting down the engine, he heard the two one-thousand-pound bombs hooked to his wings clank to the deck. He freed himself from his safety harness, scrambled from the cockpit onto the nose of the A-4E, then crawled hand-over-hand along the lancelike refueling probe jutting from the nose of his aircraft.

As he did so, a voice, tense but controlled, with a vaguely southwestern twang, came across the ship's intercom, alerting thousands of confused crewmen below decks that they were about to be hurled into every sailor's worst nightmare, a fire at sea.

"Fahr, fahr, fahr—fahr on the flight deck, fahr on the flight deck. All hands, man your battle stations. All hands, man your battle stations."

Dangling above the burning fuel, McCain knew he had no options. He dropped into the fire and rolled rapidly through the blaze till he cleared it. Slapping at his flight suit with gloved hands, he put out the flames while sprinting to the far side of the flight deck. Fighting to keep his composure, he saw a handful of men near the edge of the fire aiming a hose at the growing conflagration. A chief petty officer, armed only with a portable fire extinguisher, rushed toward the burning planes, his common sense overwhelmed by concern for the trapped pilots. Through the smoke McCain saw the pilot of the A-4E next to his trying to escape the same way he had. As the pilot rolled through the flames, McCain started toward him. He had only taken a step or two when the first bomb cooked off.

Red-hot shards of jagged metal screamed across the flight deck. A fiery rain pelted the terrorized crew. McCain was blown backward, tiny bits of shrapnel embedded in his thighs and chest. A larger piece of metal slammed into his radio, which hung across his chest. Struggling to his feet, he looked onto a scene of mind-numbing carnage. Arms and legs tumbled through the air. A body with no head came to rest on the deck near him. The pilot he had been trying to help was dead. The men with the hose, dead. The chief with the fire extinguisher, dead. The crewman who wiped his visor, dead.

Planes exploded on deck. The heat triggered ejection seats, some still manned, blowing them into the burning ether. More bombs cooked off, as did more Zuni rockets, the latter shooting across the flight deck into the flames, as if intent on striking down the inferno touched off by their murderous sibling. Bomb after bomb ignited, rocking the ship, tearing ragged holes in the three-and-a-half-inch-thick reinforced steel flight deck. Burning fuel spilled through the openings onto the hangar deck below. The fire roared on, angry, vengeful, drowning out the cries for help, the shrieks of pain, the final prayers.

Forklifts shoved planes into the sea. Crewmen rolled bombs over the side. A shaken McCain went below. On the hangar deck, to which the fire had spread, someone was trying to unload bombs from a flight elevator before the flames reached them. McCain pitched in. The job done, he staggered into the ready room.

His fellow pilots were in shock. Incredibly, a video camera mounted on the carrier's superstructure was still running, carrying eerily silent real-time images. As the ship's crew battled the fire, McCain and his squadron mates watched the macabre drama unfold on closed-circuit television.

Realizing he was bleeding, McCain went down to sick bay. Crewmen, many little more than kids, lay stretched out before him, stripped naked, horribly burned, in mortal agony. Someone called "Mr. McCain." Following the voice, he moved beside a young man charred beyond recognition, who asked about a chief petty officer in the squadron. "I just saw him, he's fine," said McCain. "Thank God he's okay," said the crewman. Then he died. McCain left sick bay, his wounds untreated.

In the first five minutes after the Zuni ripped through McCain's fuel tank, nine major explosions rocked the *Forrestal.* The fire on the flight deck was brought under control that same afternoon. The fires below raged till the following evening. At one point the skipper considered abandoning ship. When it was all over, 134 men were dead or missing, hundreds more injured. The damage to the ship was put at $72 million, not counting aircraft destroyed.

In the wake of the fire, the *Forrestal* limped to the Philippines to prepare for an inglorious return to the States and a couple of years in the yard for repairs. In port, McCain and others in his squadron were assembled. An officer explained that the *Oriskany*, another carrier on Yankee Station, had been losing pilots and was looking for volunteers to fill the ranks. McCain signed up.

He did not believe in predestination, but his experiences on the *Forrestal*, flying back from the Army-Navy game, and at the bottom of Corpus Christi Bay made him wonder if he had been spared for a reason. God, with whom he maintained a cordial if casual relationship, seemed reluctant to kill him, in fact, appeared to have plans for him. And so He did. For a long time, though, they weren't very nice plans.

The *Oriskany* was coming off the line for a few weeks, so McCain took leave, hopscotching to Hawaii, then to the mainland and on to London, where his father, by now a full admiral, was Commander-in-Chief, U.S. Naval Forces, Europe—CINCUSNAVEUR in Navy parlance. Carol was still touring the Continent with the kids when McCain's mother, Roberta, reached her with news of the fire and John's imminent arrival. After a family reunion, John, Carol, and the children headed for Cannes, where a hotel was offering a free vacation to crew members from the *Forrestal*, in happier days a frequent caller to the ports of the French Riviera.

During the day, John and Carol took the kids to see the sights. After dinner they enjoyed the nightlife. At the Palm Beach Casino, Carol got a whiff of her husband's past.

"Name, *monsieur?*" asked the majordomo, obviously new to the job.

"McCain, John McCain," came the Bond-like reply. Carol remembers heads snapping up, eyes misting over, a small crowd of casino employees closing around them. Clearly, John had been there before, and just as clearly he had not been a piker.

John's orders to the *Oriskany* were delayed. Unsure of his status, the family returned to the Jacksonville area and rented a house in nearby Orange Park that belonged to the parents of a woman whose husband, Bill Lawrence, was a prisoner of war in Hanoi.

Chuck Larson and his wife, Sally, stopped by in September. Larson saw changes in his old running mate. He limited himself to a single highball before dinner, by itself worthy of notice. After the meal, McCain took Larson aside. "I'm concerned," said McCain. "I may have to get out of the Navy." Surprised, Larson asked why. McCain explained that his past had become a burden. A lieutenant commander now, he considered himself a seasoned, competent naval officer, but whenever he joined a new outfit he was dismayed to find that his reputation for mayhem had preceded him.

"I'm serious about the Navy," he said. "If I can't get people to take me seriously, maybe I'll have to try something else."

A few days later his orders to the *Oriskany* came through. He said so long to Carol and the kids, told them to expect him back by early summer.

CHAPTER SIX

The Crown Prince

As John McCain walked out of the pilots' ready room on October 26, 1967, the *Oriskany*'s strike operations officer, Lew Chatham, said, "You'd better be careful. We're probably going to lose someone on this one." Pushing past Chatham, an old friend, McCain shot back, "You don't have to worry about me, Lew."

McCain was charged up. He had been on the *Oriskany* for about a month. The day before he had taken out three MiG fighters sitting nonchalantly on the apron at the Phuc Yen airfield outside Hanoi. Until then, Phuc Yen had been an LBJ-ordained sanctuary for the Soviet-supplied MiGs, which the Americans were permitted to engage in the air but not on the ground. The attack signaled a major escalation of the air war. About time, as far as McCain was concerned. He had flown over the harbor at Haiphong several times while Soviet ships unloaded tons of war materiel, watching as it was trucked away for use against American ground troops, unable to do a thing about it because of the restrictive rules of engagement. Now the rules seemed to be changing. McCain's A-4E Skyhawk was part of a twenty-plane mission getting ready to hit the power plant in Hanoi, another target previously off-limits.

LBJ's forbearance during the two and a half years since the first American ground units landed at Da Nang had given the North Vietnamese time to beef up the air defenses around their key cities, Hanoi and Haiphong. Hanoi was now more heavily defended against air attack than any city in history. McCain was about to learn what that meant.

Closing on the target, he weaved through air bursts and hurtled past SAM missiles that looked like airborne telephone poles. His instrument panel lit up, telling him a SAM had locked onto his aircraft. He punched out some chaff to confuse the missile's guidance system, then rolled in and released his bombs. He was pulling out of his dive when a SAM took off his right wing, sending his plane into a violent downward spiral.

Plunging toward the ground at about four hundred knots, he reached up with both hands and pulled the face curtain. The canopy blew off as small internal rockets shot him skyward, still in his seat, arms flailing wildly from the plane's uncontrolled gyrations. His right knee was broken, probably from smashing into the instrument panel on ejection. He also broke both arms, apparently when he hit the outside air.

Knocked out on ejection, he regained consciousness as he hit the tepid water of a small lake in the center of Hanoi. He sank to the muddy bottom, about fifteen feet down, then kicked back up, gasping for air.

As he sank again, he tried to manipulate the toggles of his life vest to inflate it but discovered that his arms were useless. He pushed up from the bottom a second time but couldn't make it to the top. Fighting to hold his breath, he managed to pull the toggle with his teeth; the vest inflated, and he bobbed to the surface.

He floated around for a minute or two before some soldiers swam out and pulled him into shore. An angry crowd of several hundred Vietnamese had gathered, all seemingly armed. Stripped down to his skivvies, he was kicked and spat on, then bayoneted in the left ankle and left groin. Suddenly the pain from the injuries he incurred on ejection, muted until then, flared through his body. He raised his head, was stunned to see that his right calf was nearly perpendicular to his knee, in an unnatural direction.

As he surveyed the damage, an onlooker slammed a rifle butt down on his shoulder, smashing it. Other Vietnamese responded differently. A man yelled at the crowd to leave him alone. A woman held a cup of tea to his lips as photographers took propaganda pictures. Then uniformed soldiers threw him in the back of a truck for the short ride to Hoa Lo prison, North Vietnam's main penitentiary.

John Hubbell, in his sweeping chronicle of the Vietnam prisoner of war experience, *P.O.W.*, would later write, "No American reached Hoa Lo in worse physical condition than McCain."

At the prison, christened the Hanoi Hilton by its American inmates, McCain was placed on a stretcher on the floor of a cell. After his wounds were bandaged, he was told he would receive no further medical treatment until he agreed to provide military information.

For the next few days he lapsed in and out of consciousness. He was fed small amounts of water and food by a guard. He kept the water down, but vomited the food. His captors, demanding military information, told him that as a war criminal he was not protected by international covenants governing the treatment of prisoners of war. He responded as he had been trained, with name, rank, serial number, and date of birth. Infuriated, his interrogators kicked him and pounded him with their fists.

"That just knocked me out, so the interrogations were fairly short," recalled McCain, as if he had somehow outfoxed the North Vietnamese by getting them to beat him senseless.

Denied medication to blunt the pain, he knew after a few days that he had played out his hand. A guard came in, pulled the blanket off him, exposing his lower body. His knee was the size, shape, and color of a football. He realized he was in shock when it seemed that he could look through his skin and see the blood pooling in his knee. The illusion brought back a terrifying memory. When he was a flight instructor, another pilot had injured himself in a similar manner, by cracking his knee upon ejection. The knee had swelled the same way. The pilot had gone into shock as blood drained into the joint. Then he died.

"Look, if you take me to the hospital, then I'll give you the information you want," he told his interrogator, hoping he could put him off once his wounds were treated.

The camp doctor was summoned. He took McCain's pulse, shook his head, and whispered something to the interrogator.

"Are you going to take me to the hospital?" asked McCain.

"No. It's too late," said the interrogator.

"Look, take me to the hospital and I'll be okay," pleaded McCain.

"It's too late, it's too late," the interrogator replied as he and the doctor walked out.

In shock, panicked, aware that he had been left to die, McCain lay alone in the cell for the next several hours. Then the door opened and a camp official he came to know as the Bug walked in.

"Your father is a big admiral," said the Bug.

"Yes, my father is an admiral," McCain replied, confirming the Bug's suspicions that his countrymen had bagged a most valuable prisoner.

"Now we take you to the hospital," said the Bug.

McCain passed out as he was being transported to the primitive medical facility. He woke up in a room infested with mosquitoes and roaches. Rats scurried over a floor covered with a half inch of water, a by-product of the rainy season then in progress. But McCain was not complaining. He was snug in a metal frame bed, tubes of glucose and blood pouring into his arms.

In London, Jack and Roberta McCain were dressing for a dinner at the Iranian ambassador's residence when the hot line flashed. An admiral at the Pentagon reported that two planes had been shot down over Hanoi. John was flying one of them. No survivors had been spotted.

Jack passed the news on to Roberta. They talked about it, their faith in John's resilience battling their desire not to delude themselves. "What about the dinner?" asked Roberta. Said Jack, "We're going to go and we're going to keep our mouths shut."

Returning home, they received a call from Admiral Thomas Moorer, the Chief of Naval Operations. "We don't think there are any survivors," he said.

In Florida, Carol had already received official notification when Jack and Roberta phoned to pass on what they had heard via the old-boy network.

"Carol, I think Johnny's dead," said Roberta, her voice hollow, devastated. "I think we'd better just accept it."

"I don't think we have to," said Jack.

Said Carol, "I don't intend to. It's not possible."

On October 28, *The New York Times* reported John's downing in a front-page story by Saigon correspondent R. W. Apple, Jr. The headline read, "Adm. McCain's Son, *Forrestal* Survivor, Is Missing in Raid."

After two weeks in the hospital, McCain was shifted to another part of the building where a doctor attempted to set his right arm, broken in three places. He passed out several times during the ninety-minute procedure, performed without anesthesia. The doctor tried repeatedly to manipulate the two floating bones into place, only to have one or the other slip out of alignment. Frustrated, he gave up and slapped on a plaster cast that ran from McCain's waist to his neck. The arm, still unset, jutted forlornly from his body like a television antenna after a windstorm. No effort was made to set his left arm.

The cast still wet, he was moved to a bright, reasonably clean room. An hour later he was visited by a dapper North Vietnamese known as the Cat, the commander of all POW camps in Hanoi. Earlier in the day McCain had been told that a visiting Frenchman wanted to stop by to see him and perhaps take a message back to his family. Fine, said McCain, anxious to let Carol and his parents know he was alive. Now the Cat told him that the Frenchman was a television correspondent who planned to film their conversation.

"I don't want to be filmed," said McCain.

"You need two operations, and if you don't talk to him, then we will take your chest cast off and you won't get any operations," the Cat retorted. "You will say you're grateful to the Vietnamese people, and that you're sorry for your crimes."

McCain said he wouldn't do it.

The Frenchman, François Chalais, arrived with two cameramen. He questioned McCain for several minutes. On the film, shown soon after on CBS Television, McCain looked drugged and fearful, though he answered Chalais's questions cogently. He later ascribed his appearance to fatigue and pain resulting from the abortive bone-setting procedure. Off camera, the Cat prompted him to say that he was grateful for the humane treatment he had received and to demand an end to the war. He refused. When the Cat pressed the point, Chalais stepped in: "I think what he told me is sufficient." He then asked McCain if he had a message for his family. McCain said he loved them and that he was getting well. The Cat again insisted he say that he hoped the war would be over soon so he could go home. He wouldn't do it. Chalais came to his rescue once more, saying he was satisfied. As a parting question, Chalais asked him about the prison food. "Well, it's okay, but it's not Paris," said McCain, the elemental wise-ass strain surfacing briefly.

Once the cameras had departed, he was returned to his old, roach-infested room, where interrogators made frequent visits. Incensed by his refusal to cooperate, they resorted to brutality, slapping and punching him. Once they hit him on his right arm, causing him to emit a bloodcurdling scream. They backed off, as if wary of the hospital authorities. McCain decided that officials at the hospital, if not especially competent, were at least protective of him while under their care. After that, he let loose a loud scream of pain whenever the interrogators became too physical.

For the rest of his hospital stay he was never bathed, never cleaned, never shaved, although his knee was operated on. He was told he needed more surgery on the knee but that he wouldn't get it because of his "bad attitude." American doctors later told him the North Vietnamese had simply cut all the ligaments and cartilage, which meant for nearly his entire time in prison he had only 5 to 10 percent flexion in his knee.

Even with medical care, such as it was, and the apparent desire of his captors to keep him alive, McCain was fading. One night an official came in and said, "The doctors say that you don't get better, that you get worse." McCain replied, "You need to put me with some Americans, because I'm not going to get better here." The following night he was blindfolded and taken by truck from the Hilton to a prison on the outskirts of Hanoi nicknamed the Plantation.

Bud Day, an Air Force pilot, wasn't in much better shape than McCain. After his capture in August 1967, Day was kept in a small underground bunker for several days. He escaped and struck out for the South. After an epic journey that lasted about two weeks, he was recaptured less than a mile from an American military base, the *whop, whop, whop* of U.S. Army choppers clearly audible as he was led back into a captivity that would last another five and a half years. His dash for freedom would eventually win him the Congressional Medal of Honor, one of only two POWs so honored, but the short-term result was public interrogation and torture.

His arms virtually useless after being hung on torture ropes for three hours, he was thrown into a prison called the Zoo, where his roommate, a fellow Air Force major named Norris Overly, began nursing him back to health.

In late December 1967 the Bug, upbeat, told Day that he was small potatoes, a nothing, that the North Vietnamese didn't care about him. He explained that they had just captured two full colonels. "And," said the Bug with a self-satisfied smirk, "we've got the Crown Prince."

The Crown Prince? Day didn't break the code until the next afternoon when he and Overly were moved to the Plantation. Then he remembered Hanoi radio a few weeks earlier boasting about the capture of "air pirate McCain, son of Admiral McCain." Now it made sense. Jack McCain had lectured to Day's class at the Armed Forces Staff College in 1963. Day hoped he would get a chance to meet the admiral's son. Outside his cell, he heard a commotion. The door opened and a prisoner strapped to a board was set down on the floor.

"I've seen some dead that looked at least as good as John," Day would later say. McCain weighed less than one hundred pounds. His hair, flecked with gray since high school, was nearly snow white. Clots of food clung to his face, neck, hair, and beard. His cheeks were sunken, his neck chickenlike, his legs atrophied. His knee bore a fresh surgical slash, his ankle an angry scar from the bayonet wound. The body cast added to his deathly appearance. He seemed to have shriveled up inside it. His right arm, little more than skin and bone, protruded like a stick. But it was McCain's eyes that riveted Day.

"His eyes, I'll never forget, were just burning bright. They were bug-eyed like you see in those pictures of the guys from the Jewish concentration camps. His eyes were real pop-eyed like that. I said, 'The gooks have dumped this guy on us so they can blame us for killing him,' because I didn't think he was going to live out the day."

Suddenly McCain was talking. His voice was weak, little more than a whisper, but Day and Overly were the first Americans he had seen in two months and he had a lot to tell and much he wanted to know. The discussion began in late afternoon and kept going until the early hours of the morning. McCain talked compulsively. He wanted to know about the prison camps, how they were run, what other Americans were being held and where.

At first, Day thought of Overly and himself as gently ushering McCain toward the death they both felt was imminent, as if they were priests performing last rites.

"As the day went on, though, I started to get the feeling that if we could get a little grits into him and feed him and get him cleaned up and the infection didn't get him, he was probably going to make it," said Day. "And that surprised me. That just flabbergasted me because I had given him up.

"I can remember thinking that night, My God, this guy's got a lot of heart. You've been involved in sports and games and things where people kind of rise to an occasion, and that was him. He was rising. And if he hadn't been, he'd have been dead. If he had not had that will to live and that determination, he'd have been dead."

At about three in the morning, in mid-sentence, with Norris Overly massaging his leg, McCain fell asleep. To Bud Day, it was as if God had just switched off the light.

Bud Day helped, but it was Norris Overly who put John McCain together again. First he poured the little water allotted him onto a towel and scrubbed McCain's face, though Day recalled that "the crud and the scuzz were so thick on him that it really didn't help much." Soon Overly was massaging McCain's leg at least two hours a day. He also fed McCain all his meals, leaning him against the wall in his body cast, and helped him relieve himself.

"Overly had to get him up and sit him on the john," said Day. "The john was one of these paint buckets, just a big old metal bucket all rusted up. He would sit him on this thing and get him on there and wipe him. You know, he couldn't do the first thing for himself."

By the second or third day Overly managed to soften up the encrusted filth on McCain's face so that he could scrape it off and shave him. That seemed to boost his spirits. McCain's leg, which had become infected, responded to soap and water. Before long Overly had him on his feet. By early January 1968 he could walk by himself for a few minutes at a time.

Treatment at the Plantation was not overly harsh. At times, Day suspected the Vietnamese were trying to curry favor with McCain and, to a lesser extent, Overly. One day an officer asked McCain if he wanted anything special to eat. He said no, he would eat what everyone else ate. Day concluded that the Plantation was a camp for prisoners the Vietnamese considered candidates for a rumored early-release program. McCain seemed tailor-made for the role. Shipping a senior admiral's son home could harm the morale of other, less well-connected POWs and American fighting men in general. Unknown to McCain, Day, and Overly at the time, Jack McCain had just been named commander-in-chief of all U.S. military forces in the Pacific, including Vietnam—CINCPAC for short—which stood to intensify the propaganda advantage. But the younger McCain would not play along.

"What they were looking for from John was some kind of sign that he was reliable," said Day. "But he didn't give them any kind of a clue that he would help them in any way."

Norris Overly was a different story. One evening he told McCain and Day that the Vietnamese might send him home. "I don't think that's the right thing to do," said Day. Said McCain, "I wouldn't even consider any kind of a release. They'll have to drag me out of here." The only reason to release him, he said, would be to embarrass his father, and he wasn't going to let that happen.

Day and McCain were not indulging in machismo. The Code of Conduct for American Fighting Men, developed by the armed forces after the Korean War, governed the actions of prisoners of war. Key provisions included a prohibition on accepting parole or special favors from the enemy, a requirement that reasonable efforts be made to escape, and, by extension, that any releases prior to the end of hostilities be in order of capture, that is, first in, first out. By early 1968 more than three hundred Americans were in North Vietnamese prison camps, dating back to Navy Lieutenant (jg) Everett Alvarez,

Jr., shot down on August 5, 1964. With certain exceptions, accepting a release under any other conditions was tantamount to breaking faith with fellow prisoners.

The next day Overly was moved out. McCain and Day heard on the grapevine that he and two other prisoners were being prepped for release. On the morning he left, Overly—outfitted in a cheap blue suit—stopped back to see his ex-cellmates. "What did it cost you?" asked Day. He meant the release, not the suit. "Nothing, not a thing, didn't do a thing," said Overly. Neither Day nor McCain pressed the point. Overly and two others—Air Force Captain John Black and Navy Ensign David Matheny—left later that day, February 16, the first participants of what the prisoners left behind dubbed the Fink Release Program. Five years later, when McCain was freed with the rest of the POWs, Overly called him. They spoke briefly. They have talked just once since.

McCain and Day lived together for another month and a half after Overly left. They would struggle arm in arm out to the bathing area or to get their food. As they did so, two other prisoners, Jack Van Loan and Read Mecleary, would tease them, gallows humor tailored to the POW experience: "Hire the handicapped, they're fun to watch." They got along well, with one brief falling-out. One day they killed upwards of four hundred mosquitoes, smashing them against the wall of their cell. They thought they had set a new prison record, only to learn that two other POWs were claiming a one-day kill count of over a thousand. Their jubilation soured, angry words were exchanged.

Day was ten years older, but McCain was the more worldly, regaling his cellmate with tales of youthful carousing and womanizing. He was also more politically sophisticated, having kept his ear to the wall when his parents entertained senators, congressmen, and other bigwigs at their Capitol Hill home. Day said McCain helped him understand how Washington really worked, with emphasis on the human dimension. "I had no idea that the whole damn Kennedy family was banging Marilyn Monroe and those sorts of things," said Day.

They talked about politics and the home front, stimulated by propaganda broadcasts piped into their cells from six in the morning until nine at night. These reports laid great stress on the antiwar movement and political unrest at home.

"Dr. Spock, Dave Dellinger, every wacko that had ever come down the pike and hated the country was on gook radio telling you how bad the United States was and how great Communism was," said Day. "We would talk about the fact that there was no punishment that would adequately deal with these kinds of scuzz that are eating your country, taking all the benefits, and then tearing it apart from the inside."

Vietnamese interrogators encouraged the POWs to repudiate LBJ. In general, they refused to do so, viewing it as unpatriotic and a violation of the Code of Conduct. Privately, Day, McCain, and many others felt Johnson had abandoned them. But one emerging American political figure intrigued Day and McCain: the new governor of California, then completing his first year in office. "We talked about Ronald Reagan being President back in 1967," said Day. "We talked about it frequently."

One day Jack Van Loan peered through a peephole in his cell door and saw a crowd of North Vietnamese dignitaries trudging through the courtyard toward the cell that McCain and Day shared. Nodding sagely, they entered the cubicle. A few minutes later Van Loan heard McCain cut loose with a string of obscenities that knifed through the silence of the cellblock.

"It was some of the most colorful profanity that you would ever hope to hear," said Van Loan. "He was calling them every name in the book and telling them that he was not going home early, that he wasn't going to ask for amnesty and not to ask him that again and to get out—and, furthermore, screw you and the horse you rode in on. John was just shrieking at them.

"Those guys came tumbling back out of there. I mean, they were backing up, and John was just fighting back as best he knew how. They came out of there like tumbleweeds. I was laughing and crying at the same time. They would have lugged him out of there that day and let him go. And here's a guy that's all crippled up, all busted up, and he doesn't know if he's going to live to the next day, and he literally blew them out of there with a verbal assault. You can't imagine the example John set for the rest of the camp by doing that."

As the spring of 1968 approached, McCain proudly showed one of his interrogators how well he was getting around with the ancient pair of wooden crutches he had been using. That night, guards removed Bud Day from the cell, leaving McCain by himself. He was alone for the next two years.

CHAPTER SEVEN

Do You Want to Go Home?

As the weeks in solitary stretched into months, John McCain was indefatigable in trying to make contact with other Americans, routinely defying the edict against communicating with other prisoners. Fellow POWs remember him in those days as an ungainly scarecrow suspended from crutches, loudly taunting his jailers as he limped past on his way to interrogation sessions.

"Fuck you," he yelled at the guards as they hurried him along, aware that other prisoners could see him and were loving every minute of it. "Fuck you, you goddamned slant-eyed cocksuckers."

His antagonism had a macabre looniness to it, like the game but overmatched Black Knight in the movie *Monty Python and the Holy Grail.* Squirming in the dirt, all four limbs lopped off, the Knight shouts after his departing adversary, "Oh, oh, I see. Running away, eh. You yellow bastard!"

Fighting back, even as an exercise in impotence, did a lot for McCain. It got him through the night, kept him sane, helped him maintain his self-respect. Physically, he knew he'd be a wreck if he ever got out of prison, probably crippled. But he was determined to emerge from his incarceration as Salinger's Sergeant X hoped to survive World War II, with all his f-a-c-u-l-t-i-e-s intact.

His Vietnamese guards were willing participants in his self-help program. They responded to his insults by knocking him down, flinging him against the wall, or punching him in the head. Despite the pummelings, McCain suspected he was getting special treatment. The guards seemed under orders to go easy on him unless he grossly violated the rules, at which point they were free to hammer him. Even then they kept their brutality within limits. It was a fine distinction. The Prick, as McCain named his major tormentor, might kick him as he lay on the floor of his cell, but he noticed the jailer never kicked him in his bad right leg. And although the Prick sometimes booted him in the head, he stayed away from his face. McCain knew he was escaping the Prick's full fury; he just didn't know why.

In June 1968, McCain learned the reason. By then he had been undergoing interrogation for months. The sessions fell into a predictable pattern. He refused to cooperate. The North Vietnamese told him he would be tried for war crimes and never go home.

One night the pattern abruptly changed. He was summoned to an unfamiliar room. It had soft chairs and a glass coffee table supported on each end by marble elephants. Usually he was interrogated in a bare cell with a stool for the prisoner and a chair and desk for the questioner.

Major Bai, known to the prisoners as the Cat, was waiting for McCain. As commander of the Hanoi prison system, he orchestrated the effort to break the spirit of American prisoners, by co-opting them if possible, with torture when necessary. A second Vietnamese, known as the Rabbit, stood by to serve as translator.

Cookies, a pot of tea, and cigarettes were on the table. McCain helped himself as the Cat began speaking through the translator. To McCain the conversation had a rambling quality. They talked of McCain's father, other members of his family, the war. Two hours went by. McCain, puzzled, couldn't figure out what the Cat was up to.

Then the Cat mentioned that Norris Overly and the other two freed prisoners had been welcomed home as heroes.

"That's interesting," said McCain, unimpressed.

"Do you want to be released?" said the Cat.

McCain, momentarily speechless, fought to keep his composure.

"Frankly, I don't know," he finally said. "I don't know."

"You go back and think about it," said the Cat.

In his cell, he tapped on the wall, raising his neighbor, Bob Craner. Craner listened to McCain's tale, then told him to take the release. McCain said he didn't think it was right to do so. They went back and forth without resolving the question.

McCain faced a dilemma. He was trying to adhere to the POW interpretation of the Code of Conduct that said prisoners could accept release only in order of capture. That meant Everett Alvarez and a lot of others should go home before he did. But the Code, as construed by the prisoners in North Vietnam, provided an exception for the seriously sick and injured, saying they should receive priority. The exception was driving McCain crazy. He was in wretched physical condition. Crippled, emaciated from months of dysentery, he doubted he could last another year in captivity.

Three nights later the Cat sent for him again. Same pleasant room, more hours of aimless conversation. Finally, from the Cat, "Do you want to go home?" McCain: "No."

He explained the Code of Conduct and said Alvarez should be the first to go. The Cat said the Code did not apply to war criminals. Then he announced that Lyndon Johnson had ordered him home. That got the Cat nowhere, so he took out a letter from Carol to McCain. She said she wished he had been one of the three prisoners who had come home. Until then, none of her letters had reached him. He took his wife's sentiments for what they were, an expression of love, not an exhortation to break faith with his comrades.

The Cat told him that the doctors said he couldn't survive much longer unless he returned to the States for treatment. That unsettled him since he had been agonizing over the same issue himself. But the assertion rang false. He hadn't seen a physician in months.

"Guess they're keeping in touch with my case by long distance," he said.

"Do you want to go home?"

"No."

Three days later, July 3, the Cat again summoned McCain, this time to one of the regular interrogation rooms. The Cat and the Rabbit sat at a table, McCain on a low stool in front of them. The Cat fumbled nervously with a fountain pen.

"The officer wants to know your final answer," said the Rabbit.

"My final answer is the same," said McCain. "It's no. I cannot accept this offer."

"That is your final answer?"

"That is my final answer."

The Cat, incensed, all traces of civility gone, crushed the pen in his hand, splattering the room with ink.

"They taught you too well," he said in perfect English. "They taught you too well."

Rising brusquely, knocking over his chair, he stormed out of the room, slamming the door behind him.

McCain and the Rabbit stared at each other. "Now, McCain, it will be very bad for you," said the Rabbit.

Shit, thought McCain.

For the next few days he lived in terror, trembling at each sound in the corridor, knowing beyond question that his refusal to accept a release meant the good times were over. But nothing happened. A sense of relief began to take hold. He didn't trust it.

He was right. A week later he was braced in a stark room before Slopehead, the camp commander. Ten guards were standing by, including McCain's old pal, the Prick.

Slopehead told McCain he was a "black criminal" who had broken all the camp regulations. He must confess his crimes. McCain said he wouldn't.

"Why are you so disrespectful of guards?" asked Slopehead.

"Because the guards treat me like an animal," snapped McCain.

The Prick gleefully led the charge as the guards, at Slopehead's command, drove fists and knees and boots into McCain. Amid laughter and muttered oaths, he was slammed from one guard to another, bounced from wall to wall, knocked down, kicked, dragged to his feet, knocked back down, punched again and again in the face. When the beating was over, he lay on the floor, bloody, arms and legs throbbing, ribs cracked, several teeth broken off at the gumline.

"Are you ready to confess your crimes?" asked Slopehead.

"No."

The ropes came next. McCain had never been in torture ropes, but he had heard about them from Bud Day and others. He was moved to another cell where his arms, battered, broken, and bruised in one way or another since the day he was shot down, were lashed behind his back, then cinched tightly together to intensify the pain. He was left on a stool. Throughout the night, guards came in, asked him if he was ready to confess, then smashed their fists into him when he told them no.

The next several days fell into a harrowing routine. The ropes came off in the morning. Beatings were administered throughout the day, usually by one guard, sometimes two. On occasion two guards would hold him up while a third hammered him senseless. At night the ropes were reapplied.

After a couple of days, he got some water. He was also given a bucket so he could relieve himself. Often he was so battered he could barely crawl to the bucket. Still plagued by dysentery, he often regained consciousness to find himself lying in his own waste. During one beating, staggered by a fist to the face, he slumped to the floor, smashing his left arm into the bucket, breaking it again. But he was back in torture ropes that night.

Each time the guards came in, they asked if he was ready to confess. After about a week, he knew he could not hold out any longer. Years later he would write, "I had learned what we all learned over there: Every man has a breaking point. I had reached mine."

Guards moved him to a separate building and set him to work on a confession. Like Americans before him, he tried to write in generalities, working in misspellings, grammatical errors, stilted phrases, and Communist jargon—constantly referring to Ho Chi Minh as "beloved and respected leader"—anything to make clear that it was a

forced confession. He and an interrogator wrote and rewrote for about twelve hours. He was told to say that he bombed a school. The final draft was written by the interrogator. In it, McCain said, "I am a black criminal and I have performed deeds of an air pirate. I almost died, and the Vietnamese people saved my life, thanks to the doctors. . . ." Aching and exhausted, he signed it.

Back in a cell, cut off from Bob Craner and other Americans, McCain told himself that he had held out as long as he was capable, longer than most men. But he could find no solace in excuses. No matter how he tried to sugarcoat his actions, he could not avoid the conclusion that he had dishonored his country, his family, and himself, betrayed his comrades, and besmirched the flag.

The cockiness was gone, replaced by a suffocating despair. He looked at the louvered cell window high above his head, then at the small stool in the room. He took off his dark blue prison shirt, rolled it like a rope, draped one end over his shoulder near his neck, began feeding the other end through the louvers.

A guard burst into the room, pulling McCain away from the window. The guard then administered another beating. For the next few days he was watched day and night.

"I don't know whether I would have actually gone through with it or not," said McCain as he sat in his Senate office two decades later. "I have no idea. I kind of doubt it."

But could it have happened? "It could have." He did not know at the time of his aborted suicide attempt that virtually every American who refused to cooperate with the North Vietnamese, including those widely viewed as the most courageous—Bud Day; Jim Stockdale, who disfigured himself by battering his face with a stool rather than make a public confession; Jeremiah Denton, who spelled out t-o-r-t-u-r-e in Morse code by batting his eyes at a television camera—had all been broken, often more than once. Now he knows, but it doesn't make any difference.

"I still believe that I failed," he said. The words came slowly, as if his father and grandfather were in the room, measuring him, not

pleased with what they were seeing. "I'm convinced that I did the best that I could, but the best that I could wasn't good enough."

As John McCain flirted with suicide, Jack McCain was two thousand miles away in Hawaii assuming command of the Pacific Theater. As CINCPAC, he was now the senior military man in the operational area that included Vietnam.

Flying to his new headquarters in Honolulu, he and Roberta picked up Carol in Jacksonville so she could attend the change-of-command ceremony. It was held in Pearl Harbor, aboard the *Oriskany*, the carrier John was flying off when he was shot down.

Those who knew Jack McCain during those years said he never brought up John's plight. When others did, he diplomatically changed the subject. But they also recall that he spent every Christmas for three years running with the Marines on the DMZ so he could be closer to his son.

During the dark and brutal days following McCain's refusal to accept early release, Charlie Plumb and Kay Russell were in a cell about twenty yards from him. They didn't know who their mystery neighbor was, but they could tell he was in sorry shape. Day after day they saw rags thrown out the cell door. Before the camp dogs got to the rags, Plumb and Russell could see they were covered with blood, pus, and scabs. They tried various ways to contact the unknown prisoner but received no response. Plumb finally got a chance to walk past the cell. As he did so, he whistled a few bars of "Anchors Aweigh."

Toooot Toot Toot Toot
Toot-toot
Toot Toot Toot Toot.

After a second or two there came a feeble response.

Toooot Toot Toot Toot
Toot-toot.

Plumb and Russell now knew their neighbor was a Navy man, but they still could not figure out who he was. One day, in addition to the rags, a pile of hair, human hair, much of it brilliant white human hair, was piled outside the cell.

"There's only one guy in the world with phosphorescent hair," said Plumb.

"John McCain must be down," replied Russell.

News traveled slowly in prison. By then, McCain had been a captive for nearly ten months.

CHAPTER EIGHT

'Tis the Season to Be Jolly

C*hristmas Eve, 1968. Hanoi.*

"You are going to a church service," a guard told John McCain.

McCain had been in solitary since Bud Day was removed from his cell nine months earlier. He was fifteen months into his captivity, deathly pale, eyes sunken, arms twisted, "as though he had suffered polio," according to author John Hubbell.

He hobbled into a spacious room gaily decorated with flowers. About fifty POWs were seated on benches, spaces between them to discourage conversation. An aging Vietnamese clergyman presided at a makeshift altar. A small choir of Americans was singing seasonal hymns. A noisy pack of photographers jostled for position at the rear and sides of the room. Movie cameras rolled, flashbulbs popped.

McCain decided to ruin the picture. Acting as if he owned the place, he smiled and waved at other prisoners. "No talking, no talking," warned the guard as he escorted him to his seat.

"Fuck that," said McCain. Turning to the nearest American, he said, "Hey, pal, my name's John McCain. What's yours?"

"McCain, stop talking," cooed a smiling guard called Soft Soap Fairy, aware that he was on camera.

"Fuck you," said McCain, louder than before. "This is fucking bullshit. This is terrible. This isn't Christmas. This is a propaganda show."

McCain hastily briefed his new friend. "I refused to go home. I was tortured for it. They broke my rib and rebroke my arm . . ."

"No talking!"

"Fuck you!" said McCain, momentarily interrupting his briefing. Resuming, he said, "Our senior ranking officer is—"

"No talking!" said the Prick, who had rushed to a spot just outside camera range to try to control his favorite prisoner.

"Fu-u-u-u-ck you, you son of a bitch!" shouted McCain, hoisting a one-finger salute whenever a camera pointed in his direction.

Returned to his cell, he awaited the retribution of his jailers. Nothing happened that night or the following day. It was, after all, Christmas. The next day the anticipated pounding materialized, like a present delayed in the mail.

C*hristmas Eve, 1969. Hanoi.*

Christmas carols over the loudspeaker, every other song "I'll Be Home for Christmas," the Dinah Shore version. McCain, still in solitary, was squatting in his cell when the door swung open. The Cat entered.

McCain was wary. A year and a half earlier the Cat had unleashed his goons when McCain refused to take early release. This time the Cat was in a reflective, seemingly sentimental mood, as if he wanted nothing more than conversation.

He showed McCain the small diamond embedded in his tie clip. McCain, the gracious host, complimented him on it. "Yes," said the Cat, "I received this from my father, and my grandfather before him had this tie clip." He pulled out a cigarette case, told McCain it was made from the fuselage of an Air Force Thud bomber.

"I know you miss your family," said the Cat.

"Well, I miss them, but I think this war is going to last for a very long time," replied McCain.

"Yes, you are right," said the Cat. "That's why you should have accepted my offer."

"Someday you'll understand why I could never accept that offer," said McCain.

"I may understand more than you think," said the Cat.

The conversation meandered here and there for about an hour, long enough for McCain to smoke a dozen of the Cat's cigarettes. The Cat reminisced about his family, the war, this one against the Americans and the previous one against the French, where he had been, what he had done. He asked about Christmas and how it was celebrated in America, explained Tet to McCain, what it meant, the customs surrounding it.

McCain concluded that the Cat had no hidden agenda, that this was just a time-out, akin to the brief fraternization between German and Allied troops during the first Christmas of World War I.

The Cat got up to go.

"Merry Christmas," he said.

"Thank you," said McCain.

Christmas Eve, 1969. Philadelphia.

Carol and the children were spending the holidays, the third without John, at her parents' home. At one point she burst into tears in front of the kids.

"You don't let us cry, so you're not allowed to cry, either," said Andy.

"Okay, you're right," said Carol.

After dinner she decided to drop off some presents at her friends, the Bookbinders. The task completed, she started home. It was snowing and the roads were icy. She turned onto a lonely country road. Approaching an intersection, she misjudged the stopping distance, hit the brakes, skidded, and rammed into a telephone pole.

She was thrown from the car into the snow. Alone, in unbearable pain, she went into shock. Some time later, police responding to a routine report of an abandoned vehicle found her unconscious body by the side of the road.

At Bryn Mawr Hospital, physicians pumped blood into her. "If you can hear us, wiggle your fingers," a doctor said. She did, or thought she did, until she heard the doctor say, "If you can hear us, blink your eyes."

She passed in and out of consciousness for the next day or so. She overheard doctors discussing whether or not to amputate her left leg. Terrified, she tried to scream, No, don't do that. I'll be fine. But it was several days before she could speak.

When her condition was stabilized, the doctors put her in the picture. Both legs were smashed, her pelvis and arm broken. Internal injuries included a ruptured spleen. She was told she might never walk again, but amputation was ruled out.

She spent the next six months in the hospital, undergoing a series of operations. She made friends with a doctor and his wife. After several months they brought her to their home for the afternoon, all eighty pounds of her, complete with cast, braces, wheelchair, and catheter.

Over the next two years she had twenty-three operations. By the time the surgeons finished with her, she was five foot four, four inches shorter than before the accident. She was confined to a wheelchair, one leg in a cast, the other in a brace.

Back in Jacksonville she began physical therapy twice a day at the naval hospital. The operations continued, but by late in the year the cast was off and she could get around on crutches.

Soon after the accident, the doctors had said they would try to get word to John about her injuries. No, she said, he's got enough problems, I don't want to tell him.

And she never did.

Christmas, 1970. Hanoi.

Guards transferred McCain from Thunderbird into a section of the Hilton called Camp Unity. They put him in a large room with upward of fifty other Americans, among them Bud Day. McCain couldn't believe his good fortune. It was the perfect Christmas present. In the thirty-three months since he and Day were separated in March 1968, he had spent thirty-one months in solitary.

CHAPTER NINE

Long Tall Sally

Among the American prisoners in North Vietnam, the appetite for knowledge was insatiable, not merely as a diversion but as an intellectual stimulant, a device to keep their minds from going to seed.

Orson Swindle, a tall, rangy Marine fighter pilot out of Georgia Tech, mastered six thousand words of German, thanks to a prison friend. Jim Warner, a Marine flyer who later worked in the Reagan White House, learned integral and differential calculus from his fellow inmates, then wrote a calculus textbook on sheets of cigarette paper. One day Jim Stockdale received a message from Bob Shumaker, relayed by finger code by Nels Tanner: "If you get stuck alone, remember that *e* to the *x* is equal to the sum, from *n* equals one to *n* equals infinity, of the expression *x* to the *n* minus one, over *n* minus one, factorially."

The POWs had one mental exercise in common. They committed to memory the name of every prisoner they knew of, which eventually included almost all of the nearly six hundred aviators in captivity. This mind game was serious business. Suspicious of Vietnamese claims that they had made public an accurate prisoner list, the Americans wanted to be ready for any opportunity to smuggle out a complete roster. Instead of counting sheep, John McCain dozed off reciting names to himself.

At Camp Unity, McCain and Swindle joined forces to teach a

course in English and American literature. Their lectures had a Classic Comics flavor, but they prepared as rigorously as college professors. The course included the works of Fielding, Melville, Kipling, Conrad, Hemingway, Fitzgerald, and Maugham. McCain, on his own, taught a social studies class. Never one to underplay his hand, he called it The History of the World from the Beginning.

There were less academic pursuits. McCain and Swindle pooled their knowledge of movies to entertain the troops, telling the story and doing bits and pieces of dialogue. The shows became an evening ritual, Monday Night at the Movies, Tuesday Night at the Movies, and so on. The regulars would arrive early, squat down in front, lay out a stash of cigarettes, their own and those they were able to scrounge from nonsmokers, and wait for the performance to begin. Whatever the other drawbacks, at least you could smoke at the movies in Hanoi.

"I did over a hundred movies, some of which I'd never seen," said McCain. A favorite was *One-Eyed Jacks*, in part because it contained a popular all-purpose epithet, "scum-sucking pig," which many POWs deemed dead-solid perfect for LBJ and various antiwar figures.

In early 1971 the prisoners at Camp Unity defied the North Vietnamese and held a church service, then staged a near-riot when three of their leaders were marched off in irons. Once it was over, Bud Day, the ringleader, and his partners in crime, McCain among them, were shipped off to Skid Row, a punishment camp.

The living conditions, rather than the behavior of the guards, accounted for the camp's reputation. The rooms were tiny, about six feet by three feet, the food terrible, the sanitation even worse. Jaundice and dysentery were rampant. Several prisoners came down with hepatitis. "Really bad," said McCain. "I mean, there were turds floating around in the well."

McCain and the rest of the Skid Row crew were returned to the more commodious Camp Unity in November 1971. McCain spent most of his remaining imprisonment there, though he was moved for a time to a small camp near the Chinese border called Dogpatch and spent the weeks before his release back at the Plantation.

The prisoners coasted through the last year or so of their captivity. The guards were generally tolerant, the food improved, and the men rallied physically. Two years before, McCain weighed 105 pounds, was covered with boils, and suffered from dysentery. Now he was fit enough to work out daily. Soon he was doing forty-five push-ups and a couple of hundred sit-ups, more than he could do before he was shot down.

Normal human needs, submerged by years of physical deprivation, reasserted themselves. Men talked warmly about their families and how much they missed them. McCain dreamily told his friends about his wife, the sleek ex-model, "Long Tall Sally," as he affectionately referred to Carol.

Orson Swindle remembered the John McCain of this period: "He looked sort of funny when he talked to you. He just couldn't move his arms very much, nothing above his shoulders. Yet the rascal was over there doing push-ups. They were a funny sort of push-ups, sort of tilted. And he would run in place. We occupied a lot of our time with exercises, and he was stiff-legged, bouncing as best he could running in place. And an absolute chain-smoker. I've seen John have two or three cigarettes lighted at the same time."

Some things never change. Despite the dismal conditions, most of the POWs took pains to maintain a soldierly appearance. After washing their shirts and trousers, they stretched them out on the stone floor, using the flat of the hand to press out the wrinkles and iron in sharp military creases. Once the garments had dried, the men carefully folded and stored them under their bedding. Not McCain. He tied knots in the legs of a pair of trousers, then jammed the rest of his clothes down into them, as if he were stuffing a scarecrow. Swindle, echoing McCain's Annapolis roommates, told him he was the sloppiest man he had ever met.

Richard Nixon resumed sustained bombing of North Vietnam in April 1972, three and a half years after LBJ declared a bombing halt. The POWs were overjoyed by Nixon's action.

"We knew at the time that unless something very forceful was done that we were never going to get out of there," McCain later said. "We were fully aware that the only way we were ever going to get out was for our government to turn the screws on Vietnam. So we were very happy. We were cheering and hollering."

It was Nixon's decision, but Jack McCain, as CINCPAC, actually issued the orders that dispatched the bombers to the skies over Hanoi, in effect directing the bombardment of the city where his son was held captive.

Jack hid the strain well, though not from his wife, Roberta. She remembered that after John was shot down, her husband would retire to his study for an hour every morning and night, get down on his knees, and read his Bible. "He was," she said, "in agony."

Nixon suspended the bombing when the Paris Peace Talks appeared on the verge of a breakthrough in the fall of 1972. But the talks broke down, and in mid-December, Nixon resumed heavy air attacks on Hanoi, Haiphong, and other major North Vietnamese cities by B-52s based on Guam. Though no B-52s flew on Christmas Day, the attacks became known as the Christmas Bombing and ignited a fresh storm of controversy at home.

There was little second-guessing among the guests at the Hanoi Hilton when the bombs began to fall about an hour after dark on December 18. Though the closest landed thousands of yards away, the explosions shook the ground of the prison compound and caused plaster to fall from the ceilings. The prisoners cheered, and cries of "Let's hear it for President Nixon!" swept the cellblocks.

At first the North Vietnamese had a large stockpile of SAMs on hand, capable of knocking down a B-52 at thirty thousand feet. When they scored a hit, the explosion lit the sky, and the aircraft plunged to earth like a gigantic flare in free-fall. But as the bombardment continued day after deadly day, the SAM supply dwindled.

"The bombers kept coming, and we kept cheering," Jim Stockdale would later write. "Guards who were normally enraged by loud talk, guards who normally thrust their bayoneted rifles through the bars and screamed at us if we dared shout during air raids, could be seen silently cowering in the lee of the prison walls, their faces ashen in the light reflected from the fiery skies above."

In Stockdale's view, the North Vietnamese could hardly find comfort in a burning B-52 tumbling from the sky. "For the North Vietnamese to see that and the bomber stream continuing to roll right on like old man river was a message in itself—proof that all that separated Hanoi from doomsday was American forbearance, an American national order to keep the bombs out on the hard military targets. We prisoners knew this was the end of North Vietnamese resistance, and the North Vietnamese knew it, too."

Nixon halted the bombing on December 30. Formal negotiations resumed in Paris on January 8, 1973. On January 23 the President announced that an agreement had been reached to end direct American involvement in the war. The provisions called for the accord to be read to all the prisoners. They were formed in ranks for the ceremony. On orders from their superiors in the prisoner chain of command, they displayed no emotion when the section providing for their staged release was read. The cease-fire went into effect January 28.

Henry Kissinger, the chief American negotiator, later told McCain that when he was in Hanoi to sign the treaty documents, the North Vietnamese said he could take one man back to Washington with him: John McCain. Kissinger said he refused the offer. McCain thanked him.

The initial group of prisoners was flown out of Hanoi on February 12, 1973. In line with the "first in, first out" rule, they were led to the plane by Everett Alvarez, in captivity since August 1964. Jim Stockdale and Jeremiah Denton followed close behind.

McCain, slated to leave with the third group, was moved back to the Plantation on January 20. He and his comrades were fitted with trousers, shirts, windbreakers, and shoes. The guards left them alone, the food got better, but time dragged despite card games, sex talks, and the occasional flare-up.

Playing bridge, Orson Swindle and his partner trounced McCain and his partner.

"I was just teasing the hell out of John," said Swindle. "And he got mad with me, and he got all puffed up because he hates to lose. . . . He had this peg leg of his, he's limping and everything. He's just fuming. And this goes on for a couple of days. He wouldn't even speak to me."

A few nights later guards called off the names of several prisoners, including Swindle's, and told them to roll up their gear. They were going home. McCain, stricken, rushed over to Swindle, told him he was his best friend, apologized for being a shit.

"Don't even talk to me, you little shrimp," said Swindle, cutting him no slack.

Swindle was released on March 4. A few days later he found himself in a hospital bed in Jacksonville, not far from where Carol was living in Orange Park.

"I want to see Carol McCain," he told his doctors. To prepare her for the shock of seeing John, he explained.

"He'd been hurt, and it showed," Swindle later said. "I just wanted to tell her that John's okay. His mind is great. He's a little broken up, but the therapy is going to cure that."

The next day he was told that Carol was on her way to see him. He climbed out of bed to greet her, peered down the long corridor, spotted her as she came through a set of double doors. From the deep dip in her gait he could see she was severely crippled. He was stunned, knew John had no idea anything had happened to her.

"God," he said to himself, "how much do we have to endure?"

A day or so before he was released on March 14, McCain was summoned by a team of North Vietnamese officials. He noticed a tape recorder in the room.

"The doctors have been asking about your condition," said one of the officials.

"That's interesting," replied McCain.

"You know, the doctors that operated on you," the official said.

"Oh, yes," said McCain.

"We wonder if you would like to say a word of thanks to the doctors for the operation on your leg," the official continued.

"Well, not exactly," said McCain, "but I'm extremely curious since I haven't seen the assholes for five years why they should have their curiosity aroused at this point."

McCain and the official stared at each other.

"I know they've been awfully busy," said McCain, a ball-buster to the end.

On receiving the news that John was free and had landed in the Philippines, Carol called the kids into the house, which she had filled in her husband's absence with all sorts of animals—dogs, cats, birds, fish, gerbils.

"Your daddy is coming home," she said. "He is out. They cannot get him anymore."

Andy and Doug cheered. Sidney, who was six, looked puzzled.

"Where will he sleep?" she asked.

"He will sleep in my bed, with me," replied Carol.

Sidney thought that over for a few seconds.

"And what will we feed him?" she asked.

CHAPTER TEN

Reentry

Free at last, a smiling John McCain hobbled down the steps of an Air Force C-141 at Clark Air Base in the Philippines on March 14, 1973. He was greeted at the foot of the ramp by Admiral Noel Gayler, who had relieved his father as CINCPAC the previous year. *The New York Times* ran a picture of his descent from the plane on its front page the next day, attesting to his celebrity status among the returning POWs.

A team of debriefers was standing by to break the news of Carol's injuries. Before they could do so, a well-meaning officer, unaware that John knew nothing of his wife's injuries, said, "Carol's been doing fine since her accident."

Later in the day, after he had been put in the picture, he called Carol in Jacksonville.

"There's something I've got to tell you," she said.

"I already know," said John.

"What do you know?" asked Carol.

"I know you had an accident."

"John, it was really bad. You might be upset when you see me."

"Well, you know, I don't look so good myself. It's fine."

At Clark he was poked and prodded by doctors and fitted with a false tooth, easing his snaggle-toothed appearance. When not closeted with doctors, he read hungrily, trying to fill in the five-and-a-half-year gap in his life. He already knew about the bad things that had happened since he was shot down in October 1967—the Kennedy and King assassinations and Watergate, news his captors were only too eager to provide. He had learned indirectly of the 1969 moon landing, the camp loudspeakers having blared out a 1972 campaign speech in which George McGovern said Nixon could put a man on the moon but he couldn't put an end to the war. Beyond that, he was pretty much in the dark.

After a few days at Clark, he was flown home to Jacksonville. Appropriately enough, he got there on a holiday, Saint Patrick's Day. For years Carol and the kids had lived from one holiday to the next. Maybe he'll be home by the Fourth of July, or Thanksgiving, or Groundhog Day, she would say, breaking time into more easily digestible chunks for the children. He was on crutches when he arrived, as were Carol and fourteen-year-old Doug, who had broken a leg playing soccer. The *Jacksonville Times-Union and Journal* headlined its story of the homecoming: "No Limps in Joy of McCain Family Reunion." Carol laughed when she saw it: "I thought, of course, we would live happily ever after."

Carol rented a small beach house at South Ponte Vedra, about forty-five minutes from their Orange Park home, so that she and John could have some time alone. She gently questioned him about prison. At first he did not want to talk about it. Finally, he said, "Do you really want to know what happened?" Said Carol, "I really do." Over the next few days he told her all of it.

"What didn't you buy while I was in Vietnam that you'd really like to have?" he asked her one day. Without hesitation she replied, "A house at the beach." A few days later, on a walk along the oceanfront, they stopped in front of a small cinderblock bungalow. Beaming, John said, "I just bought it."

In the years to come they would add a bedroom with a large fireplace, and a porch, then a deck. On a visit, POW friend Bob Craner helped John build a railing to make it easier for Carol to get over the dunes to the beach. Carol thought of the beach house as heaven, the nicest present she had ever received. Eight years later she sold it, unable to imagine ever setting foot in it again.

Unlike most Vietnam veterans, McCain and the other POWs were welcomed home as heroes. To many Americans they were. To others they symbolized the national catharsis that effectively marked the end of the nation's participation in the Vietnam War. There were parades in their honor, speeches lauding their gallantry, a visit to the White House. In a memorable UPI photo, McCain is seen in dress whites, awkwardly draped over his crutches, a spectral stick figure shaking hands with the President, Richard Nixon.

As in Hanoi, McCain at home was one of the best-known prisoners. In May, two months after his return, he wrote an article on his imprisonment for *U.S. News & World Report.* The magazine devoted thirteen pages to the piece, entitled, "Inside Story: How the POWs Fought Back." It ran with a sidebar, "Three Generations of a Famous Navy Family," with pictures of his father and grandfather.

McCain ended his article by saying, in words that hinted at the politician to come, "I had a lot of time to think over there, and came to the conclusion that one of the most important things in life—along with a man's family—is to make some contribution to his country."

The tone of the article was significant, too. There was anger toward his captors, but he seemed remarkably free of bitterness toward those of his countrymen who had opposed the war. Unlike many other returning POWs, he did not get apoplectic over the dramatic changes in social mores, either.

"Now that I'm back, I find a lot of hand-wringing about this country," he wrote. "I don't buy that. I think America today is a better country than the one I left nearly six years ago."

In the weeks and months that followed his homecoming, he led parades, gave dozens of speeches, received scores of letters from young people, many containing POW bracelets bearing his name that the senders had worn during his captivity. He called the outpouring of goodwill toward him and the other ex-prisoners "staggering, and a little embarrassing."

The public adulation did not fully explain his measured reaction to American society of the 1970s. He was, probably without realizing it, in the process of reinventing himself. Although the irreverent, fun-loving aspect of his personality remained intact, he was older and more mature. As his heroism in prison became more widely known, he began to move beyond the long shadows cast by his father and grandfather and his own zany reputation. Most important, he recognized himself as a survivor and wondered anew what that meant. Prison could now be added to the crash into Corpus Christi Bay, the fiery holocaust on the *Forrestal*, the last-second ejection over the Eastern Shore, the power lines in Spain. God, it seemed, was keeping him around for a reason.

The Lord's plan, whatever it was, did not appear to include remaining in the Navy. Both his arms, objects of sustained abuse in prison, were in wretched condition. He could raise neither above shoulder level. One shoulder socket had been smashed beyond repair by a rifle butt. The major problem, though, was his right knee, which he could bend at most five degrees.

After the short interlude with Carol at the beach, he entered the naval hospital in Jacksonville. The doctors decided to leave most of his injuries alone. Too much time had passed; little could be done about them. He had two operations on his knee, removing scar tissue and otherwise trying to free up the joint. At the end of his hospitalization, which lasted about three months, he was only able to bend it ten degrees, and the prognosis was not good. In the case of McCain and the other returning POWs, however, the Navy was careful not to be seen as rushing men who had endured so much into premature retirement.

For McCain it was not enough to stay in the Navy. He wanted to fly again. The doctors told him to forget it, that flying was out of the question, but he was determined to prove them wrong even if he had no idea how he was going to do it.

The answer came in a phone call he received that summer. By then he was a student at the National War College at Fort McNair, in southwest Washington.

You don't know me, said Diane Rauch, but I'm a physical therapist and I want to help you.

McCain had been taking physical therapy at Bethesda Naval Hospital, but the trek from his home in Alexandria to Fort McNair and the hospital north of Washington was taking a toll. Moreover, he did not see himself benefiting much from the treatment, which the doctors said would provide only twenty-five degrees of flexion at best. Diane said she could do better and suggested he talk to her other patients, including Sonny Jurgensen, the Washington Redskins quarterback, whom she had treated for a shoulder injury. McCain was impressed, but there was a problem. The Navy would not pay for a private therapist when it had a facility of its own in the area providing a similar service.

I know, said Diane. I'll do it free. I'd consider it an honor.

She did more than that. When she learned another member of the family was in bad shape, she told her partner, Barbara Devine, who volunteered to treat Carol free of charge as well.

Over the next year, Diane worked on John's frozen knee for two hours a day, twice a week. She called her procedure manipulation/mobilization. McCain called it the pain method. After he had spent a half hour in the whirlpool, Diane braced her shoulder behind his knee and slowly tried to bend it. He never screamed, just said, "That's it, honey," when her efforts became unbearable. After a few minutes, she repeated the process, bending the knee a dozen times a session. She was a hard taskmaster, but she relaxed one of her standing rules for him: He was the only person she ever let smoke in the whirlpool.

Progress was slow, the pain excruciating—ten on a scale of ten, according to Diane. On good days he gained two degrees of new flexion. Sometimes a week or more went by with nothing to show for it. But by the end of eight months, he could bend his knee a full ninety degrees.

The McCains repaid the favor. Diane was separated from her husband, a Navy admiral, so they introduced her to a POW friend, Bill Lawrence. Of all the men he knew in prison, McCain most admired Lawrence. At Annapolis he had been a star athlete and brigade commander. In Vietnam he was a quiet presence, the man everyone leaned on when times were bad. Returning home after nearly six years, he learned that his wife had divorced him and remarried. Diane Rauch and Bill Lawrence were married in August 1974. Four years later he became superintendent of the Naval Academy.

Near the end of his time at the War College, determined to regain flying status, McCain went to Pensacola for a medical screening. He demanded that the doctors strictly adhere to the detailed list of physical parameters, not simply look him over and decide on the basis of what their eyes told them that he could not fly again. He could bend his knee ninety degrees, the minimum requirement for pilots. Some of his other ailments did not seem to be listed at all, probably because it stood to reason that no one so afflicted could hope to pilot a plane. Somehow, he was cleared to fly. He later joked that he probably wouldn't have been able to get his arm up high enough to pull the curtain if he ever had to bail out again.

At the War College, John McCain decided to find out what historical forces had combined to land him in a North Vietnamese prison. He designed a personal tutorial on Vietnam. For the next year he read whatever he could find about Vietnamese society, politics, and the wars, the one the Americans were just finishing as well as the French debacle that preceded it.

He read the classics, Bernard Fall's *Street Without Joy* and *Hell in a Very Small Place*, Graham Greene's *The Quiet American*, everything on Dien Bien Phu.

He also looked closely at American decision-making, as described in David Halberstam's landmark chronicle *The Best and the Brightest* and in the supersecret government documents known as the Pentagon Papers, leaked to the press in 1971 by Daniel Ellsberg, a Pentagon official who ardently supported the war early on but later had a change of heart.

McCain never turned against the war or apologized for his part in it. Nor did he portray himself as a pawn in the grip of forces beyond his control. "Nobody made me fly over Vietnam," he said publicly on more than one occasion. "Nobody drafts you into doing those kinds of things. That's what I was trained to do and that's what I wanted to do."

Some of his judgments were harsh, but he confined them mostly to the power structure. Political and military leaders had grossly underestimated the will and resiliency of the enemy. Senior military men had been delinquent in other ways. Most if not all recognized that the strategy employed was not merely flawed but doomed to failure. "The military leadership wouldn't stand up and be counted," he said. As far as he was concerned, the top generals and admirals should have resigned in protest, preferably en masse, his father included.

As for members of the antiwar movement, he did not buy their reasoning, but he endorsed their right to demonstrate against government policy. "The freedom they were exercising was what I was fighting for," he said.

He even took a live-and-let-live attitude toward draft dodgers. "They have to judge whether they conducted their lives in the best fashion, not me," he said. "God knows I've made enough mistakes in my life and did enough things wrong and continue to do enough things wrong without being a judge of others."

To the extent he admitted any anger, it was toward a system that put the burden of service on the poor and the powerless, then through mismanagement, duplicity, and political cowardice allowed nearly sixty thousand young men to die for vaporous national goals: "Those who were better off economically did not carry out their obligations, so we forced the Hispanic, the ghetto black, and the Appalachian white to fight and die. That to me was the greatest crime and injustice of the Vietnam War."

The year at the War College helped McCain come to terms with Vietnam. At the end of his tutorial he felt he understood enough about the war to set it aside and move on. He was determined not to become a professional POW, partly because it was not his nature, mostly because it meant living in the past, which did not interest him. "I don't talk about prison because it bores the shit out of me," he once said.

As much as any POW, McCain transformed his prison experience into a positive force in his life, one from which he drew strength and, eventually, power, but which by an awesome act of will he refused to dwell on. "Just as I profited from my first year at the Naval Academy, which I didn't enjoy, I profited from my time in prison, which I didn't enjoy." At times it came back to haunt him. Usually, though, what he felt came out in small ways, often in an eruption of temper out of all proportion to the provocation.

"You either go in one of two directions," he later said. "Either you go forward and try to rebuild your life—not just the material part, but the spiritual part, too—or you look back in anger. If you look back in anger, it can be not only nonproductive, but self-destructive."

He added, "It's all been part of my life, but it was just a part of my life, and it's over."

There was one exception: the confession tortured out of him during his first year in prison. "It's the only blemish," he said. "It's something I'll never get over."

• • •

John McCain's relationship with Ronald Reagan began in the spring of 1973, about two months after his release. He and Carol were in Los Angeles, where McCain was waiting to testify against Daniel Ellsberg, under indictment for passing the Pentagon Papers to the press. McCain had found the documents riveting, basing some of his strongest judgments about the war on their contents. But he considered Ellsberg's disclosure of the papers an act of unspeakable treachery and readily agreed when prosecutors asked if he would describe for the jury how the enemy could have used the information against Americans.

He never testified. A report in late April linking the Nixon White House to the 1971 burglary of the office of Ellsberg's psychiatrist was followed in early May by the government's admission that it had failed to provide all its wiretap information to Ellsberg's lawyers. On May 11 the judge dismissed all charges, saying government misconduct had "incurably infected the prosecution."

Freed from trial duties, the McCains flew up to San Francisco where Ross Perot, the Texas billionaire and a 1953 Academy graduate, was hosting a gala homecoming weekend for POWs at the Fairmont Hotel.

Nancy Reynolds, a special assistant to Governor Reagan, was in the hotel lounge with a group of ex-prisoners and their wives when someone at the table, as if spotting a movie star, shouted, "There's Johnny McCain."

McCain was on crutches; Carol had crutches and a wheelchair. Even so, Reynolds had never met a happier, jauntier, more delightful couple. "It was like meeting two people you know you'll never forget," she said. McCain struck her as a natural celebrity: "He walks into a room, and it's *bing, bing, bing* and everybody's sort of dazzled."

Reynolds was not at the Perot party by chance. From the late 1960s on, Ronald and Nancy Reagan had taken a personal interest in the POWs. Reynolds served as staff liaison with the families. At one picnic in their honor, a young boy, Todd Hansen, said to the governor, "Will you bring my daddy home?" Reagan was speechless until Todd asked a follow-up question that got him off the hook: "Will you take me to the bathroom?"

The Reagans' concern for the POWs seemed genuine. "I can't wait to get my arms around each of those men," Nancy Reagan sobbed as the first group touched down on American soil. The Reagans hosted a total of four parties for the men and their families, two in Sacramento, two in Los Angeles. Mrs. Reagan planned all the details herself, down to the place settings. At one party a POW gave her the tin cup and spoon he had used in prison. She burst into tears on the receiving line.

Back in the office after the Perot weekend, Reynolds told the Reagans, "You have to meet the McCains." She arranged for the two couples to get together a few days later when both would be in Los Angeles.

The governor, singing the praises of California wine, ceremonially uncorked a bottle of Wente Brothers Gray Riesling when John and Carol arrived at the Reagan home in Pacific Palisades. Even with Reagan and his wife doing all they could to put them at ease, the McCains were uncomfortable at first, not quite sure what they were doing there.

When everyone was settled, the Reagans began peppering John with questions about prison. For the next two hours they led him through a chronology of his experiences. "They wanted to hear every detail," said Carol. John fretted over wearing out his welcome, but each time he made overtures to leave, the Reagans said, "No, no. Stay right where you are."

"Did you ever want to kill yourself?" asked Reagan, a piercing question of the type he would rarely ask as President.

"Sure, but that's easy," said McCain, shading the truth. "That gives you a way out if you kill yourself."

The McCains became favorites of Reagan and his California crowd. They all knew John had suffered terribly, but he made it hard for them to feel sorry for him. When pressed to talk about prison, he spoke about the heroism of others or transformed the Hanoi Hilton into an updated version of *Stalag 17*, a bunch of wild and crazy guys outsmarting a crew of bumbling, if sadistic, jailers.

A favorite story concerned a prisoner who built himself a motorcycle only he could see. When he finished, he took it out each day for a spin around the courtyard. At times it broke down, and he would have to repair it. Give me a wrench, he would demand of the guards, give me a screwdriver. Crazy, crazy, the guards would say, shaking their heads. One day, though, he hit a curve too sharply, taking a nasty spill. Racing over, the guards assisted him to his feet, picked up the motorcycle, and helped him remount.

In 1974, his last year as governor, Reagan invited McCain to speak at the annual prayer breakfast in Sacramento. "Nancy cries when we send out the laundry," said Reagan in his introduction, "so I want to tell you, she'll never make it through listening to a talk by our next guest, Commander John McCain."

Never glancing at a note, McCain told a prison parable, of being in solitary, a hole in the ground, unbearable heat, suicidal thoughts intensifying. By chance he discovered some scratchings on the wall, the words of a previous inmate: "I believe in God, the Father Almighty."

Reagan was right. Mrs. Reagan had the Kleenex out within five minutes. She wasn't alone. "There must have been three hundred or four hundred people, maybe more than that, all these people sobbing," said Nancy Reynolds. "Not just sniffling. Ronald Reagan was sitting up there bawling.

"We were all dazzled," she continued. "He was a natural speaker, a natural storyteller. He was attractive. He was very funny." In short, as she was beginning to realize, a natural politician.

For McCain, Reagan was the real thing, a politician who stood for something, who insisted the men who fought in Vietnam were deserving of honor. Equally important, he declared that a nation should never send its sons to die in a war it was unwilling to win.

"He loved him, he loved Ronald Reagan," said Carol. "He was music to John's ears."

In November 1974, twenty months after his release from prison, McCain accepted an invitation from the South Vietnamese government to join an American VIP contingent visiting Saigon. Having completed his studies at Fort McNair, he was intrigued at the prospect of seeing the country with a more educated eye.

The old colonial capital seemed frozen in time. The restaurants were still magnificent and the shops continued to do a brisk trade. The sweeping veranda of the Hotel Continental, symbolic of a century of French rule, remained a pleasant and sophisticated gathering place for afternoon cocktails, assuming you could ignore the muffled reports of artillery fire in the distance.

He met with South Vietnamese officials and found their brave talk hollow. Any real hope South Vietnam had for sustaining itself was about to end as the newly elected congressional class of 1974, dominated by antiwar Democrats, readied itself to severely scale back American aid. The situation, he believed, had been preordained by the failure of the Paris peace accords to require the withdrawal of North Vietnamese troops from the South. To his mind, Nixon and Kissinger had done their best to keep faith with the American commitment, but under intense domestic pressure they had agreed to terms that guaranteed a North Vietnamese victory.

Before departing, he spoke at the South Vietnamese war college. He offered words of encouragement that he did not feel, though he was not certain, based on his brief stay, that things were as bad as they seemed. Hang in there, he told the assemblage. Had he trusted his instincts, he might have been tempted to offer different advice, that is, You can't count on us, run for your lives.

A few months later, as North Vietnamese forces poured across the DMZ, he knew his instincts had been right, that the United States had ceased to be a reliable ally.

"These weren't guys in black pajamas," he said. "It was a conventional invasion of the South while our Congress cut the aid and cut and cut again."

In the fall of 1974, McCain was transferred to Jacksonville as the executive officer of Replacement Air Group 174, the long-sought flying billet at last a reality. A few months later he assumed command of the RAG, which trained pilots and crews for carrier deployments. The assignment was controversial, some calling it favoritism, a sop to the famous son of a famous father and grandfather, since he had not first commanded a squadron, the usual career path. McCain ignored the howls. He had been given his chance and intended to make the most of it. He did. At the end of his tour the RAG received a Meritorious Unit Citation, its first ever.

At the change-of-command ceremony, Jack McCain, retired but still wielding his big cigar, shared the dais with his son, as did Roberta. Bud Day was there, too. An old family friend, Admiral Ike Kidd, spoke. Kidd's father had died at Pearl Harbor, where he won the Medal of Honor. In Kidd's remarks, he evoked echoes of the past, praising Jack's service, and Slew's before that. As for John, the admiral said he had earned himself a place of honor alongside his father and grandfather. Carl Smith, a friend and fellow officer, later said he never saw McCain so moved as on that day.

There was a dark side to the Jacksonville tour. The storybook marriage that had survived separation, pain, and prison began to fray. Off-duty, usually on routine cross-country flights to Yuma and El

Centro, John started carousing and running around with women. To make matters worse, some of the women with whom he was linked by rumor were his subordinates. In some ways the rumors were an extension of the John McCain stories that had swirled in his wake since Academy days—some true, some with an element of truth, others patently absurd. Asked about them, he admitted to having a series of dalliances during this period, but flatly denied any with females, officer or enlisted, under his command.

Though officially frowned upon, romantic relationships between officers of different grades are not uncommon and for the most part are free of a superior-subordinate element. Many have led to marriage. But fraternization between officers and enlisted persons is considered over the line, not because of caste discrimination, but because the color of authority is too vivid, almost impossible to soften.

At the time the rumors were so widespread that, true or not, they became part of the McCain persona, impossible not to take note of. What is true is that a number of POWs, in those first few years after their release, often acted erratically, their lives pockmarked by drastic mood swings and uncharacteristic behavior before achieving a more mellow equilibrium.

More troubling, sad beyond words, was the failure of the marriage. If there was one couple that deserved to make it, it was John and Carol McCain. They endured nearly six years of unspeakable trauma with courage and grace. In the end it was not enough. They won the war but lost the peace. Hemingway writes of people becoming stronger at the broken places, which is a heartening thought, and sometimes true. All too often, though, it's simply bullshit.

John and Carol would not discuss the breakup of their marriage in any detail. McCain spoke vaguely of time having taken its toll. "I had changed, she had changed," he said. "People who have been apart that much change." He added, "I think she has reason to be bitter." Carol was less vague, but equally terse: "The breakup of our marriage was not caused by my accident or Vietnam or any of those things. I don't know that it might not have happened if John had never been gone. I attribute it more to John turning forty and wanting to be twenty-five again than I do to anything else."

The conventional view is that John came home not to the Long Tall Sally of his overheated prison imaginings but to a real woman—older, shorter, crippled—and before long began to stray. No doubt it was more complicated. Like most marriages that fail, theirs was a drama that involved two people who themselves could only make educated guesses about what went right and what went wrong.

Carol was mistaken on one point. Vietnam did play a part, perhaps not the major part, but more than a walk-on. McCain was no different from most veterans of that war. As he went through life, Vietnam kept scrambling onstage and chewing up the scenery no matter how often he thought he had written it out of the script.

CHAPTER ELEVEN

Guerrilla Warfare

In early 1977, as John McCain was finishing up his command tour in Jacksonville, Admiral James Holloway, the Chief of Naval Operations, learned McCain was slated for a low-profile staff billet. The assignment seemed unimaginative, a waste of talent. McCain's a well-known guy, people like him, the CNO told the Bureau of Naval Personnel, let's put him where he can do us some good. McCain soon had orders to Washington as the number two man in the Navy's Senate liaison office. Several months later, after his selection for captain, he took over the office.

The Navy, like the other services, maintains liaison offices in the House and Senate. A large part of the job is constituent service, determining, for example, why a sailor from a lawmaker's state or district is being court-martialed or why his wife has not received his allotment check.

Liaison officers also act as go-betweens, facilitating the exchange of information between legislators and the Pentagon. On overseas congressional trips they serve as escorts, arranging for transportation, lodging, at times even lugging suitcases.

McCain's father, a liaison officer two decades earlier, had greatly expanded the position, becoming a lobbyist in uniform and a presence on the Hill. Most of Jack McCain's successors, however, reverted to the standard role of medal-bedecked attendants, their chief duty the care and feeding of senators and congressmen.

John McCain reversed the trend again, giving new, at times unusual twists to the job, along the way limbering up for the political career he would launch five years later.

Under McCain, the Navy's small liaison office on the first floor of the Russell Senate Office Building became a late-afternoon gathering spot where senators and staffers, usually from the Armed Services and Foreign Relations committees, would drop in for a drink and the chance to unwind.

The magnet was McCain, a fun-loving, irreverent, mildly impetuous figure whose judgment members trusted on military matters because of the long naval tradition that he embodied and his own well-chronicled experiences.

Though invariably courteous, he was without awe, rarely minced words, kowtowed to no one. For all the Hill's caste consciousness, he was soon moving on an equal footing in a bipartisan circle of junior senators and staffers.

"I never ran across any people in the military liaison offices that were at all like John," said Albert "Pete" Lakeland, a senior Foreign Relations Committee staffer. "In fact, I really didn't even get to know any of the others. They handled baggage, and that was it."

His closest friends were two of the younger, more independent senators, Democrat Gary Hart of Colorado and Republican William Cohen of Maine.

Hart had managed George McGovern's 1972 antiwar presidential campaign, but it did not become an issue in the friendship between the two men. "Never crossed my mind," said McCain.

In fact, though McCain held Congress in part to blame for the Vietnam debacle, there was no discernible evidence that he nursed a grudge, let alone a corrosive anger on the order of many other veterans.

"John McCain was as easy, as open, and as accepting of the United States Congress, both as an institution and as individuals, as any military officer that I've seen in twenty-five years," said William B. Bader, majority staff director of the Foreign Relations Committee.

McCain did not view lapses in taste and personal behavior as heralding a national Armageddon either, his live-and-let-live attitude in sharp contrast to the grim moralizing of another former POW, Alabama Senator Jeremiah Denton. Bader thought of McCain as emerging from prison as Saint Francis of Assisi, Denton as the Grand Inquisitor.

Not all McCain's senatorial friends came from the junior ranks. During four years on the Hill, he developed special relationships with some of the Senate's most powerful figures, most notably Texan John Tower, an ex-Navy man and the ranking Republican on the Armed Services Committee.

"He was very much loved by John Tower," said James Jones, a Marine officer serving under McCain on the Navy liaison staff. "I think that John McCain is the son that John Tower never had."

His popularity was wide and deep, his friendships nonideological. His affection for Tower, a Vietnam hawk, was mirrored by his admiration for Jacob Javits, sponsor of the Vietnam-inspired War Powers Resolution, which sought to limit the ability of presidents to wage undeclared wars.

"John McCain, as a Navy captain, knew on a personal basis more senators and was more warmly received than virtually any lobbyist I have ever known in this town; they loved to see him," said James McGovern, a Navy lieutenant on the liaison staff, later undersecretary of the Air Force.

McCain was much in demand for overseas escort duty, especially by members of the Armed Services and Foreign Relations committees. He was fun to be around, his wit appealing, his natural exuberance infectious. In an Athens taverna he danced on a table with Senator Joseph Biden's wife, Jill, a red bandanna clenched in his teeth. In Seoul he told Bill Cohen that a seemingly empty room in their hotel was filled with Korean security men. Cohen laughed. McCain dared him to walk in. As Cohen tried to enter, a dour Korean stepped out of the shadows and blocked his path. "Just looking around," said the senator, retreating sheepishly. At the Peking Opera, Cohen marveled at the brilliant costumes, the acrobatic performances, and the enthusiasm of the audience. Said McCain as they departed the theater, "That's the most fun I've had since my last interrogation."

An episode on a flight to China in the spring of 1979 left Bill Bader wondering if there might be more to McCain's appeal than his reputation as an engaging traveling companion. During the trip no fewer than five senators, all antiwar Democrats, wandered separately to the rear of the plane where McCain was seated and invited him to join them up front. After watching the parade for several hours, the perplexed Bader puzzled it out. The senators, he decided, were making their peace with John McCain.

On the same trip senators and staffers were touring a factory complex outside Shanghai. McCain and Bader, losing interest in the official blather, began wandering around the outbuildings. They poked their heads into one, a primitive infirmary, its metal-frame beds covered with gray blankets, a red stripe running through them. Bader turned to McCain. He was ashen. "John, what is it?" asked Bader. Murmured McCain, "Those were the blankets we had in Vietnam."

Bader had rarely seen that side of McCain. If he talked of prison at all, it was almost always in a joking way, as with the wisecrack to Cohen at the opera. Bader later concluded that his long incarceration, for all its hardships, had lent a different dimension to McCain, made him more than he might otherwise have been.

"I knew two hundred John McCains," said Bader, a Navy bombardier-navigator during the Korean War. "And I still know them. They're vaguely paunchy, overgrown boys. If John McCain had not had this Vietnamese experience, of prison, of solitude, of brutality, he would have just been one more Navy jock."

McCain and Pete Lakeland were in Honolulu, at a CINCPAC reception for a Foreign Relations Committee contingent on its way to China. They were having a drink together when someone tapped

Lakeland on the shoulder. He swung around, exchanged a few words. When he turned back, he spotted McCain across the room introducing himself to an attractive young blond woman.

Lakeland was surprised. He knew that McCain, by then separated from Carol, liked women, but casual pickups were not his style. Something clearly was going on. McCain and the woman spent the entire reception together, talking, laughing, an island to themselves. Whenever Lakeland walked toward them, McCain maneuvered his back to him, as if he didn't know him.

The party was closing down when Lakeland finally broke through the invisible barrier that McCain had erected around his new acquaintance.

"Hey, John, are you going back to the hotel, or what are you doing?" said Lakeland, peeved at his friend.

"Oh, Pete, I want you to meet Cindy Hensley," said McCain. He explained that Cindy was visiting Hawaii from Phoenix with her parents. He added, "We're going out for dinner." Lakeland waited. "You wouldn't like to join us, would you?" asked McCain. "No, no," said Lakeland. "I'll see you. Have a good time."

Walking back to his hotel, Lakeland realized that whatever he had witnessed, it had not been a casual pickup. "John was smitten," he said. "He was instantly, compellingly attracted to her."

The senatorial contingent left for China the next morning. Throughout the journey McCain talked about Cindy, insisting she was someone special, becoming testy when teased about earthy motives. Midway through the trip he called her in Phoenix. She was in the hospital, recuperating from minor knee surgery. Earlier in the day an arrangement of flowers had been delivered to her room, the card signed "John." She thanked him effusively. "It was nothing," he said. "I just wanted you to know I was thinking about you." Two years later she found out that McCain's only involvement with the flowers had been to take credit for them. Another John, an old friend in Tucson, had sent them.

Over the next year or so they got together often, in Washington, in Arizona where Cindy lived, in Fort Walton Beach, Florida, where they stayed with an old McCain friend, Jerry Dorminy, the owner of the Hog's Breath Saloon.

At twenty-five, seventeen years McCain's junior, Cindy had the youthful good looks of a beauty queen without the shallowness that goes with the stereotype. Her widely spaced blue eyes communicated intelligence, her demeanor casual elegance, the product of the best schools and the better southwestern country clubs. She was rich but not idle rich. When McCain met her, she was teaching disabled teenage children of migrant farm workers, defying superiors who forbade her to make home visits because they were not considered safe.

The family money came from beer. Her father, Jim Hensley, hocked everything he had in 1956 to come up with $10,000 to buy a small Anheuser-Busch distributorship. Two decades later he had turned it into the largest in the country. The Hensleys, said one observer, had "more money than most small countries."

McCain's detractors, and some of his friends, would later say that he saw Cindy as the ultimate target of opportunity and locked on to her with single-minded, even cynical calculation. It was fine that she was young and beautiful, so it was said, but the real attraction was that she was the daughter of a rich, well-connected businessman from a state that seemed to offer opportunities to someone with McCain's emerging political ambitions.

"Absolute bullshit," said Jim McGovern. "One thing I can say about John McCain is, he ain't calculating."

The scenario is hard to take seriously. Was it even remotely possible that the impulsive, hot-blooded McCain who used to take his Navy pay in cash had suddenly been reborn as a gold-digging manipulator, coolly mapping out a marriage of convenience? Even if he contemplated such a union, he had to realize that divorcing Carol, an essential part of his alleged game plan, could easily sidetrack his political career at any point down the line. The courageous, crippled wife cast aside for a wealthy and beautiful younger woman—how understanding were the voters likely to be in a conservative state with a large, politically active, fundamentalist Christian community? Especially when many of his friends, people who knew and liked him, already held against him the failure of his marriage to Carol.

McGovern had a simpler explanation: hormones. That fits. But Cindy may have represented more to McCain.

"I think John very much saw her as reclaiming the life he had lost," said Pete Lakeland. "I think that was the real theme, that Cindy stood for everything he didn't have in prison. This was the sweet, innocent, pure American dream."

It was as if McCain had decided to start life over again. "I think he was determined that his future was not going to be controlled by those five and a half years and his POW experience," said Lakeland. "He saw Cindy as the focus for his regeneration."

As the Navy's emissary to the Senate, McCain was mindful of what he perceived to be the best interests of the service even if on occasion those views were not shared by the Carter administration or, officially at least, by the Navy itself. In more than one instance, he went his own way on issues in which administration policy seemed driven by politics, expediency, ignorance, or some combination of those factors. He knew he was taking risks. He didn't care. After five and a half years in prison he had no intention of meekly falling in line. Too many generals and admirals had done that during Vietnam, ruining their reputations, ill-serving the nation, getting a lot of kids killed.

McCain's reluctance to follow in their footsteps was demonstrated most graphically in the battle between the Carter administration and Congress over an aircraft carrier. Of merely passing interest today, at the time the confrontation between the two branches of government was intense, triggering a presidential veto one year and embarrassing acquiescence the next. McCain's role in all this was a small one, but not all that small and not all that defensible. In his way he was a double agent, in the main arranging trips, guiding Navy department officials to meetings with senators, on the side waging guerrilla warfare.

The carrier issue flared in 1978 when Jimmy Carter decided the fleet did not need a new supercarrier to replace the *Midway*, an aging flattop built during World War II. The Navy, unhappy with Carter's judgment but having no choice in the matter, went along with the Commander-in-Chief. McCain did not.

For the next two years, McCain, assisted by Jim McGovern, quietly but effectively lobbied for the new carrier in secret defiance of Navy Secretary W. Graham Claytor, for whom he worked, and President Carter.

Retired Rear Admiral Mark Hill, chief lobbyist for the Association of Naval Aviation, the organization that spearheaded the drive to push the carrier through Congress, remembers McCain's activities well.

"John McCain was a stalwart little soldier in that fight," said Hill. "He never wavered. He was supporting the big carrier, and he did a lot of stuff behind the back of the Secretary of the Navy. . . . He was gutsy enough to say, Screw my boss."

McCain did not flaunt his opposition to the administration's policy. At first, when senators or staffers asked his opinion, he explained the President's position. If they pressed, he told them that he thought the carrier was badly needed and why.

As time went on, he intensified his efforts, still keeping a low profile. He talked with senators on overseas trips or when they dropped by his office, to their aides, even their friends. Jim McGovern, with McCain's encouragement, wrote a position paper laying out the case for the carrier. No letterhead, no signature, wide distribution.

McCain was also serving as a forward observer for the pro-carrier forces, relaying target data from his perch in the Senate to Mark Hill and like-minded lobbyists about which senators were wavering, where their concerns lay, what arguments might sway them.

"John McCain had his ear to the ground closer than anybody else," said Hill. "He was an absolutely essential nerve center."

Over the objections of President Carter, Congress in 1978 approved $2 billion for a new nuclear carrier. To kill it, an outraged Carter had to veto the omnibus $36 billion defense authorization bill, which contained the funds for the ship. Congress sustained the veto.

"Admiral, we're not going to give up, are we?" McCain asked Hill when the veto override failed. "No way," Hill replied. The following year, with McCain and Hill once more lobbying furiously, Congress again funded the carrier. This time Carter signed the legislation.

McCain saw nothing disloyal in what he and McGovern did: "It wasn't like I said to Jim, Let's overturn the President, let's go do battle with the administration. We both believed the carrier was pretty important. . . . We knew all of the uniformed Navy agreed with us. . . . We didn't ever portray it as anybody's views but our own, but because we had credibility with people, they listened to us."

How did Carter administration officials react? "They didn't even know what hit them," said McCain. "It had never happened before and it's never happened since."

McCain's reasons, as he later explained them, included his personal dismay with the state of the post-Vietnam military, which he ascribed primarily to Carter, but to Congress as well. "We had enlisted petty officers with families on food stamps. We had ships that couldn't leave port. The problems were just incredible."

There were other reasons. McCain himself was evolving. He loved working in the Senate, but he was not content with being a bit player, solving constituent problems for senators, running their errands, handling their baggage.

Said McCain: "We [meaning he and McGovern] recognized that you can do that job, be a caseworker, see that Seaman Smith gets his hardship discharge, or you can get involved in issues of substance, and that's what we did.

"The Vietnam experience made me want to be involved more in public service," he said on another occasion, "*and seeing things happen right.*" It was a breathtaking assertion, worthy of two fellow Academy men, Oliver North and McCain's classmate John Poindexter, after a few years in the White House.

Laboring away in the Senate as a junior captain, McCain knew his Navy career was about over. His annual physicals were not good, and he hadn't been slated for a major sea command, the usual stepping-stone to flag rank. He figured he might make rear admiral, but vice admiral, let alone full admiral like his father and grandfather, seemed out of the question.

He began thinking of retirement and life after the Navy. He considered staying in Washington as a civilian lobbyist, probably for a defense contractor, but the prospect didn't interest him. He knew that John Tower wanted him on the Armed Services Committee staff, which was more appealing. Finally, though, he admitted to himself that what he really wanted to do was enter politics.

It was not a new idea. Back in 1976, when he was stationed in Jacksonville, he thought about running for the House, tested the waters, decided the incumbent congressman would be too hard to beat. If the prospect had merely intrigued him then, his time in the Senate had whipped his ambition into a lather.

It was a time of change. His marriage to Carol had been effectively over for some time. After a number of trial separations, they were legally separated in January 1980 and divorced a month later. In May he married Cindy Hensley in Phoenix. Senator Bill Cohen was his best man, another senator, Gary Hart, an usher. The newlyweds honeymooned in Hawaii. A few weeks earlier they learned each other's real ages, thanks to the local paper, which routinely published marriage license data. Cindy, worried that John might think she was too young for him, had told him she was three years older than she was. John, fearing the opposite, had shaved four years from his age.

Carol, despondent, in need of diversion, had gone to work as

Nancy Reagan's personal assistant a few months earlier, traveling the campaign trail with the future First Lady throughout the primaries.

Carol's friends in the press corps helped buoy her spirits with black, convoluted humor. On the day John and Cindy were married, reporters on the press bus serenaded her with endless refrains of "Those Wedding Bells Are Breaking Up That Old Gang of Mine." When Reagan made a patriotic speech at the Alamo, asking his audience what had become of the heroes of yesteryear, Lou Cannon of *The Washington Post* slipped up behind her and quipped, "Yeah, Carol, just where is that son of a bitch?"

CHAPTER TWELVE

The Candidate from Hanoi

In early 1981, a few months into Ronald Reagan's presidency, Washington political consultant J. Brian Smith got a call from a client, Senator Bill Cohen, asking him to get together with a Navy captain named John McCain and brief him on Arizona politics. Smith, who did not know McCain, was busy and tried to bury the request, but Cohen called back a few days later and pressed him. Smith agreed to meet McCain for lunch.

Avoiding the usual noontime haunts, they met at The Broker, a tasteful Swiss-run restaurant about a mile from the Capitol. As Smith listened skeptically, an animated McCain explained his plan. When he retired from the Navy, he said, he was going to move to Arizona and run for Congress. "What district?" asked Smith. "I haven't figured that out yet," said McCain, as if it were a mere detail. "Well, when are you going to run? In eighty-four?" asked Smith. "No. Eighty-two," said McCain.

"I was astounded," Smith later said. Charmed and entertained as well. To this day he cannot recall ever laughing as much as he did that afternoon. McCain talked nonstop, interrupting himself every five minutes to say, "You think I'm crazy, don't you, Jay?"

McCain had a simple scheme. He would run for the new seat Arizona would get in 1982 because of population growth over the previous decade. He figured the seat would be in the Phoenix area, where he and Cindy were about to move. Smith, who had experience in Arizona politics, was not so sure. His contacts were telling him the seat would probably be carved out of the southern portion of the state, near Tucson. But that was nothing compared to the larger issue, that McCain didn't live in the state, had never lived in the state, yet had the audacity to believe he could be elected to Congress barely a year and a half after taking up residence there.

Jack McCain died on March 22, 1981, aboard a military transport while flying from London to the United States. The Navy contacted Carol when officials couldn't find John. By chance she knew how to reach him, called, and gently broke the news. The plane bearing Jack's body had stopped to refuel in Bangor, Maine, so John and Cindy were able to meet the aircraft when it landed at Andrews Air Force Base outside Washington.

John McCain retired around the same time. Before he left Washington, John Lehman, the new Secretary of the Navy, awarded him the Legion of Merit at a private ceremony in his Pentagon office. John Tower hosted a huge farewell reception for McCain in the Senate Caucus Room, where John Poindexter, Oliver North, and Robert McFarlane, the three Annapolis men swept up in the Iran-Contra scandal, would meet their congressional accusers six years later.

In late March, John and Cindy boarded a plane that would take them to their new home in Arizona. Earlier in the day, Jack McCain had been buried at Arlington Cemetery. After the funeral, John stopped by the Navy offices in Crystal City and turned in his active duty identification card. He was optimistic as he prepared to depart Washington, but the relinquishing of his ID card coupled with the great sadness surrounding his father's interment dampened the leave-taking. For virtually the first time in this century, he realized, no member of the McCain family wore the uniform of an officer in the United States Navy.

• • •

"For God's sake, be very discreet," Jay Smith had admonished McCain before he left for Arizona on the outbound leg of what he hoped would be a round-trip back to Washington.

The worst thing you can do, Smith warned his new client, is let people know you plan to run for public office. "It would be viewed as very opportunistic," he said. "Let's face it, it is, but let's not have it viewed that way."

Smith advised McCain to get himself known around the state. He went at it like a full-time job, raising his profile in a remarkably brief period of time. Cindy was his advance man. When she was tied up, he did it himself. "Hi, I'm John McCain," he would greet some homegrown power broker. "I'm new to the state, and I'd like to come over and say hello." He became active in the state Republican Party, helping with fund-raising, local campaigns, and phone banks. Service clubs like the Rotary and Kiwanis, always looking for luncheon and dinner speakers, were only too happy to provide a forum for the war hero and Washington insider who had generously volunteered his services. Soon he was speaking twice a week, usually on defense and foreign policy issues. Meanwhile, Cindy's father, beer baron Jim Hensley, gave him a public relations job that took him to conventions around the state where he built up his contacts as he promoted the King of Beers. Smith was amazed by McCain's energy and enthusiasm. We have a secret weapon here, he told himself. Too bad he doesn't have anyplace to run.

Those first nine months in Arizona put McCain's discretion, never his long suit, to a severe test. His time in prison had intensified his natural impatience. He was, in effect, a stealth candidate, racing around auditioning for a job that didn't even exist. To make matters worse, he couldn't tell anyone about it. Instead, he talked in vague terms, coy claptrap. I want to get involved politically, I've been interested in public service all my life.

Smith's sources, meanwhile, turned out to be right: The new congressional district was in Tucson, too far for McCain to jump without indelibly branding himself a carpetbagger. The Phoenix-area seats were all held by strong incumbents, among them John Rhodes, a fellow Republican, and Morris Udall, an entrenched and popular Democrat.

In January 1982, Rhodes called a press conference amid rumors that he might announce his retirement. Since he resigned as House minority leader a year earlier, there had been speculation that he might not run again for the First Congressional District seat he had held for three decades. The district fell completely into the Phoenix metropolitan area and included suburban Tempe, Mesa, and portions of Scottsdale. John McCain lived just outside the district, in central Phoenix, a stone's throw away.

This is how Jay Smith remembers the day John Rhodes announced his retirement from Congress.

Smith is in Washington, on the phone with McCain in Phoenix. McCain has a second phone to his ear, an open line to someone he has sent to the Rhodes press conference. Rhodes says he is stepping down. McCain gets the word, passes it on to Smith. Jubilation. Whoops and cheers careen across phone lines from the Salt River to the Potomac. Then, from McCain, Okay, what now?

They discuss plans. Smith hears McCain talking to someone else, realizes Cindy has just walked into the room. "Did you buy it? Did you get it? Did you find it?" Smith overhears McCain ask his wife. Murmuring in the background. McCain, back on the line: "She got it. Great. Yea!"

"What's that?" asks Smith, perplexed.

"We just got a house in the First District."

• • •

Jay Smith later called it "the Super Bowl of all campaigns . . . the toughest, the hardest, the most amazing."

One of the most difficult parts, for Smith, was restraining McCain. He wanted to declare his candidacy for the First District seat the same day Rhodes called it quits.

"Calm down," said Smith. "This is a long-distance run. It's not a forty-yard dash. There's time."

At Smith's urging, McCain announced the formation of an exploratory committee while he went through the motions of weighing his decision. A time-honored political ploy, the pose created artificial tension—Who is he? What's his story? Will he run?—that McCain milked for weeks of free publicity.

McCain understood the strategy, but he didn't like it, making Smith's life miserable. "He just wanted to go," said Smith. "If he could have found a way to have the election held that week, he would have done it."

By the time he declared his candidacy in late March, three other candidates—two state legislators and a politically active veterinarian—had entered the race for the GOP nomination. All were given a good chance to win, McCain next to none. The September 7 GOP primary would decide the nominee, tantamount to election in the solidly Republican district.

With McCain officially in the race, Smith could finally employ his secret weapon, his candidate's immense energy. He launched him on a grueling schedule of door-to-door campaigning, saying, "You want to win? This is what you've got to do." Smith had tried this tactic with other candidates, found their enthusiasm for door-knocking held up only so long as reporters were following them around.

McCain was different. "Let's go hit the bricks, Brad boy," he'd tell his driver, Brad Boland, each morning as he reported to headquarters to pick up the day's voter lists. Through the late spring and summer, when temperatures in the Phoenix area routinely climb above one hundred degrees, he campaigned door-to-door six hours a day, six days a week, personally knocking on twenty thousand Republican doors. By the end of the campaign he had gone through three pairs of shoes—Cindy had the third pair bronzed—and developed skin cancer, which has since required four minor surgeries.

At first it was drudgery, the glazed look and the dismissive question: "What are you selling?" He would later joke that he began the campaign with 3 percent name recognition with a 3 percent margin of error. If he felt discouraged, he never let on, showing up each morning, grabbing Brad boy, and hitting the bricks. One day he noticed that fewer people were asking him what he was selling. Instead they brightened and said, "Oh, yeah, John McCain," when they saw him perched on their doorstep.

Part of his evolution into a plausible candidate was due to the targeting. He may have been new to the area, but so were a lot of others. The population of the district had increased nearly 50 percent between 1970 and 1980. Smith directed him to those areas in which the newcomers were concentrated.

In addition, he raised $313,000 for the primary, more than half of it, $167,000, in loans from himself. The amount wasn't staggering, but it was more than his three better-known rivals had to spend, and it lent credibility to his dark-horse candidacy. More important, it permitted him to run a modern, high-tech campaign, complete with slickly produced television commercials.

TV spots for congressional races often look like a cross between used-car commercials and hair-weaving ads, but McCain's, produced by Smith & Harroff, Jay Smith's consulting firm, were several cuts above the norm. They promoted him as "a new leader for Arizona," a man who "knows how Washington works," picturing him at a table with Nancy and Ronald Reagan or standing beside his friend John Tower, the popular Republican senator from Texas. His POW days were recounted, then voters were told "he's come to Arizona to serve again." Although no more substantial than the usual election-year

U.S. Naval Academy—
Three Generations of a Navy Family
John Sidney McCain III,
Class of 1958.
John Sidney "Jack" McCain, Jr.,
Class of 1931.
John Sidney "Slew" McCain,
Class of 1906.
(U.S. Naval Academy)

Midshipman John McCain's boxing style was to charge to the center of the ring and throw punches until either he or his opponent went down. *(U.S. Naval Academy)*

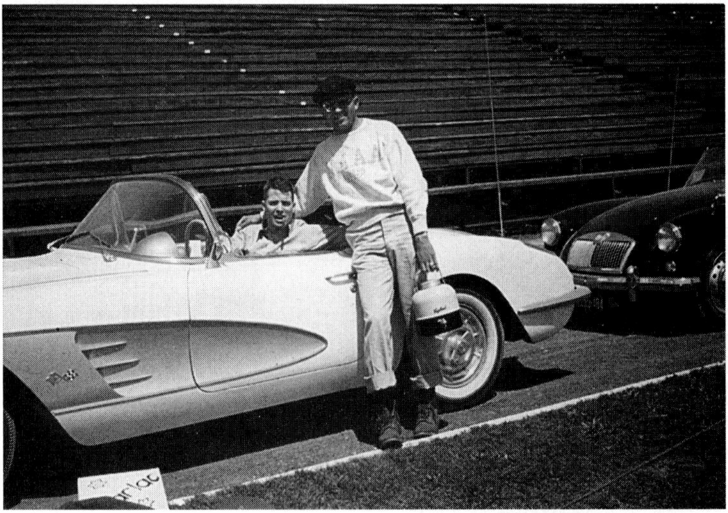

Joined by his roommate, Frank Gamboa, Midshipman First Class John McCain sits in his new Corvette on the day before his June 1958 graduation from the Naval Academy. *(Frank Gamboa)*

Midshipman John McCain poses with his father, Captain John S. McCain, Jr., at the wedding of his sister, Sandy, in 1956. *(Office of Senator John McCain)*

Lieutenant Commander John McCain is pulled from a lake in Hanoi and taken captive by the North Vietnamese after his A-4E Skyhawk was shot down by a surface-to-air missile on October 26, 1967. He broke both arms and his right knee upon ejection. *(Office of Senator John McCain)*

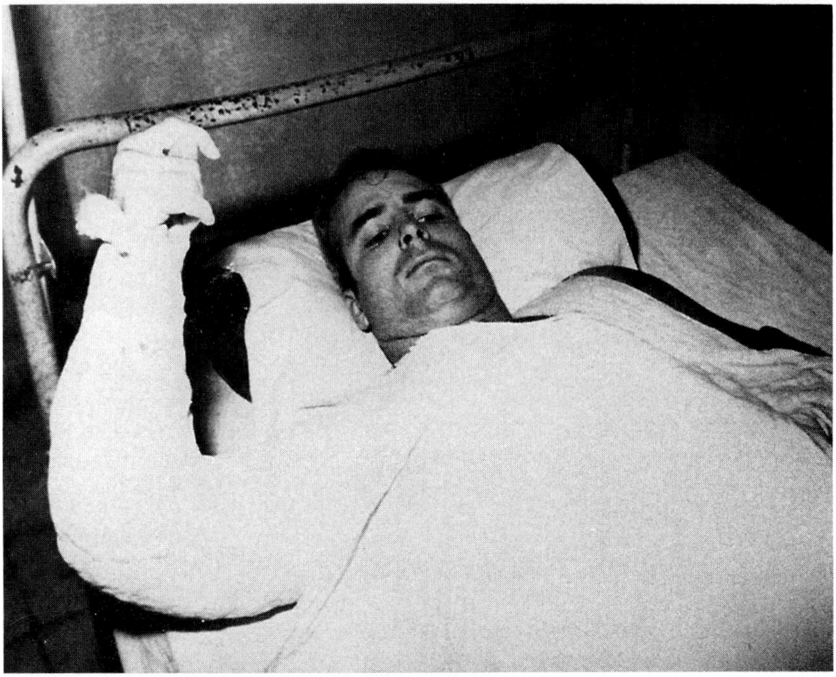

John McCain in a hospital in Hanoi shortly after he was shot down. *(AP/Wide World Photos)*

John McCain's wife Carol and the couple's children—sons Doug and Andy, and daughter Sidney—observe Thanksgiving during John's captivity. The McCains later divorced. *(Office of Senator John McCain)*

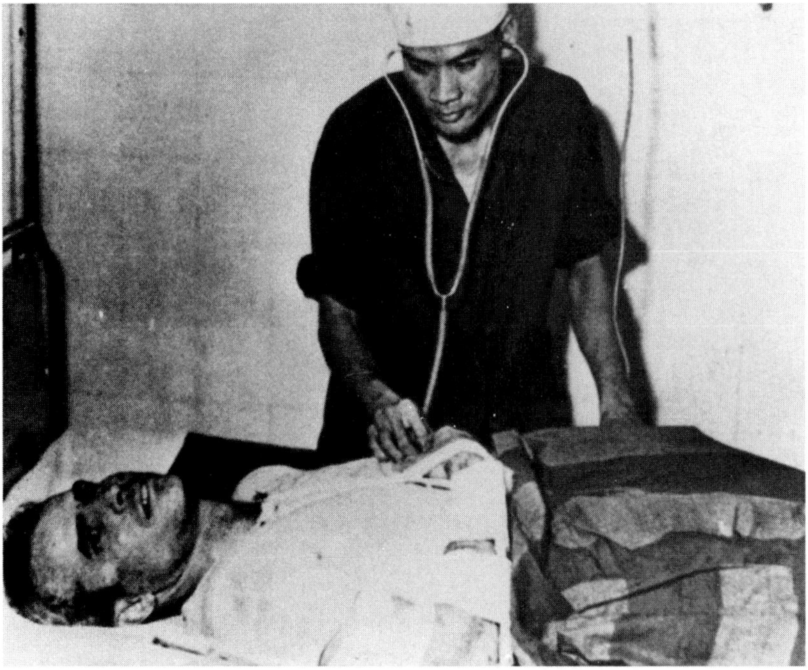

John McCain's North Vietnamese captors became concerned with his injuries after they learned his father was one of the most senior admirals in the U.S. Navy. Before then, they left his wounds largely untreated. *(Office of Senator John McCain)*

Admiral John S. McCain, Jr., visits American troops at the Con Thien combat base near the Demilitarized Zone at Christmas in 1970. During three of his son's five and a half years in captivity, Admiral McCain had overall command of all American forces in the Pacific, including those in Vietnam. It was said that he made annual Christmas visits to troops near the DMZ in part so that he could feel closer to John. *(David Burnett/Contact Press Images)*

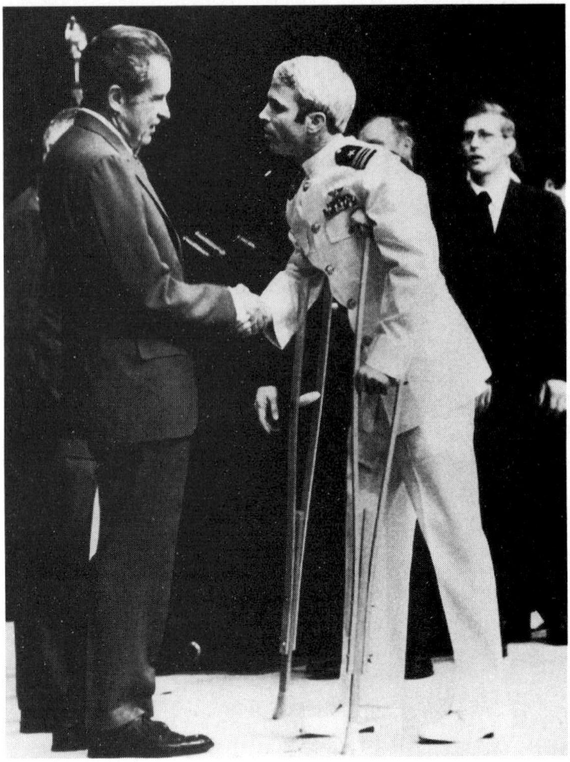

President Nixon greets Lieutenant Commander John McCain at a May 1973 White House reception for returning POWs. *(UPI/Corbis-Bettmann)*

Congressman John McCain talks with Walter Cronkite of CBS News during his return to Vietnam in the spring of 1985. *(CBS Photo Archive)*

Congressman John McCain deep in conversation with President Reagan in 1986. *(Office of Senator John McCain)*

Senator John McCain, who stood fifth from the bottom of his Annapolis class in 1958, congratulates a graduating midshipman after delivering the commencement address at the Naval Academy in May 1993. *(U.S. Naval Academy)*

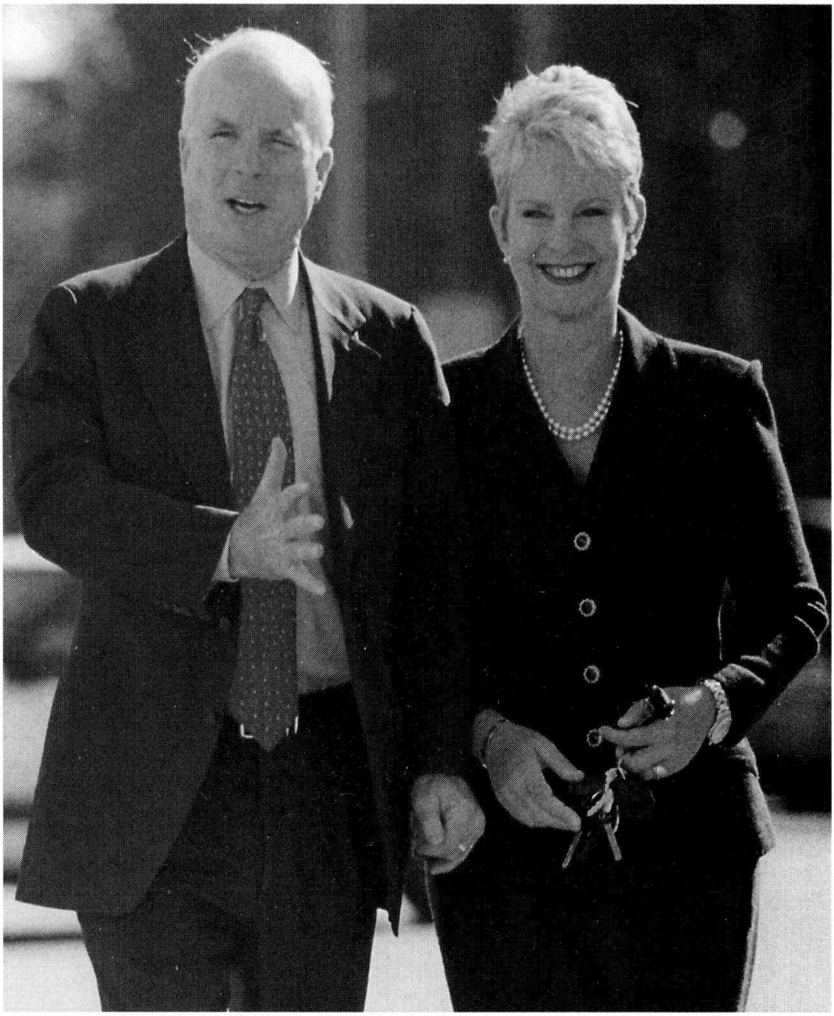

John McCain and wife Cindy, whom he married in 1980, arrive at a Phoenix polling station to cast their ballots on Tuesday, November 3, 1998. Seeking reelection to a third term, McCain won in a landslide. *(AP/Wide World Photos)*

hype, the spots introduced McCain to prospective voters in an upbeat, engaging, and effective way. Soon kids were stopping him on the street and asking for his autograph. Drivers honked. Not everyone knew his name. They recognized him as the guy with the white hair from television, the one who spent all those years in a North Vietnamese jail.

There was something else. During his campaign and now in the White House, Ronald Reagan was changing the way America looked at its servicemen, past and present, including veterans of the nation's longest war, Vietnam. As evidence of the shift in perceptions, a memorial to Vietnam veterans was nearing completion on the Mall in Washington. In the fall, hundreds of thousands of veterans and their families would converge on the nation's capital for the dedication, cheered on by many of their old adversaries in the press and the public at large. For many, the dedication of the memorial would symbolize reconciliation and healing and the long-delayed greeting of heroes. And among that elite fraternity there were few who swayed to the rhythm of the Nightingale's Song as effortlessly as John McCain. It was as if it had been written for him.

The carpetbagger issue plagued him from the start of his campaign, became the killer question at the candidates' forums to which the four hopefuls dragged themselves two and three nights a week. You've just lived here a year, how can you know Arizona or the district? Aren't you just an opportunist? At first he explained that, having never lived anywhere permanently, he moved to his wife's home state when he retired from the Navy, just as many others had settled in Arizona in recent years. It was a weak response, and he knew he was getting beat up.

One night he turned it around. This time his face grew red as he listened to the familiar question.

"Listen, pal," he replied, "I spent twenty-two years in the Navy.

My father was in the Navy. My grandfather was in the Navy. We in the military service tend to move a lot. We have to live in all parts of the country, all parts of the world. I wish I could have had the luxury, like you, of growing up and living and spending my entire life in a nice place like the First District of Arizona, but I was doing other things.

"As a matter of fact, when I think about it now, the place I lived longest in my life was Hanoi."

The audience sat for several seconds in shocked silence, then broke into thunderous applause. "The reply was absolutely the most devastating response to a potentially troublesome political issue I've ever heard," said political columnist John Kolbe, of the *Phoenix Gazette*.

With Ronald Reagan's election, Carol McCain became head of the White House Visitors Office, arranging tours and the like. She was working late in her East Wing office one night when she received a phone call from State Senator Jim Mack, one of the other candidates in the First District race. Mack said a friend told him Carol had some "negative material" on her ex-husband that she might be willing to share. Carol was outraged, refused to discuss her marriage with Mack.

"I told him I believe in John McCain," she said in an interview with columnist Kolbe. "He's a good person. I wish him every bit of success. I was appalled Senator Mack would ask such personal questions. I can't imagine a gentleman doing that."

The unmasking of Mack by the *Gazette* was not enough for Jay Smith. We've got to put a stop to this kind of thing, he told McCain. You'd better talk to him. McCain needed little prodding. The next time the candidates got together, he maneuvered Mack away from the others.

As recounted by Smith, McCain said to Mack, "I understand you called my ex-wife. I want you to know that, campaign aside, politics aside, you ever do anything like that again, anything against a person in my family, I will personally beat the shit out of you."

McCain was a nervous wreck on Election Day, the one day in a campaign when the candidate is superfluous. He was in the way, driving campaign staffers crazy as they went about the mechanics of getting out the vote. Go home, go anywhere, Smith told him, just let us do our jobs.

He went to a movie, *Star Wars*, couldn't sit still, got up every ten minutes and paced in the lobby. It was worse that night as the votes started rolling in, showing him with an early lead. He stayed home until ten, then went down to headquarters. By eleven the momentum had swung in his direction. The final totals: McCain, 32 percent; Russell, 26 percent; Mack, 22 percent; Carlson-West, 20 percent.

At the victory celebration, he ascribed his win to the months of intensive door-to-door campaigning, told the press he would be out again early the next morning, a statement he later regretted (though he made good on it) because he never got to bed that night.

Those were his public comments. Privately, according to Jay Smith, "He started talking about running for the Senate."

The general election, as expected, was no contest: McCain bested his Democratic opponent, William Hegarty, by thirty-five percentage points. It was a remarkable political story: elected to Congress eighteen months after moving to the state, less than a year after taking up residence in the district. In those moments of victory, had he ever looked back on how far he had come since saying so long to the Prick, the Cat, Soft Soap Fairy, and his other friends in Hanoi?

"No," he replied. "The moment I landed at Clark I started putting the Vietnam experience behind me."

In prison McCain and Orson Swindle discovered that as kids they had both been fans of "Felix the Cat" cartoons. When Felix got in trouble, they laughingly recalled, he would raise his paws and roll his eyes, a picture of innocence. They started doing the same thing when one or the other seemed too full of himself.

Years later, as McCain was moving into his first congressional office, Swindle poked his head in the door. "This is for you," he told the new lawmaker, presenting him with a large Felix doll. "You put this somewhere where you can look at it. And don't you ever forget where you came from and get too big and get too wrapped up in all this crap."

Pointing at Felix, Swindle added, lightly but not too lightly, "This is reality."

CHAPTER THIRTEEN

The Shadow of Vietnam

When he arrived in the nation's capital in January 1983, the Washington press quickly pegged the new congressman from Arizona as a predictable conservative, thus a reliable vote for the administration. The label didn't bother John McCain. He had known and liked Ronald Reagan for a decade, admired him even longer, never more so than during the first two years of his presidency. McCain's estrangement and divorce from Carol and his remarriage to Cindy had cooled the personal relationship, but politically he and Reagan were on the same wavelength.

There was one major exception that first year. John McCain wasn't buying anything coming out of the White House about Lebanon, where U.S. Marines and a largely American fleet offshore were trying to preserve the shaky independence of a small state riven by factionalism and threatened by its more powerful neighbors, Syria and Israel. To McCain, Lebanon looked too much like a ghost from the past. Not long past. His past.

On September 28, 1983, three days after the latest in a series of cease-fires had been hammered out—this one under the fearsome shadow of the battleship *New Jersey*—the House prepared to vote on a war-powers measure that would permit the President to keep the Marines in Lebanon for another eighteen months. During a seven-hour debate long on references to Vietnam, one of the few congressmen who had been there took the floor.

"The fundamental question is, What is the United States' interest in Lebanon? It is said we are there to keep the peace. I ask, What peace? It is said we are there to aid the government. I ask, What government? It is said we are there to stabilize the region. I ask, How can the U.S. presence stabilize the region?"

Do you really think naval forces off the Lebanese coast are going to so intimidate the Syrians that they will engage in meaningful negotiations? he asked his colleagues. For this to occur, he said, the Syrians must believe we will use the full military power at our disposal.

"Are we prepared to use this power? I do not think so, nor do I believe the Syrians think so."

He knew a quagmire when he saw it. "The longer we stay in Lebanon, the harder it will be for us to leave," he said. "We will be trapped by the case we make for having our troops there in the first place."

McCain concluded by saying the American presence would not make a difference, that the same things which had been occurring for the past several years would continue to happen—more factional violence, more innocent civilians killed and wounded—whether the Marines were there or not. "I am not calling for an immediate withdrawal," he said. "What I desire is as rapid a withdrawal as possible."

In office barely nine months, he cast his vote against the resolution, one of twenty-seven Republicans to defy Reagan. The final tally in the House was 270 to 161. Speaker Thomas P. "Tip" O'Neill led the fight for the White House, bringing 129 other Democrats with him. The Speaker's fears were calmed by a promise from Reagan to seek congressional authorization for any "substantial expansion" in the size or mission of the Marine contingent.

A few weeks later the liberal *Rolling Stone* magazine, a product of the social and political upheavals of the 1960s, flayed O'Neill and the Democrats who followed his lead in an article entitled "Profiles in Cowardice." But the author, William Greider, tipped his hat to McCain: "In the House of Representatives, a respected veteran of Vietnam . . . chose to remind his colleagues of that war's lessons. . . .

It takes enormous courage for an old military man to deliver a message like that."

For McCain, the vote against keeping Marines in Lebanon signaled a willingness to go against the grain when the issue seemed of sufficient gravity to warrant challenging the wisdom of his party's leaders, the President included. He would do so with sufficient frequency in the years ahead that he earned a reputation as a maverick. He displayed this quality on both domestic and foreign issues. Most likely to draw his fire? Instances in which he feared that a president, Republican or Democrat, might be placing American servicemen in peril without clearly defining their mission.

Which should come as a surprise to no one. Orson Swindle had urged him when he first took office as a congressman not to forget where he came from. He never has, as evidenced by the commencement address he delivered in June 1994 to the Marine Corps Command and Staff College in Quantico, Virginia.

He told the graduates that they faced new, uncharted dangers in the post–Cold War era and that the old bipolar world "where our enemy was indeed evil, but not irrational," was gone. "If I am nostalgic for it at all, it is only a middle-aged man's nostalgia for the time where his youth was spent," he said. "My world, after all, had its moments of cruelty and terror, some of which it was my fate to witness personally."

It was a moving speech, striking chords of honor, patriotism, and the historic gallantry of the Corps, but he delivered it in a businesslike manner. As he neared the end, though, his voice caught in his throat, and for a moment it seemed as if he might not be able to continue.

> I have memories of a place so far removed from the comforts of this blessed country that I have learned to forget some of the anguish it

once brought me. But my happiness these last twenty years has not let me forget the friends who did not return with me to the country we loved so dearly. The memory of them, of what they bore for honor and country, causes me to look in every prospective conflict for the shadow of Vietnam.

I do not let that shadow hold me in fear from my duty as I have been given light to see that duty. Yet it no longer falls to me to bear arms in my country's defense. It falls to you. I pray that if the time comes for you to answer the call to arms, the battle will be necessary and the field well chosen. But that is not your responsibility. Your honor is in your answer, not your summons.

CHAPTER FOURTEEN

The White Tornado

John McCain was an interloper, his election to Congress in 1982 an aberration, a prelude to the crushing defeat that awaited him two years down the line. By then real Arizonans—defined by McCain's political rivals as anyone who had lived in the state longer than he had—would rally behind a single candidate and boot him out of office. Or so it was said.

To the consternation of real Arizonans, Republicans and Democrats alike, McCain refused to play along. Instead, he settled on a strategy to solidify his political base, working at it as if the 1982 campaign had never ended.

He promised to return to his congressional district every weekend, a ridiculous pledge entailing a four-thousand-mile round-trip. He made good on it, though, racing to catch the last flight to Phoenix late on Thursday, when the House normally completed work, then riding the red-eye back Monday night so that he was in his office on Tuesday morning when the legislative week began in earnest. He did it forty-seven weekends that first year, a pace he barely eased in the years that followed.

He was not merely accumulating frequent-flyer miles. The weekends were spent in grueling and frenetic political activity. He marched in parades, met with constituents, spoke to political and service clubs, weighed in on local issues, held town meetings. When possible, he and Cindy reserved Sundays for themselves. To cement his ties to the state, they made a cold-blooded political decision. She would reside in Phoenix, in their new First District home, not Washington.

He was welcomed to Capitol Hill as a celebrity. On his arrival he was elected president of the GOP freshman class, a largely honorary title but enough to cut him out of the herd. A month in office, he was the subject of a long, admiring profile in *The Washington Times* entitled "From Hanoi to the House." Though his interests lay in foreign affairs, defense, and national security policy, he took a seat on the House Interior Committee, which handles water, land reclamation, and similar issues close to the heart of Arizona voters. In deference to the state's large retired population, he joined the Select Committee on Aging.

His support for Reagan was genuine and pleased the folks back in Phoenix. He created a mild furor in the district with his September 1983 vote on Lebanon. The criticism lasted a month, until October when the Marine barracks in Beirut was bombed, killing 241 American servicemen, and coffin-laden troop transports began the long, mournful journey home.

The base-building strategy paid off. On primary day 1984 he was the only Republican on the ballot. He won the general election against Democrat Harry Braun, 78 percent to 22 percent, a landslide. Time to turn his attention to the Senate and the seat that would be up for grabs two years later.

In December 1984, a month after the election, Walter Cronkite invited McCain to join him on a trip to Hanoi where the former CBS News anchorman was to film segments for an April documentary commemorating the tenth anniversary of the end of the Vietnam War. The McCain portions of the nationally televised special were described in *The Arizona Republic* as "a true American hero returning to his prison camp." A politician's dream, if it didn't turn into a private nightmare.

The anticipated benefits were enormous. Though well known in his congressional district, McCain was less familiar to voters elsewhere in the state whose support he would need if, as expected, he ran for the Senate. The documentary would help remedy that problem. The broadcast would also highlight his war record, which Arizona voters knew only vaguely. It might also attract campaign contributions from donors in and out of the state.

As if the potential payoff wasn't great enough, Hanoi raised the stakes, allowing McCain to hit an even greater jackpot. Miffed by McCain's promise to bring up the issue of Americans missing in action, Vietnamese officials refused to grant him a visa. For nearly two months Arizona citizens followed the saga of McCain's off-again, on-again return to Hanoi. From the sidelines, political consultant Jay Smith and other McCain aides provided running commentary. "It's a sticky situation," Smith told *The Arizona Republic*. "He was a thorn in their side." Vietnamese officials, Smith added, considered him "a very bad man."

In January, still lacking a visa, McCain took matters into his own hands, flying to Bangkok to link up with the CBS film crew in the hope that his heavily reported presence there would persuade the Vietnamese to relent and admit him. They didn't, the PR adroitness that they had employed to such devastating effect during the war deserting them. McCain cooled his heels in Bangkok for four days, then flew home, saying he had to get back for the christening of his daughter Meghan, the first of three children he would have with Cindy.

As McCain was making his way home from halfway around the world, a political adviser, Grant Woods, said, "If I had to orchestrate it, it couldn't have worked out better. He's the first congressman they wouldn't let in."

Woods was wrong. It could have worked out better. And it did. In February the Vietnamese issued the visa, and McCain, a four-man film crew, and Walter Cronkite, the most trusted man in America, arrived in Hanoi.

With cameras rolling, the two men strolled along the edge of the lake into which McCain had plunged eighteen years earlier. As curious Vietnamese gathered around, they inspected an elaborate stone monument erected years earlier to celebrate McCain's shoot-down and capture. It depicted a figure resembling the crucified Christ, slumped forward, head bowed, arms stretched skyward as if attached to torture ropes. Cronkite informed the Vietnamese onlookers that his white-haired companion was the man identified in the inscription as "McCan . . . the famous air pirate."

The friendly crowd closed around the two men, pumping McCain's hand and shouting his name. "They felt they were meeting some kind of hero," Cronkite later said. McCain told Cronkite that Hanoi was the only place in the world where he was better known than the famed newsman.

At the former prison the POWs called the Plantation, they had tea with their Vietnamese hosts in a room adjoining a cell in which McCain had been tortured. "He was obviously not comfortable and anxious to get out of there," said Cronkite.

On camera he was an accomplished tour guide, smoothly conducting Cronkite here and there. In one of his old cells, he explained that the shutters were always kept closed and described how he and Bob Craner had communicated through the walls by tap code. Now, though, he seemed less smooth, a bit harried. When the camera caught his eyes, they looked wider than usual, almost doelike, with highlights that for a split second betrayed a terror long held at bay. Then the moment passed.

"Honor, Duty, and a War Called Vietnam," as the heavily promoted special was entitled, was thoughtful and moving, the kind of high-quality production for which CBS and Cronkite had long been known. McCain was prominently featured throughout the hour-long broadcast. The opening segment concluded with the stroll along the lake as Cronkite, in a voice-over, said, "It has been almost eighteen years since former Navy pilot John McCain parachuted into that small Hanoi lake. Tonight he will see it again, and the monument the Vietnamese built to commemorate his capture. He also will walk back into the cell where he spent much of his five and a half years as a prisoner of war. Tonight John McCain returns to his battlefield as we return to others in the war America did not win."

It was billed as a battle of titans. Bruce Babbitt, the youthful, enormously popular Democratic governor, versus John McCain, the ambitious, headstrong, and energetic Republican champion with the trademark shock of white hair. The prize: the senatorial seat that had been held for the better part of three decades by Barry Goldwater, one of the most influential figures in postwar American politics.

That was the popular perception in the weeks immediately following the 1984 election, but the McCain camp was already maneuvering to smother the high expectations of Arizona's political junkies.

The key to victory, McCain's advisers decided, was to keep Babbitt out of the race. If they could do that, and avoid a primary battle that might splinter the party, McCain could expect to be sworn in as the junior senator from Arizona in January 1987.

"It became the campaign within the campaign to convince Bruce Babbitt not to run for the Senate," said Jay Smith.

Babbitt, though clearly interested in running for Goldwater's seat in 1986, was said to view the Senate as a stepping-stone to something loftier, a presidential bid in 1988 when Ronald Reagan's second term ended. A Senate race made sense for him only if he could avoid a costly, draining campaign. He also needed to win. A loss would doom his presidential aspirations. McCain and his political team embarked on a course to persuade Babbitt that the risk of defeat was simply too great.

They employed various tactics to feed Babbitt's anxieties. To remove any doubts Babbitt might have about the resolve of his prospective rival, McCain and his lieutenants spread the word in political circles that nothing could keep him out of the race, that he saw it as a win-win situation. He would run a spirited campaign and broaden his appeal around the state. If he lost, he would challenge the incumbent Democratic senator, Dennis DeConcini, when he came up for reelection in 1988.

He also intensified the frenetic activity that marked his first term, extending it now all across the state. "John McCain is still driven," wrote Richard de Uriarte in the *Phoenix Gazette*. "No rural hamlet too remote to visit. No fund-raiser he can't attend. No interest group he can't romance. No civic organization he can't address. No social event he won't grace with his Boy Scout earnestness. No constituent meeting he can't fit into his schedule."

Then there was the money. McCain had raised $522,000 for his 1984 congressional campaign, compared to a paltry $2,700 by his opponent, Harry Braun. There seemed little doubt that he could raise millions for a senatorial race, especially with the well-heeled national Republican Party trying to beat back a strong Democratic drive to regain control of the Senate. To Babbitt this meant he would be facing not only a vigorous and attractive opponent but a well-financed one as well.

By early 1985 any thought Babbitt may have had about using the senatorial race to prep for a 1988 presidential run had been exposed as a pipe dream by the man dubbed by the press "the White Tornado."

On March 18, 1985, Babbitt ended months of speculation by announcing that he would not run for the Senate the following year. He called it a personal decision, the best thing for himself, his wife, and his two young sons. "At this time in my life and our lives, it's not right for us," he said. He denied that McCain had bullied him out of the race.

McCain, in Washington, scrambled the troops as soon as he learned the news, alerting Cindy, who was in town, and Jay Smith. All three converged on National Airport late that afternoon for a flight to

Phoenix. He officially declared his candidacy for the Senate the next morning.

To Smith, an election that wouldn't go to the voters for another year and a half had already been decided: "We knew McCain was going to be the next senator if he didn't shoot himself in the foot. He tried to, but even he couldn't do it."

Occasionally John McCain's rat-a-tat style and his bubbling self-confidence grated on people, but they were a minority. Thanks to his natural magnetism, he had made friends easily all his life. And he could always draw a crowd. Nothing changed when he settled in Arizona. Looking back, though, he might have been better off had he been a late bloomer, a nerd, a geek, anything but a guy used to being the center of attention. That way, when everyone started gathering around, he might have asked himself an important question:

What do all these people want from me?

One of his earliest and closest friends in Phoenix was Darrow "Duke" Tully, the swashbuckling publisher of *The Arizona Republic* and its sister paper, the *Phoenix Gazette*. Of all McCain's friends, Tully seemed to need the least from him—or anyone else for that matter. If anything, the reverse was true. Tully's position made him one of the most powerful men in the state, a peerless ally for an ambitious politician like McCain. "I tell Arizona what to think," Tully was once quoted as saying.

The relationship between Tully and McCain was grounded in their common military backgrounds. Both were war heroes, Tully having compiled a long list of decorations as an Air Force fighter pilot in Korea and Vietnam. Unlike McCain, Tully gloried in his past exploits, regaling acquaintances with tales of his crash-landing in Korea, his hundred combat missions over North Vietnam, filling his home, office, even his bathroom with military memorabilia. A lieutenant colonel in the Air Force Reserve, he often attended social events in uniform, medals adorning his chest, surrounded by senior officers from Arizona's many military bases.

Two days after Christmas 1985 the headline on the *Republic*'s lead story read, "Publisher Tully Quits; Made Up War Record." A day earlier, Tom Collins, a local prosecutor, had shocked the state by revealing that Tully had never been in the Air Force. Tully had lived a delusion for thirty years, conjuring up war stories, awarding himself medals, periodically promoting himself to higher ranks. Though he was a skilled private pilot, there had been no crash-landing in Korea, no combat missions over North Vietnam, only a bizarre "Mitty-like fantasy," as the *Republic* called it.

As Tully's world disintegrated, he was scorned and ridiculed. Bumper stickers appeared saying, "I Flew with the Duke." A local topless-bottomless club promoted "The Duke Tully Memorial War Heroes Party."

McCain was astounded by Tully's sham, but he did not join in the piling on. "He was my friend and he is my friend," said McCain. "Politics does not take precedence over friendship, but that certainly does not mean that I condone what he did. The whole thing smacks of tragedy."

He was right. Beneath the deceit lay a tragic tale of a bookish child growing up in the shadow of an athletic older brother, a Marine lieutenant killed in a midair collision during World War II, and of a grieving father who for the next thirteen years lavished his love on the dead son before finally climbing a tree, looping a rope around his neck, then shooting himself.

McCain said he never suspected that Tully was engaged in an elaborate masquerade, an admission the *Republic* reported under the headline "Tully's Lies Rang True to Combat Flier McCain." The story seemed the ultimate in chutzpah, as if McCain were somehow remiss in failing to unmask the man who had run the paper for seven years in full view of scores of ace reporters and crackerjack editors who never smelled a rat.

As for Tully, he wanted something out of his relationship with

McCain, and he got it. The friendship reinforced his lies, allowed him to bask in reflected glory. Whatever the root of Tully's problem, Torie Clarke, a McCain aide, described him accurately, if indelicately, as a jock sniffer.

For McCain, the Tully episode proved little more than an embarrassment. But he had other friends with more concrete needs that would be harder to meet and more difficult to explain. And one of them, a savings-and-loan mogul named Charles Keating, would soon ask too much.

In May 1985, McCain's sole potential rival for the GOP senatorial nomination, five-term congressman Bob Stump, a Democrat turned Republican, announced he would not enter the race. Stump's decision meant McCain had achieved the twin goals of his campaign strategy a year and a half before the election: no bruising primary fight and no Bruce Babbitt toting the Democratic standard.

Babbitt's decision two months earlier not to run for the Senate shifted the political spotlight to other well-known party members. None seemed eager to take on the carpetbagger. McCain finally got an opponent in October, Richard Kimball, a tall, grim thirty-seven-year-old often described as a Robert Redford look-alike.

Kimball had a respectable political pedigree. A native Arizonan, he was the son of a former state senate majority leader and had served four years in the legislature himself. Unlike McCain, he had a successful statewide campaign under his belt, having been elected to the three-member Corporation Commission, which regulates public utilities. In that post he had championed consumer causes, demanding that utilities use resources in an efficient manner as a precondition to rate increases.

He was not by any measure a political heavyweight. To some he came across as an odd, occasionally fey personality. In a campaign profile the *Republic*'s Don Harris reported that when Babbitt named two members to the Corporation Commission to fill unexpired vacancies, leaving Kimball as the lone elected member, the trio was dubbed "two lame ducks and a daffy duck."

In his announcement speech in October, Kimball lambasted Duke Tully, whose ticket to Fantasyland had not yet expired, and portrayed McCain as a pawn in the publisher's power game. The attack gained him some attention, but Tully's fall two months later deprived him of a villain and his campaign was effectively becalmed for the next three months.

Supposedly, Kimball was boning up on issues and preparing position papers, but when he unveiled the first in February, *Republic* political columnist Pat Murphy found the fifteen-page document riddled with fractured syntax, aimless phrasing, and misspellings—"barrow" for "borrow," "lisensing" for "licensing," and "physical" for "fiscal." Someone penciled in the correct spelling of "fiscal" before the paper was released, but *Gazette* columnist John Kolbe swore in print that Kimball used the word "physically," as in "We can be physically responsible without abandoning social issues," several times when he interviewed him.

By early 1986 Kimball had regressed from a credible dark-horse candidate to a figure of fun. Murphy concluded that Kimball's missteps were part of a devilishly clever scheme to transform himself into the artless James Stewart character in *Mr. Smith Goes to Washington.* Kolbe, less charitably, diagnosed Kimball's problem as "terminal weirdness."

Kimball shared his name with the David Janssen character in the old TV series "The Fugitive," even using a stick figure of a running man as his logo. The graphic would have been more appropriate for his opponent. McCain, taking nothing for granted, was campaigning as if running against Goldwater rather than trying to succeed him. "I think the worst enemy of any politician is overconfidence," he said. "Remember President Romney and President Muskie?" The press, in state and out, did not share his caution. A *New York Times* op-ed piece in May 1985, entitled "The Changing Faces of Politics in Arizona," focused on McCain, tagging him as the "likely heir" to Goldwater's seat. George Will, in a glowing February 1986 column, said McCain "almost certainly" would win the seat. In May, *Baltimore Sun* syndicated columnists Jack Germond and Jules Witcover said McCain "threatens to become an instant institution in Arizona politics." By May he enjoyed a two-to-one margin in the polls over Kimball. A *Gazette* writer actually urged McCain to ease his frantic pace, saying Arizonans had too much invested in him for him "to drive himself to an early grave."

Meanwhile, nothing seemed to work for Kimball. He lagged behind McCain in the polls and fund-raising. He tried to turn his underfunded, long-shot candidacy into an advantage, declaring he represented the people, not the big corporations, but he remained underfunded and no less a long shot.

As far back as January, however, the *Gazette*'s Kolbe had spotted an unsettling flaw in McCain—his temper—and warned that it could derail his campaign. "It is because McCain's temper flares up so unpredictably, often over such inconsequential trivia, that his friends fear it could jump up and bite him at an inopportune time—such as late October," wrote Kolbe.

This was a variation of Jay Smith's belief that once Babbitt dropped out, no one could hurt McCain but McCain himself. Both Kolbe and Smith were right. McCain, meanwhile, flew into private rages each time Kolbe mentioned his temper in print. "I don't have a temper," he thundered at staffers as they struggled to keep straight faces. "I just care passionately."

The first issue to slow McCain's progress cropped up in June when Kimball allies unearthed a tape recording of remarks he had made in February to students at the University of Arizona. In a wisecracking style tailored to his youthful audience, he urged the students to register and vote, suggesting they emulate the heavy voting patterns of the elderly if they wanted their voices to be heard. "Most of the people coming here presently are senior citizens moving to Leisure World, I mean Seizure World," he said, drawing some politically incorrect laughs. On a roll, he continued, "I mentioned about Seizure World a few moments ago. . . . The last election in 1984, 97 percent of the people who live there came out to vote. I think the other 3 percent were in intensive care."

Typical McCain wisecracks, neither vicious nor terribly original. Residents of Leisure World, an east Mesa retirement community, had heard worse jokes and probably coined many of them. But there was hell to pay. Democrats jumped on McCain, accusing him of insensitivity toward the elderly. Puffed up with indignation, Kimball pronounced himself offended by the joke. "It leaves me humorless," he said.

McCain had stumbled. He might have quickly righted himself, John Kolbe maintained, by issuing an apology, admitting he had said a dumb thing, and moving on. Instead, he kept the issue alive by reacting at length each time anyone said the magic words Seizure World, trotting out his record of support for the elderly, and complaining that he had been quoted out of context. "We're hard-pressed to think of a context in which it would sound better," quipped Kolbe.

Finally drawing blood, Kimball moved to exploit the wound. In July at a convention of public employees, he described McCain as "bought and paid for" by corporate fat cats and labeled his contributor list "a *Who's Who* of high-dollar special interests looking for political protection." Hammering home the charge, he pointed to $100,000 in contributions from defense-related companies and their political action committees, $53,500 from petroleum-related businesses, $43,300 from utilities, and over $50,000 from real estate interests and developers.

Few campaigns are complete without such charges. They are standard, predictable, and legitimate grist for the political mill, especially when one candidate is being outspent four to one by his opponent. What was not predictable was McCain's response. He called a press conference and angrily denounced Kimball for waging "one of the most sloppy and dirty campaigns in Arizona history."

McCain's overblown reactions to Kimball's taunts threatened to throw him off his game. He was beginning to resemble a rabbit-eared rookie unable to ignore the trash talk from the opposing team's dugout. Jay Smith patiently explained the facts of life to him. When you're an underdog, you try to get under the skin of your opponent. So you needle him, make him react to you. If you get lucky, he says something stupid. That's what Kimball's doing to you, and you're playing into his hands. McCain nodded in agreement and held his peace—until the next time.

Throughout the summer, Kimball agitated for debates, dared McCain to meet him face-to-face. The McCain team had decided they did not want to debate until mid-October. A radio station tried to set up a debate and pressed McCain for a commitment. "I want to do it, Jay," said McCain, infuriated by Kimball's charges that he was ducking him. "Look, we're not going to let this turkey run the campaign," said Smith. "We'll do it on our terms. When you debate, it is going to be when it's good for us, it's going to be on statewide TV, and we're going to kick his ass." McCain persisted: "I don't want people to think I'm afraid of him." Said Smith, "John, nobody cares."

By mid-September, Kimball had closed to within thirteen percentage points. The McCain camp was worried and looked to the first of three televised debates, scheduled for October 17, to halt Kimball's advance. McCain was tense as the showdown approached. His advisers insisted that all he had to do was look senatorial and avoid a major blunder.

To prepare for the debate, McCain went into seclusion two days beforehand at his cabin in Sedona with aides Jay Smith, Grant Woods, and Wes Gullett. Smith played Kimball, hurling charges willy-nilly at McCain. Seizure World. Bought and paid for. Reagan puppet. PAC-man. Tool of defense contractors. Never saw a weapons system he didn't like. McCain was slow hitting his stride, seemed inarticulate, blocked. By the morning of the debate, though, he felt confident, as if he had broken through a wall.

That afternoon Smith checked out the debate site, a high school auditorium. He immediately sensed a problem. The two candidates were to be positioned in such a way that McCain, a good six inches shorter than the lanky Kimball, would appear even shorter to viewers because of the camera angles. "I don't want John to look like a pygmy," Smith angrily told the producer. The producer suggested placing a riser behind McCain's podium for him to stand on. Smith reluctantly agreed.

The debate began with brief opening statements. Kimball appeared earnest and intent, if somewhat brittle. McCain seemed polished and affable, though from time to time his eyes dropped disconcertingly to his note cards. Once into the questioning, stylistic differences emerged. McCain, fully in control, fielded the questions smoothly, made his points coolly. Kimball, by contrast, grew angrier and more self-righteous by the minute. Instead of Robert Redford, he looked like Alan Alda as Hawkeye Pierce in moments of high dudgeon, but without the offsetting charm and humor. Near the end Kimball almost seemed to be snarling, as if ready to reach through the television screen and grab the throat of any viewer who disagreed with him.

Kimball had openings but failed to capitalize on them. His responses were long and confusing, fat paragraphs without topic sentences. Although he was neither mean-spirited nor arrogant, everything he said seemed to come out that way. "I understand John's confusion about my Central American policy," he said at one point. "This is the first time he has been allowed to be in my presence in this campaign." Translation: McCain had been dodging him.

Kimball got to McCain once. In an exchange over whether McCain had voted for a weapons system called the Bradley Infantry Fighting Vehicle, Kimball said, "You come in here and you treat people for suckers. You stand on a soapbox to make yourself appear to look taller." McCain's eyes flashed, his only response on camera. Afterward, though, he was furious. "Wanted to kill him," reported Jay Smith.

Kimball devoted most of his closing statement to reasons why voters should reject McCain, without offering even a marginally compelling reason why they should elect him. McCain finished up by citing his experience and accomplishments. He then recalled how the terminally ill Lou Gehrig had bowed out of baseball by calling himself "the luckiest man on the face of the earth."

"I feel the same way," said McCain. "For twenty-two years I was privileged to serve our nation in the U.S. Navy, the way my father and grandfather did. And unlike many thousands of our young men who gave their lives in Vietnam for the cause of freedom, I was lucky to be given a second chance, a second chance to serve my country, a second chance to give something back to this nation which has given so much to me and to all of us. With your help I can be of even greater service to Arizona and America in the U.S. Senate."

The press called the debate a tie. McCain fumed when he saw himself perched on a footstool on the front page of the *Republic*. Jay Smith, convinced McCain had murdered Kimball, wondered if he should revise his prediction of McCain's vote total upward from his pre-debate figure of 57 percent. He decided he should, but kept it to himself. The election was more than two weeks away. With John McCain, anything could happen.

On Election Day, McCain followed the tradition he had established back in 1982 by going to the movies. He saw *Crocodile Dundee*. Jay Smith, mindful of the huge fund-raising advantage McCain enjoyed over Kimball—$2.6 million to $550,000—told his boss *The Color of Money* would have been more appropriate.

The polls had barely closed when the networks declared McCain the winner. The final margin was twenty percentage points, 60 percent to 40 percent. McCain headed to the downtown hotel where his supporters and the press had gathered. Earlier in the day, local TV producers told Smith that they had placed a riser at the spot where McCain was to deliver his anticipated victory speech. Make sure he stands on it, Jay. Our cameras will never pick him up if he doesn't. Smith promised to do so, but in the flurry of Election Day activities it slipped his mind.

Arriving at the hotel shortly after McCain, Smith saw reporters and well-wishers huddled together on the stage. From the midst of the throng he heard a familiar voice floating upward, thanking the voters for sending him to the Senate. Familiar but disembodied. McCain had seen the riser and kicked it aside. The White Tornado had become the Invisible Man.

The final days of the campaign were ripe with foreshadowing.

On November 2, two days before the election, R. W. Apple, Jr., of *The New York Times* all but conceded McCain the Senate seat, saying he "now seems poised to emerge as a significant figure in national politics."

The following day the *Republic* carried a less flattering article on its lead local page. It said that McCain and six other congressmen who had received campaign contributions from Charles Keating had aided a Keating thrift—Lincoln Savings and Loan Association of Irvine, California—in a bitter battle with the Federal Home Loan Bank Board.

On Election Day, November 4, as the fifth man from the bottom in the Naval Academy Class of 1958 was being swept into the United States Senate, the number one man in that same class, White House National Security Adviser John Poindexter, was on the verge of ruin. A bizarre tale drifting out of the Middle East said that the Reagan administration had been trading arms to Iran in return for Americans held hostage there. Poindexter was about to be engulfed in the Iran-Contra scandal, the Watergate of the 1980s.

• • •

True to R. W. Apple, Jr.'s preelection prediction, McCain on moving to the Senate in January 1987 quickly established himself as an important new figure on the national political scene. The Senate had swung Democratic, but he had bucked the tide of GOP losses. By the following spring he was receiving serious mention as a running mate for George Bush, who had nailed down the Republican presidential nomination.

CHAPTER FIFTEEN

Halos and Horns Redux

In November 1986, two weeks after John McCain's election to the Senate, Attorney General Edwin Meese walked into the White House pressroom and directly implicated Vice Admiral John Poindexter—along with fellow Naval Academy graduates Oliver North and Robert McFarlane—in the Iran-Contra affair, a mushrooming scandal that threatened the future of the Reagan presidency.

At the time, Poindexter was Reagan's national security adviser. McFarlane was his predecessor, North the trusted aide of both men. From the start, Iran-Contra had a kaleidoscopic quality, the pattern fracturing and re-forming with each new wave of revelations. The lone constant in those early days was the presence at the heart of the scandal of the three Annapolis men.

Iran-Contra needs no lengthy retelling. Its shape and most of the details are now familiar, though it retains the power to shock and befuddle. The United States, it seemed, had been secretly selling arms to Iran in the hope of obtaining the release of American hostages held in Lebanon. Supposedly the overriding goal was to create a strategic opening to the oil-rich Middle Eastern state, ruled since 1979 by the revolutionary regime of the Ayatollah Ruholla Khomeini. To many, the arrangement smacked of trading arms for hostages, something the United States had said it would never do.

The other shoe dropped a few weeks later. Meese revealed that both he and the President had just learned that North, with Poindexter's knowledge, had taken some of the profits from the Iranian arms sales and diverted the money to a guerrilla band in Nicaragua—the Contras—that was attempting to overthrow the pro-Communist regime there. This seemed to fly in the face of a congressional measure that its sponsors would argue prohibited any U.S. support for the rebels. That measure, and its precise impact, would later be widely debated. Moreover, in the months ahead, the circle of knowledge and involvement would grow considerably. But in those first weeks the glare of the national spotlight shone almost exclusively on Poindexter, North, and McFarlane.

A few days after the diversion was exposed, Poindexter was called to testify before the House Armed Services Committee. It was the lame-duck period in Washington and John McCain was still a member of the panel, his swearing in as a senator still a month away.

Having heard that Poindexter planned to take the Fifth Amendment against self-incrimination, McCain invited his old classmate to stop by his office prior to his appearance before the committee. The two men had not been close either at the Academy or in ensuing years, but there was mutual respect for each other's accomplishments. Poindexter arrived with his attorney, Richard Beckler, a former naval officer and one of the city's most prominent criminal lawyers.

After his guests had been seated and served coffee, McCain said, "John, you can't become the first admiral in the history of the United States Navy to plead the Fifth."

Beckler, responding for Poindexter, promised that the admiral would explain everything in detail at the right time, but not that day.

McCain, unappeased, pressed the matter: "John, you can't do it."

Poindexter said little, impassively sipped his coffee. The scene had an Alice-in-Wonderland quality, the Annapolis screw-off preaching to the model midshipman. A few minutes later, Poindexter walked into the committee room, was sworn in, then asked a question. He refused to answer on the grounds that his reply might incriminate him.

Several months later, during a break in Poindexter's lengthy testimony at the congressional Iran-Contra hearings, NBC's Tom Brokaw asked McCain to explain his classmate's self-proclaimed decision not to tell Reagan about the diversion of arms sale profits to the Contras.

"I know John to be a man of the highest integrity," said McCain. "At the same time it is difficult to comprehend why he would not inform the President of activities of that magnitude. . . . I think he made a terrible mistake."

Afterward, an infuriated Mark Hill, by then cochairman of the Poindexter legal defense fund, called McCain in his Senate office and demanded to know how he could make such a statement.

Didn't you do the same kind of thing, working behind the President's back, when we were trying to get Congress to fund the carrier? asked the retired rear admiral.

McCain called Hill an old goat.

Over the next five years, Poindexter lived a nightmare, one that finally ended in December 1992 when the Supreme Court declined to reinstate his conviction on five Iran-Contra charges that an appeals court had previously reversed. The shape of Iran-Contra had changed considerably by the time the high court acted. Poindexter's culpability had been established in the eyes of many Americans, but there was greater comprehension of the difficult situation in which he had found himself.

McCain, meanwhile, was enmeshed in a scandal of his own during three of those five years. One of the so-called Keating Five, he and four other senators found themselves fighting for their political lives because of their relationship with savings-and-loan mogul Charles Keating.

In January 1993, their separate ordeals over, Poindexter and McCain found themselves at the White House where President George Bush was presenting the Medal of Freedom, the nation's highest civilian award, to Ronald Reagan.

At the reception following the ceremony, John and Cindy McCain joined Poindexter and his wife, Linda. They talked about the bad times both families had endured. McCain said something about how the Keating Five experience had given him a new perspective on a lot of things. Poindexter took the remark as a concession by McCain that perhaps he had been too harsh in his comments to Tom Brokaw during the Iran-Contra hearings. The commiseration was brief, neither man given to a mournful replaying of the past. Looking to the future, they spoke expectantly of the thirty-fifth reunion of the Class of 1958, coming up in the fall.

CHAPTER SIXTEEN

Bahama Mamas on the Beach

John McCain did not become the Republican vice-presidential nominee in 1988, but as the Bush years began he continued to gain political momentum. He led the fight to win confirmation of his old mentor, John Tower, as Secretary of Defense, losing the battle but earning new stature in the Senate.

In early October 1989 he won a grueling and notable legislative victory, defying both the Republican and Democratic leadership and forcing the repeal of a catastrophic health insurance law that was passed the previous year.

The final vote came in the early-morning hours of Saturday, October 7. Torie Clarke, his press secretary, had a freshly butchered 110-pound pig in the bathtub of her first-floor flat in Georgetown, shipped in from Iowa for a backyard barbecue that afternoon. Planned as a gathering of friends, it would now do double duty as a victory celebration. But McCain never showed up. Something bad was in the air.

Sunday, October 8, 1989, marked the zenith of McCain's astounding rise and the start of his even more rapid descent. That morning he was on CBS's *Face the Nation* discussing events in Panama. *The Washington Post* and the *Los Angeles Times* both ran op-ed pieces written by him on the health insurance issue. But back in Phoenix *The Arizona Republic* led with a story tying him to Charles Keating, the embattled savings-and-loan kingpin. Keating, his family, and associates had contributed $112,000 to McCain's House and Senate campaigns. Keating, who resided in the Phoenix area, had also been McCain's friend. The main story was accompanied by two sidebars fleshing out the details of the relationship. The Keating story had been exploding around McCain for months, bracketing him like mortar fire. Now the gunners were firing for effect.

"I'm really sorry I didn't come to your party," said McCain as he met a hungover Clarke outside the CBS News bureau that morning. "I was too depressed. I thought I would be a wet blanket."

"John, you couldn't be a wet blanket if you tried," said Clarke, laughing.

She was wrong. The next three years were among the most dispiriting of his life as he struggled to clear his name. He alternated between anger and depression, the resilience his Vietnamese captors had failed to beat out of him only fitfully evident. What had been perhaps the most happy-go-lucky of senatorial offices was soon gripped by paranoia and an ever-deepening despondence. Everyone down to the lowliest intern still called him by his first name, but the excitement and the joy of working for a senator with seemingly boundless prospects was gone, replaced by the aroma of impending political death.

He talked about not running again when he came up for reelection in 1992. By then his three younger children would be old enough to understand the vicious attack ads that he had every reason to believe the opposition would mount. He did not know if he was up for the fight. Having barely survived five and a half years in prison, he seemed totally unprepared for the horror to arise and come at him again in a different form.

"This is the worst thing, the absolute worst thing that ever happened to me," he said at one point early on as aides gathered in his office.

"It can't be the worst thing," said one of those present, amazed at his use of the superlative.

"No," he said, "this is worse."

Carelessly choosing his friends, as he had in the case of publisher Duke Tully, McCain had stumbled into a scandal of immense proportions. Tully had been a ridiculous figure, his fall little more than a minor embarrassment for McCain. Charles Keating, it turned out, had built his financial empire on the life savings of elderly retirees, men and women who watched helplessly as their dreams were snuffed out along with the assets of Keating's Lincoln Savings and Loan Association.

The story was complicated, but the press found a tag line that simplified it. McCain and four other senators with ties to Keating were dubbed "the Keating Five." The label stuck, imputing to all the same degree of guilt even though it soon became evident that at least two, McCain and former astronaut John Glenn of Ohio, were far less culpable, if they were culpable at all.

Stripped of the veneer of sleaze that coated the affair, McCain's defense of his actions was solid and credible. It didn't matter. The Keating Five label endured, shabby journalistic shorthand that made up in simplemindedness what it lacked in precision, five faces symbolizing a scandal that stood to cost taxpayers untold billions as a result of rampant thrift failures—$2.6 billion because of Lincoln alone, the costliest bailout ever. Stories routinely carried mug shots of the five senators, adorned with boldface dollar figures showing the amount Keating had raised and contributed to their political organizations. News reports invariably referred to five "powerful" senators. At the time of the meetings that lay at the heart of the charges, McCain—the lone Republican in the deck—had been a senator for less than four months.

The most serious charges revolved around two meetings in April 1987 at which the senators—four at the first, five at the second—allegedly pressured officials of the Federal Home Loan Bank Board to make concessions that might help Keating save his ailing savings and loan. The implication was that the meetings delayed action against Keating, further depleting the accounts of depositors. Lost in the uproar was McCain's defense.

According to undisputed testimony before the Ethics Committee, he was drawn into the case on March 17, 1987, when he received a letter from Keating complaining of his treatment by bank board examiners. To support that contention, Keating sent along two letters, the first from Alan Greenspan, the respected economist who since 1989 has chaired the Federal Reserve Board, the second from Arthur Young & Co., one of the big five accounting firms. Greenspan supported Keating's assertion that Lincoln's financial structure was sound. The Arthur Young letter questioned the duration of the examination and called the examiners "openly hostile and inflexible" toward Lincoln.

Persuaded that serious questions had been raised about the conduct of the examination, McCain agreed to the suggestion of fellow Arizona senator Dennis DeConcini to explore the issues further with Edwin Gray, the federal bank board chairman, on April 2. DeConcini first proposed that he and McCain fly to San Francisco to meet with the regulators, but McCain declined, believing such a trip smacked more of pressure than fact-finding.

Nine days before the meeting, on March 24, McCain met with Keating, who demanded that McCain negotiate with the bank board on his behalf. McCain refused. His responsibility as a senator was to ensure that constituents were treated fairly, he said, not act as their agent. He was already furious with Keating, having heard that the banker had called him a "wimp" earlier that day on learning that he had rebuffed DeConcini. McCain told Keating he resented the remark. Angry words were exchanged. The meeting, and a six-year friendship, ended with a red-faced Keating storming out of his office.

In the immediate aftermath, McCain considered backing out of the meeting set for the following week with bank board chairman Gray. McCain decided to attend, he said, because Keating's American Continental Corporation, Lincoln's corporate parent, was a major employer in his state, providing jobs to some two thousand persons in the Phoenix area.

Four of the senators—McCain, Glenn, DeConcini, and Alan

Cranston of California—attended the April 2 meeting with Gray in DeConcini's office. Gray later asserted that he felt intimidated, but his actions do not seem to support that claim. He testified that he did not even ask his staff what the meeting was about. Once there, he professed ignorance of the status of the Lincoln examination. He did not air his charges publicly for two years. Moreover, it was Gray, not the senators, who suggested the more controversial follow-up meeting with bank examiners, something McCain had shied away from when DeConcini suggested it. McCain, again according to undisputed testimony, asked if such a meeting would be proper. Gray assured him that it would be.

According to the bank board's own transcript, McCain's opening comment at the April 9 meeting with the examiners was as follows: "One of our jobs as elected officials is to help constituents in a proper fashion. ACC is a big employer and important to the local economy. I wouldn't want any special favors for them." He also said, "I don't want any part of our conversation to be improper. We asked Chairman Gray about that, and he said it wasn't improper to discuss Lincoln."

At that meeting—attended by Donald Riegle of Michigan as well as the original four senators—the examiners received tough questioning about the conduct of the Lincoln probe. Near the end, however, they informed the senators that they had uncovered serious accounting irregularities and that they would soon be referring the case to the Justice Department with a recommendation that criminal charges be brought against the thrift and its principal officers. That nugget effectively concluded the meeting. McCain, convinced Lincoln was being treated fairly, never again involved himself in the matter. Nor did he communicate again with Keating. If he can be faulted at all for his actions at the meeting, it would be for failing to break in when the tone of other senators' remarks bordered on negotiating for Keating—to say, Hold it. So-and-so doesn't speak for me.

His personal relationship with Keating complicated the matter.

Keating, also a former Navy pilot, had been a friend as well as an important campaign contributor and rainmaker dating back to 1981. Their families had vacationed together at Keating's home on Cat's Key in the Bahamas in 1984, 1985, and 1986, the McCains often flying there aboard Keating's corporate aircraft. In February 1989, American Continental informed McCain that he had not paid the company for some of those flights. The amount at issue was $7,215.

McCain was appalled. The notice could hardly have come at a worse time, a year and a half into the scandal. He ordered a staff review of his records, which determined that he had paid for some of his flights but not for others. To further confuse matters, the review disclosed an additional $3,755 in unpaid fares due ACC. He paid the bill, which eventually came to $13,433, in full. He then informed the Senate Ethics Committee and the press about what had transpired.

He insisted that the charges had come as a complete surprise to him. He had failed to pay in a timely manner, he said, because he did not have a reliable system in place to ensure that he received bills for personal travel, as opposed to official or campaign travel. In other words, bills were paid when tendered, but he had no tickler system for making sure he received the bills in the first place.

To support that defense, he produced canceled checks showing that he had made a number of other payments to ACC at the time flights were taken. "My payments clearly reflect my intentions to have such travel reimbursed in a timely fashion," he told the Ethics Committee. "They prove that I was sensitive to my responsibility to reimburse for corporate air travel and that I did not intend to avoid payment."

His defense rang true. Although he took full responsibility for the oversight, he was very much like his father in that he left matters of personal finance to others. Unmentioned was another factor. With his Navy pension and Senate salary, he was financially comfortable. Cindy was rich. There was no reason to try to skip out on a $13,000 tab.

Finally, there was the Fountain Square Project. In 1986, Cindy and her father, James Hensley, invested in a shopping center under development in Phoenix. They were among several limited partners in a project in which a subsidiary of Keating's American Continental Corporation was the general partner.

McCain screamed bloody murder when the *Arizona Republic* published its account, even exploding at me when I told him I thought it was a legitimate story. He argued that Cindy was a businesswoman in her own right, that she and her father had made joint investments before and probably would again. He also pointed out that he and Cindy had entered into a prenuptial agreement in which their finances were to remain separate. They filed individual tax returns. He had publicly disclosed his wife's Fountain Square investment on his annual disclosure report for three years. Plus, there was no evidence that Cindy and her father had received more favorable treatment than any of the other investors.

On one side of the ledger, an argument can be made that Keating, directly or indirectly, acted in ways that benefited McCain. Just raising $112,000 for his campaigns establishes that. And certainly any money Cindy made helped him, prenuptial agreement or not. Where the case against McCain falls apart is on the other side. What did he do for Keating? Next to nothing.

Despite his falling-out with Keating, he was persuaded by the Alan Greenspan and Arthur Young & Co. letters that reasonable questions existed about the treatment of a major employer in his state. As a result, he went to two meetings at which he acted properly beyond perhaps his failure to clearly disassociate himself from the remarks of other senators. His questions answered, he washed his hands of the whole affair.

Two weeks after the first news stories of the scandal broke on that Sunday in October 1989, McCain met with the Arizona press in Phoenix. He promised to stay until all questions were answered, and he did. The news conference lasted seventy-five minutes. He was well prepared by his staff, which had little doubt he could handle the substance of the questions but feared he might lose his temper, the eruption blotting out all that might precede it. A day or so earlier, press secretary Torie Clarke had cautioned him against letting his anger get the best of him. "When was the last time I lost my temper with a reporter?" he snapped at her. "Two weeks ago, with —— and ——," she fired back, naming two *Arizona Republic* reporters. He grumpily conceded the point, heeded the warning, never came close to losing it during the news conference.

The early returns were favorable. The accounts ranged from neutral to positive. The editorials were even better, lauding him for his forthrightness and accessibility. But the lull was brief. In November, the Senate Ethics Committee announced the hiring of Robert S. Bennett, a prominent Washington criminal lawyer, to look into the actions of the five senators and their relationship with Keating. A month later the committee launched a preliminary inquiry. Just before Christmas, Susan Rasky of *The New York Times* reported that McCain's friends were worried about him. "Normally given to expansive gestures and almost hypertensive movement, he seems, they say, to have visibly shriveled, hunching his shoulders and clasping his arms tightly about his chest as if to ward off blows," she wrote. His efforts to lighten awkward moments merely heightened their concerns, she wrote, quoting him as telling dinner companions, "You know what Chairman Mao said—It's always darkest just before it's totally black."

His mood rarely brightened. His honor and integrity had been questioned. Cindy had been dragged into the scandal. A strong Democratic challenge in 1992, impossible to conceive of a few months earlier, suddenly seemed likely. He nevertheless stayed on the offensive, charging out ahead of the other four senators in making himself available to the press. Meeting with the regulators, he said, was a serious mistake. Though not actually improper, it gave the appearance of impropriety, if only because of the number of senators who participated. He submitted a lengthy written rebuttal of charges to the Ethics

Committee, offering to meet with the panel and answer all questions. His only request: act quickly, end this nightmare.

Instead, the probe dragged on for another year and a half. In September 1990 attorney Bennett recommended that the committee drop the charges against McCain and John Glenn but continue the investigation of DeConcini, Cranston, and Riegle. The panel—evenly divided between Democrats and Republicans—split along partisan lines and refused to do so. McCain and others suspected the Democrats of playing politics. He was the lone Republican in the pack. They couldn't just clear Glenn. He hadn't done much for Keating, but even he had done more than McCain. Instead, the committee announced that it would begin public hearings on the actions of all five senators in mid-November. "Glenn got screwed because of me," McCain would later say. Senator Warren Rudman, a New Hampshire Republican regarded as a pillar of rectitude and vice-chairman of the ethics panel, would subsequently make a similar comment about McCain: "He was screwed."

The process was taking a toll on McCain and those around him. When it was all over, Cindy, normally cool and composed, burst into tears when asked how much it had changed him. "I watched John just crumble," she said. Overnight, it seemed, he had gone from a youthful, dynamic senator to an anxious, distracted figure, slumped in a chair, finally looking his age, staring bleakly into space. For the first time in their married lives, they exchanged angry words. Each blamed the other for failing to pay for the flights to Cat's Key, a bigger issue in Arizona than the meetings with regulators. Finally, after weeks of rancor, they agreed they were both to blame and closed ranks.

In self-defense, Cindy stopped reading the papers. She also blew town. In 1986 she had founded an organization called the Arizona Voluntary Medical Team, which began by sending medical supplies to the Pacific Island of Truk. The following year she took a team of physicians there, creating a self-contained civilian medical organization akin to a MASH unit. As the scandal raged around her, she sought refuge in good works far from home, leading her corps of doctors and nurses on seven or eight trips a year, each of at least two weeks' duration. By early 1991 the team had ministered to the ill and disabled in Vietnam, Micronesia, Bangladesh, Nicaragua, El Salvador, and Kuwait. She was with her husband at the hearings, then headed off to the Persian Gulf. Three days after the Gulf War ended, as McCain was sweating out the deliberations of the Ethics Committee in Washington, she called him from Checkpoint 99 in Iraq.

McCain by then was fighting back hard, not only to meet what Rasky of the *Times* called "a seemingly unquenchable need to defend his honor" but to save his Senate seat. The televised hearings lasted eight weeks, ending in mid-January. McCain took some hits during the inquisition but rebounded so well that John R. Crawford of *Congressional Quarterly* said he had fared better than if the ethics panel had taken Bennett's advice and cleared him in advance. Bennett, in fact, used McCain and Glenn as role models of proper senatorial conduct, contrasting their actions with those of DeConcini, Riegle, and Cranston.

After six weeks of deliberations, the committee rendered its judgment on February 27, 1991. The interim had been filled with reports of political gamesmanship aimed mainly at keeping Republican McCain from getting off scot-free. Cranston was hammered; the panel concluded that he had engaged in "an impermissible pattern of conduct in which fund-raising and official activities were substantially linked." McCain, at the other end of the culpability spectrum, received a mild rebuke for exercising "poor judgment." He pronounced himself vindicated and put aside lingering thoughts of retirement.

On paper, McCain had everything going against him as he hit the campaign trail for the 1992 election. A firestorm of anti-incumbent sentiment was sweeping the nation, fueled by the savings-and-loan scandal. And McCain was not just any incumbent, an innocent bystander tarred by the sins of his colleagues, but one of the infamous

Keating Five. Moreover, in a year dubbed by pundits "The Year of the Woman," his Democratic opponent was Phoenix community activist Claire Sargent. Former right-wing Republican governor Evan Mecham was also running, as an independent, his candidacy seemingly a vehicle to take vengeance on McCain for calling on him to resign from office in January 1988 following his indictment on six felony counts. McCain could write the attack ads himself: he and Cindy lounging on the beach, sipping Bahama Mamas, as Charlie Keating stuffs thousand-dollar bills into his pockets.

The 1991 Gulf War helped restore McCain's image. His military background made him much in demand as a television commentator, nationally and in Arizona, even as his integrity was being questioned daily in hearings televised on C-SPAN. Now, the hearings behind him, he picked up the pace of his campaign. Soon White Tornado sightings were being reported all across the state. By early 1992 his poll standings had improved, and his campaign coffers were filling steadily.

Meanwhile, Mecham—who was found not guilty of the 1988 charges—seemed to be going nowhere, and Sargent was proving a lackluster candidate, her high-water mark a quip at a Washington fund-raiser: "It's about time we put someone with breasts in the Senate. We've already got enough boobs." She remained severely underfunded, a commentary on her stature when contrasted with that of her Republican opponent. Emily's List, a political action committee that supports female candidates, contributed nothing to her campaign. She worked hard but never caught fire. She chose not to lean heavily on the Keating Five scandal. No money. No attack ads. No Bahama Mamas on the beach.

As the campaign neared its end, George Bush was plummeting everywhere, even in Arizona. McCain, according to election eve polls, was expected to crush Sargent and Mecham. Taking nothing for granted, McCain spent the day before the election driving himself hundreds of miles, gorging on Whattaburgers, shaking every hand in sight.

On election night, friends and campaign workers gathered in his north Phoenix home. Four television sets were mounted side by side in the living room. The polls closed at 7:00 P.M. At 7:01 CBS declared him the winner. By 7:05 ABC and NBC had followed suit. CNN waited till 7:15. He had received a whopping 58 percent of the vote in a three-way race, but he seemed subdued. By then the dimensions of Bush's defeat had become clear.

About an hour later he headed downtown to the GOP's election night headquarters at the Hyatt Regency. He waited until Bush made his concession speech, then entered the packed ballroom to chants of "six more years." In deference to Bush's loss, he kept his remarks brief. He thanked everyone who had helped him in the campaign and promised to work to break the gridlock in Washington. As he concluded, the "six more years" chant resumed. From deep in the crowd a lone voice shouted: "McCain for President."

A few weeks later Cindy said, "He's doing a lot better now, but, no, he's not all the way back. I don't think he ever will be." Men and women he barely knew had rallied around him during the bad times, but he had been wounded by the silence of old friends. In Washington he began his second term working as feverishly as ever, seemingly content to be a good senator, his national ambitions dulled by the ordeal of the previous four years.

"I've seen the glow go out of him," said Cindy. "This is a guy that could reach for the stars, and now he can't—or he won't."

CHAPTER SEVENTEEN

The Road Back

John McCain is one of those rare political gems who has a position that will offend everybody sooner or later.

David Nyhan, *Boston Globe*, November 14, 1997

McCain rebounded from the scandal, but it was a slow process, one that took years. The road back began in Annapolis on May 26, 1993, not—as one might have imagined—with his resounding reelection to the Senate seven months earlier.

The occasion was the Naval Academy graduation at the Navy–Marine Corps Stadium. As the commencement speaker he was seated on the dais alongside the Academy superintendent, Rear Admiral Tom Lynch. Arrayed before him were 1,050 first classmen, 961 men and 89 women. The class was one short. Jeffrey Mascunana, a twenty-three-year-old midshipman from Savannah, Georgia, scheduled to graduate with his class that morning, died shortly after midnight in a bizarre accident. He and his girlfriend, Julie Ann Mace, were in Mascunana's 1983 Toyota when it veered off the road and flipped over. Julie Ann was thrown from the car and died from her injuries.

Mascunana, apparently trying to flag down assistance, was struck by a van and killed as well.

The timing of the tragedy, within hours of graduation, riveted the press and eclipsed coverage of McCain's address, which was barely reported. But for perhaps the first time since Keating had engulfed him he looked and sounded like the man he used to be. Many of his Academy classmates, some from as far away as California, had converged on Annapolis to cheer him on. And he responded, not only to his old friends, but to the midshipmen and the Academy itself, as if he was drawing strength from an institution that he had in many ways detested during his time there.

As distinguished graduates go, he was not in the classic mold, which he was quick to point out. "My four years here were not notable for individual academic achievement," he puckishly told the graduates, "but, rather, for the impressive catalogue of demerits which I managed to accumulate. By my reckoning, at the end of my second class year, I had marched enough extra duty to take me to Baltimore and back seventeen times."

As his audience whooped and applauded, he turned serious. He spoke of his father and his grandfather, then added, "For much of my life, the Navy was the only world I knew. It is still the world I know best and love most." He recalled that his father had been the commencement speaker in 1970, an occasion he said he would have loved to attend had he not been "otherwise engaged," meaning doing hard time in Hanoi.

There was, in his tone and words, a feeling that he had come home. Not for good, certainly, and not for long, but long enough perhaps for the visit to rejuvenate him and set in motion the long process of restoring that unsinkable quality that prison could not steal from him, but Keating almost did. Thus he spoke of the enduring message that the Academy seeks to impart to all its graduates.

"Here," he said, "we learned to dread dishonor above all other temptations."

He closed with a litany so personal that those close to him over the years found themselves choking back sobs.

"I have spent time in the company of heroes," he began. He spoke of aviators hurled off the decks of pitching ships. Navy gunners face-to-face with attacking kamikazes. Submariners beating back terror as they patrolled the ocean's depths. The crew of the *Forrestal* fighting to save a ship that had become a floating inferno. The First Marine Division battling its way back from the Chosen Reservoir over bleak, frozen terrain through seven North Korean divisions. Finally, he said, "I have watched men suffer the anguish of imprisonment, defy appalling human cruelty until further resistance is impossible, break for a moment, then recover inhuman strength to defy their enemies once more."

He continued, as he and his audience seemed to blend into one, "All these things and more, I have seen. And so will you."

Then he added: "I will go to my grave in gratitude to my Creator for allowing me to stand witness to such courage and honor. And so will you.

"My time is slipping by. Yours is fast approaching. You will know where your duty lies. You will know."

The Nightingale's Song, as sweet and as pure as it gets. Ronald Reagan could not have sung it better.

A year later, in July 1994, he spoke at the commissioning ceremony in Bath, Maine, for the USS *John S. McCain*, an Aegis-class destroyer named for his father and grandfather. "They were my first heroes," he said, "and their respect for me has been the most lasting ambition of my life." The principal speaker that day was former President George Bush.

By then McCain seemed to have moved out of the shadow of Keating. A month later, however, his life was rocked again, once more clouding his future. Cindy narrowly escaped indictment for siphoning off prescription drugs from the medical assistance team she had set up in 1989 to work in Third World countries. Her addiction dated back to the early days of the Keating Five scandal. *The Arizona Republic*, always among the harshest of McCain's critics, ran an editorial cartoon showing Cindy holding an emaciated black child upside down and shaking him over what appeared to be a field of corpses. "Quit your crying and give me the drugs," read the caption.

The furor took its toll on her, but in late 1997 she boasted to a reporter of being drug-free for the previous five years. She was once again active in civic and humanitarian work while raising the couple's four children, including seven-year-old Bridget, whom the McCains had adopted as an infant after Cindy brought her home from Bangladesh and presented her to John at the airport with the words, "Meet your new daughter."

By mid-1994, McCain had gained fresh stature by challenging President Clinton's policies in Somalia, loudly warning against committing troops to the Balkans, and sounding the alert on North Korea's nuclear ambitions. To some he seemed the near-perfect candidate to challenge Clinton in 1996, but he brushed aside all approaches, even after a Republican tide swept the nation in November, giving the GOP control of both houses of Congress for the first time in forty years. Instead he left the field to a collection of retreads and wannabes, along with one fresh new face, retired Army General Colin Powell, former chairman of the Joint Chiefs of Staff.

Presidential prospects aside, McCain had become the GOP's unofficial spokesman on national security issues. In the fall he took the lead in opposing American intervention in Haiti, appearing almost daily on radio and television or in the newspaper. The notion that he might someday be Secretary of State or Defense in a Republican administration was beginning to take root. And there was renewed talk about Vice President.

Vietnam was the defining event of his life, but unlike many veterans of that conflict, most of whom suffered far less than he did, he had never permitted himself to be a prisoner of it. He seemed to have fought off the anger and sense of betrayal that haunts much of his generation of combat veterans. Unlike many of them, he didn't hold grudges. Some of his best friends resided on the far crest of the generational fault line that separated those who went and those who, for whatever reason, did not. And for him as for many kindred spirits who had managed to move beyond the darker episodes of their youth and young manhood, he did not, as he has said, look back in anger. He just did not look back, except for the occasional fleeting glance, which in his case was more than enough.

He had, during these years, an oddly symbiotic relationship with Bill Clinton, whose youthful antiwar activities and draft avoidance efforts had stained him among many Vietnam veterans. McCain, by contrast, never attacked Clinton on that issue, though he was critical of him on policy matters. His position, frequently enunciated since he was often asked to comment on the Vietnam-era Clinton, boiled down to this: *Look, the American people elected Bill Clinton their president. That's good enough for me.*

But he did more than refrain from trashing the chief executive. In 1993, when veterans reacted angrily to reports that the President planned to speak at the Vietnam Veterans Memorial, McCain wrote Clinton a letter that said, in effect, you are the Commander-in-Chief and if you want to go to the memorial, I'd be honored to accompany you. Clinton declined the offer and went on his own, but in ensuing years he welcomed McCain's support, most notably when McCain, along with another highly decorated Vietnam veteran, Democratic Senator John Kerry of Massachusetts, put his considerable stature behind the President's efforts to establish diplomatic relations with Hanoi. Clinton, given his history, could not have done it alone. With McCain and Kerry beside him, protecting his political flanks, he did so at a White House ceremony in July 1995.

McCain's high-profile involvement in the issue cost him friends.

Some fellow POWs were furious, as were many other veterans and families of men still officially missing in action. Among conspiracy theorists, there could be only one explanation: McCain was a puppet of Hanoi, nothing less than the Manchurian candidate.

Throughout the 1990s, he repeatedly warned against a deepening American involvement in the Balkans. Even so, following the 1995 Dayton accords, as American troops were first being deployed to Bosnia as peacekeepers, he opposed Republican efforts to cut off funding for them and helped then Senate Majority Leader Bob Dole push through a resolution allowing the president to make good his decision to send troops. At the time, McCain was chairman of Texas Senator Phil Gramm's campaign to overtake front-runner Dole for the 1996 Republican presidential nomination. Gramm strongly opposed the resolution, but efforts to turn McCain failed. His years in Hanoi had been peppered with reports of congressional attempts to cut off funding for the war. "I've had another life," he explained to those who urged him to side with Gramm. "I know what it means when troops are put in harm's way and Congress doesn't support them." But the deployment of American peacekeepers did not end the crisis in the Balkans, as the years ahead would amply demonstrate.

Dole did win the 1996 GOP presidential nomination. In the days leading up to the national party convention in San Diego, McCain seemed a heavy favorite for the number two spot on the ticket. At the eleventh hour, Dole turned instead to Jack Kemp, the former congressman and HUD secretary, who was better known than McCain and was a special favorite of the party's conservative wing.

McCain had long been an important player on the domestic front, often on reform issues. He waged a successful ten-year battle to pass the line-item veto, which allowed the president to veto specific items of an appropriations bill without scuttling the entire measure. That 1996 victory was short-lived. Two years later the Supreme Court declared the law unconstitutional. He also brokered a compromise in 1996 to severely limit members of Congress and their staffs from accepting gifts. "If a constituent is having a barbecue, it is appropriate to have a hamburger," he said at the time. "But we do not need tickets to lavish balls to do our jobs. We do not need $100 gift baskets to do our jobs. And we do not need unlimited, expensive free meals to do our job." He had become as well the scourge of the pork barrel, those projects that senators and congressmen are forever slipping into legislation to trumpet to voters back home. Alerted by a staff member nicknamed "The Ferret," he regularly raced to the floor to finger and denounce such projects and even mounted a pork Web page that featured a pig prancing across the top of the screen.

But as Clinton moved into his second term, McCain became best known for championing two highly visible congressional initiatives—campaign finance reform and antitobacco legislation. McCain and Senator Russ Feingold, a Wisconsin Democrat, first introduced their sweeping campaign finance reform bill, which would have outlawed largely unregulated contributions known as "soft money," in 1995. "We have a system awash in money dominated by special interests, a system that cries out for repairs," he said. The measure promised to reduce the impact of big money on political campaigns and garnered broad national publicity. Even so, it seemed to be going nowhere. Reports of the widespread abuse of soft money by both parties during the 1996 presidential campaign, however, imparted fresh energy to the issue and kept it alive for a time. Clinton, under intense fire for the soft-money machinations of his reelection campaign, embraced the McCain-Feingold bill just before Election Day, a move ridiculed by the president's critics as equivalent to pleading, Stop me before I kill again. But Clinton and Senate Democrats remained solidly behind the measure while McCain's fellow Republicans, who saw themselves as losing their historic fund-raising advantage, fought it and eventually killed it. In opposing the legislation, they said it infringed on free speech and would not pass constitutional muster when challenged in court, a contention that independent observers said could well be true. And, scandals notwithstanding, the issue failed to ignite excitement at the grass roots.

In 1997, McCain assumed the chairmanship of the powerful Senate Commerce Committee. In that capacity he took the lead—and further raised his national profile—in pressing for comprehensive antismoking legislation. Besieged by Big Tobacco's congressional protectors on one side and the industry's most vehement critics on the other, he tried to find a common ground that did not abandon his ultimate goal: a measure that would put a huge dent in teenage smoking. Against daunting odds he managed over the course of two weeks of around-the-clock bargaining in 1998 to push a bill through his committee on a surprisingly lopsided 19-1 vote. Clinton and antitobacco activists such as Dr. David Kessler, former head of the Food and Drug Administration, and Everett Koop, former Surgeon General, welcomed the measure, but the opposition responded forcefully. The tobacco companies denounced the bill, saying the $506 billion price tag would bankrupt them and that the tax increases contained in the measure were regressive, falling disproportionately on the poor and the middle class. They also insisted the bill would trigger bootlegging on a scale not seen since Prohibition. McCain accused his opponents of gross exaggeration but conceded that his bill left a number of tough questions unresolved, saying they needed to be dealt with as the measure moved toward action by the full Senate. "There is no doubt this is only the first round," he said. "But without our completing the first round, there would be no second round." Tobacco companies, meanwhile, took aim at him, running TV, print, and radio ads denouncing what they labeled The McCain-Clinton Tobacco Tax, which they said would cost those who smoke two packs a day $1,460 a year. In June 1998 the tobacco industry managed to kill the bill with the help of high-powered Washington lobbyists, to whom it paid some $40 million.

Although his standing had grown, there had developed by then an undercurrent of personal dislike for McCain in some quarters on Capitol Hill and elsewhere. That animus, moreover, seemed to go beyond philosophical conflicts, relating instead to what some saw as a self-righteous quality, others as a refusal to even consider the possibility that he might have been off base. "John's problem is that he takes [differences] not as an attack on an issue, but as an attack on him," said longtime conservative activist David Keene in late 1997. Then there is his temper, reports of which he claimed were overblown but which led *Washingtonian* magazine in 1997 to label him "Senator Hothead."

A buzz about a possible presidential run in the year 2000 began in earnest in 1997. At first he seemed a fringe figure among those mentioned as possible candidates for the Republican presidential nomination, sometimes listed among the top prospects, other times ignored, perhaps because he had not clarified his intentions. At the time, associates said that he wanted to run but had no intention of subjecting himself to the indignities of a candidacy going nowhere, akin to Indiana Senator Dick Lugar's hapless effort in 1996. Throughout 1997 and most of 1998 he took few steps to improve his standing as a presidential hopeful. His top priority, he said, was winning reelection to his Senate seat in November 1998. A decision on running for president would have to wait until that campaign was over. Although he faced only token opposition, he refused to establish either an exploratory committee or a political action committee, both of which could have been used to advance his presidential prospects, particularly in terms of providing the financial and organizational underpinnings of a serious run for the nomination. Indeed, well into 1998 he had not even discussed the matter in depth with his wife. "No sense bringing on a domestic crisis before it's necessary to do so," he laughed.

In a normal election year, such a delay would be the kiss of death. Candidates, other than those with great public stature such as Colin Powell or extraordinary wealth such as magazine publisher Steve Forbes, must begin laying the foundation for a presidential run at least two years before the caucuses and primaries begin. But going into Election 2000, the GOP found itself in the unusual position of having no candidate with a clear-cut claim on the nomination, such as

Ronald Reagan in 1980 and 1984, George Bush in 1988 and 1992, and Bob Dole in 1996.

McCain won reelection to a third senatorial term in November 1998 with nearly 70 percent of the vote, a total that included 65 percent of the women's vote, 55 percent of the Hispanic vote, and 40 percent of Democrats. Two months after the election he finally announced formation of an exploratory committee, a device by which putative candidates can raise money and otherwise test the presidential waters without fully committing themselves to run.

To mount a credible campaign, most observers agreed, he had to be more than a party irritant and associate himself with issues that resonated with the party activists who dominate the caucuses and primaries. "Other than his background, he hasn't put himself on their radar screen with anything they like," said David Keene. Beyond that, he needed to make the case that he was more than a man with an inspiring resume, but one who had the leadership qualities and the vision to lead the nation into the next century.

There was another hurdle, one that stood to cripple his candidacy: money, the millions of dollars a candidate must have in the bank going into the primary season. "It's a $20 million sport," said Eddie Mahe, a Republican political consultant. But McCain over the years had not been a big-league fund-raiser, partly because he had not needed to. But he also hated doing it and detested the system that made it necessary.

Finally, there was his unpredictability, the nagging sense that, just as he had the potential to put together a winning campaign, he also had the ability to torpedo his chances.

And that applies to more than his temper. In June 1998, for example, at a Republican fund-raising dinner, he told what *The Washington Post* described with unerring precision as a vile joke. The joke, which the *Post* declined to print, came at the expense of the First Lady, her daughter, and the Attorney General. The joke went pretty much like this. Question: Why is Chelsea Clinton so ugly? Answer: Because

Janet Reno is her father and Hillary Clinton is her mother. After the papers got wind of it, he apologized in a letter to the President. Both sides described the apology as "abject, contrite, and profuse." Still, it was an unspeakable thing to say, unworthy of him, presumably lacerating for all concerned.

He was not without assets. The mid to late 1990s had been good ones for him in terms of public exposure. He made frequent appearances on CNN and the Sunday morning talk shows. In May 1997 he was the subject of an admiring *New York Times Magazine* cover story and long feature pieces in *USA Today* and several major metropolitan dailies. *Time* magazine named him one of the twenty-five most influential Americans. In February 1999 the Arts and Entertainment Network told his story as part of its *Biography* series. *The Washington Post* reported that the show was seen in 1.6 million homes, impishly noting that the figure was higher than Bob Dole's when *Biography* first telecast its profile of him, but well short of the series champion, wrestler Andre the Giant. McCain, moreover, was one of the Republicans most in demand at grassroots party events and had traveled indefatigably on behalf of GOP candidates, making important contacts and collecting valuable political chits. At the 1996 national convention he was chosen by Dole to deliver the nominating speech, and he stood shoulder to shoulder with the GOP standard-bearer to the end, earning high marks for loyalty.

There was another factor, one that few of the pundits had looked at. There were 19.1 million living veterans. In March 1999, Mary McGrory, the perceptive *Washington Post* columnist, called the veterans vote McCain's "stealth weapon." McGrory also pointed out that New Hampshire, site of the first primary in the nation, included 138,000 veterans in its population of 1 million.

In early 1999, as he moved closer to declaring his candidacy for president, McCain struggled with another issue: the Clinton-Lewinsky scandal. He had been uncomfortable with it from the beginning. Throughout the impeachment proceedings in the House and the trial in the Senate, he had said little. Even so, no one doubted how he would vote. No Republican senator with aspirations to his or her party's nomination in the year 2000 could fail to vote to convict. It was a fact of political life, one that was easier to swallow for some senators since it had been clear for weeks, if not months, that Clinton would be acquitted.

McCain did the expected, voted to convict. In his statement that February day, he said that he had done things in his private life that he was not proud of and wished that circumstances had allowed the President "to keep his personal life private." Once Clinton's dalliances with Monica Lewinsky became public, however, he had an obligation to tell the truth when under oath. "In my former profession," McCain said, "those who violated their sworn oath were punished severely and considered outcasts from our society. I do not hold the president to the same standard that I hold military officers to. I hold him to a higher standard. Although I may admit to failures in my private life, I have at all times, and to the best of my ability, kept faith with every oath I have sworn to this country. I have known some men who kept the faith at the cost of their lives."

As he moved to the threshold of entering the presidential contest, he could look back on an extraordinarily full life to which he continued to add fascinating episodes. One of them, known to few, occurred in 1994 on one of several trips he made back to Vietnam. Years earlier, in prison, he learned of a retreat that Ho Chi Minh maintained on one of the small islands scattered throughout scenic Ha Long Bay, off the port city of Haiphong. His Vietnamese hosts were flabbergasted when he asked them about the hideaway, more so when he told them he'd like to spend the night there. An hour-long boat ride ended on an island with three dilapidated French villas. After dinner that night, McCain's chief of staff, Mark Salter, remembered his boss shouting over his shoulder as he stole off with Cindy, "I'm going up to Ho's house."

Said Salter, "I had a feeling he had made a promise to himself, like 'One day I'm going to sleep in that guy's bed.' And he did it."

To Salter it was nothing less than a victory lap.

EPILOGUE

As John McCain pondered his presidential prospects in the early months of 1999, George W. Bush, the governor of Texas, surged into a lead in polls of prospective Republican primary voters. Each day brought fresh reports of prominent Republicans—governors, members of Congress, former Cabinet officials, savvy political handlers—flocking to Austin to scramble aboard the Bush bandwagon. After six years of Bill Clinton, the GOP was looking for a winner and seemed to feel it had found one in the son of the man whom the voters had unceremoniously booted out of the White House on that fateful November day in 1992. As for money, *The Washington Post* reported that Bush was assembling "the most ambitious Republican presidential fund-raising effort ever," and was looking to raise $20 million more than the previous record of $31.7 million.

None of this was news to McCain. He knew from the start that he would not be able to match Bush's fund-raising prowess or, for that matter, the rainmaking ability of some of the other candidates. Billionaire magazine publisher Steve Forbes, moreover, had spent $37 million of his own money in 1996 to wrest the nomination from Dole and was running again. Then there was the question of how many people had even heard of McCain, let alone planned to vote for him. Polls placed his name identification among likely Republican primary voters in the 50 percent range, which meant that about half at least knew he existed. Supporters, those who actually thought they might vote for him, were in single digits.

McCain could take comfort, though, in some lessons of history. At the same point in the election cycles of 1976 and 1992, some twenty months before the November general election, Jimmy Carter and Bill Clinton were in much the same shape as McCain. And, while money was a worry, McCain could look back on his tenure as national chairman of Texas Senator Phil Gramm's campaign for the 1996 nomination. Gramm led the field in fund-raising in the early stages of the contest but never made it to New Hampshire, dropping out after a woeful performance in the Iowa caucuses. Steve Forbes, despite his seemingly bottomless pockets, did not beat Dole. As for McCain's name identification problem, it was no worse—in fact it was marginally better—than his standing in early 1982 when he decided to run for Congress the first time. Then there was this: McCain had spent his life bucking the odds.

On a Saturday night in March he put weighty matters aside. The occasion was the white-tie dinner of the Gridiron Club, an annual affair that brings together Washington's movers and shakers, from the president on down, and the elite of the national press corps. The evening features a series of comical and pointed musical skits that are said by the club "to singe, but never burn." When the skits conclude, the President and a member of the party not holding the White House traditionally take turns delivering speeches in the lighthearted mood of the evening.

John McCain, the Republican speaker that night, seized the moment to engage in a favorite pastime, poking fun at himself. He walked to the podium, his chest dripping with large, phony medals, much like the old cartoons of Russian commissars. He then pronounced himself the man for president because, in addition to being "a genuine war hero," he was also an "incredibly self-effacing guy."

He continued in that vein, to gales of laughter. "As I was lying there in my prison cell in Hanoi having my legs broken by interrogators, one thought and one thought alone kept me going—that someday I would come home and do something about soft money and PACs." Each day while shaving, he said, he asked himself, "Okay, John, you're an incredible war hero, an inspiration to all Americans. But what qualifies you to be President of the United States?" His answer? The Hanoi Hilton had been perfect training for the Oval Office. "In both cases you know that every time someone walks in the door, *it's gonna be bad news.*"

It was a dangerous gambit, one that could easily have fallen flat and humiliated him. Instead, he pulled it off. The consensus: nothing less than a triumph. Godfrey Sperling, the venerable *Christian Science Monitor* columnist, called it "a boffo performance" and "more an event than just a speech."

McCain planned to announce his candidacy for President on April 6. It would be in many ways a formality because he had been running for months. But a presidential announcement is more than a declaration of candidacy for the nation's highest office. In recent decades it has become a celebration and a rallying of the troops for the long, brutal days ahead that author Jules Witcover had aptly termed a marathon. The announcement speech also afforded the candidate the best opportunity he was likely to have—unless and until he won the nomination—to explain in a coherent manner why he was seeking the presidency, to present his vision for America, and to describe how he intended to achieve it.

In keeping with recent tradition, McCain's announcement was to be an elaborate affair, a four-day jaunt from the Atlantic to the Pacific and back again. The first day was to begin in Annapolis, where he was to have breakfast with the midshipmen at the Naval Academy. From there it would be on to New Hampshire, then to South Carolina, which has the largest percentage of veterans of any of the fifty states. He was to end the day with announcement festivities in Phoenix, complete with balloons, bunting, high school bands, and about three thousand jubilant supporters. The announcement roadshow was to continue over the next three days with similar events in vote-rich California and other strategically important states.

It didn't happen, at least not like that. On March 24, NATO bombs and cruise missiles began raining down on Serbia. Diplomacy having failed, the American-led alliance had finally made good its threats of military action to halt the murderous Serbian repression of ethnic Albanians in the province of Kosovo and to force Yugoslav President Slobodan Milosevic into a negotiated settlement that provided for NATO ground forces to guarantee Kosovo's autonomy. President Clinton, in a nationally televised address, explained the air attacks as both a "moral imperative," because of atrocities that Serbian forces were inflicting on the Albanians in Kosovo, and in America's national interest. "But," Clinton added, "I do not intend to put our troops in Kosovo to fight a war."

A day earlier, as reports of impending air strikes swirled in Washington and around the world, McCain had taken to the floor of the Senate to oppose a Republican measure that he felt would tie the President's hands in dealing with the escalating terror in Kosovo. McCain said he shared the concern of many of his colleagues that the dangerous military mission about to be undertaken lacked a clear sense of what would be required to achieve NATO's objectives. But, he said, "We must take action," citing "an uninterrupted pattern of atrocities since 1992" by the Serbian army under Milosevic along with a series of empty American threats to use force that he said had gravely damaged U.S. credibility abroad.

The Clinton administration, it was widely reported, expected Milosevic to fall in line with the first whiff of cordite, as *Newsweek* put it. Instead, the air attacks seemed to stiffen the resolve of the Serbs and trigger fresh action against the Kosovars. Graphic stories, photos, and television footage of Serb atrocities monopolized news coverage in the days that followed as Milosevic's forces stepped up their campaign of "ethnic cleansing," forcing hundreds of thousands of refugees from their homes at gunpoint; some fled to neighboring states of Albania and Macedonia, while others simply disappeared.

On Monday, March 29, amid an escalation of gloomy assessments of the effectiveness of the air war, McCain issued a statement that abruptly elevated his public profile. The issue, he said, was no longer whether the United States should have intervened in the Balkans. Having done so, it was imperative to succeed, he insisted. He did not call for the deployment of ground troops but argued that the President and NATO should not unilaterally foreclose that option, as Clinton seemed to have done.

"Should Milosevic achieve his abominable goals in Kosovo, and successfully resist the will of NATO and the decent opinion of mankind, America's adversaries from Pyongyang to Baghdad will be encouraged to challenge our interests more aggressively," he said.

He added, in what was to become his signature statement on the situation, "We are in it, now we must win it."

Overnight he became the congressional voice most in demand by the press, especially the TV talk shows. And, with the Serbs intensifying their repression in Kosovo rather than backing down, McCain continued to make his twofold argument:

- The world's lone superpower, having committed itself militarily, cannot afford to be humbled by an army of forty thousand in a country no larger than Connecticut;

- Telling an adversary that he does not have to fear facing ground troops is a form of unilateral disarmament and only emboldens that adversary. In other words, you may never use ground troops, but you need to be prepared to employ them if necessary, and you sure as hell don't tell the other guy he doesn't have to worry about them.

McCain continued speaking out as the bad news and gripping pictures coming from Kosovo mounted. Some pundits were moved to contrast McCain's forceful position with the more predictable, often murky, statements from other GOP prospects. Two longtime veterans of the campaign trail, Jack W. Germond and Jules Witcover of the *Baltimore Sun*, wrote that McCain "has effectively advanced himself as a leading voice, perhaps the leading voice, among Republicans on this issue. His willingness to confront the complexity of the problem directly is a sharp contrast with the cautious responses of his rivals." The headline on an editorial in the *Des Moines Register* said the same thing, if a bit more briskly: "McCain 1, Others 0."

Then, on March 31, less than a week before McCain was to kick off his candidacy for President, the Serbs took three American soldiers captive, their grim and battered images beamed around the world on Serbian television. The next day McCain announced that he was canceling the announcement festivities scheduled to start five days later. "It is not appropriate at this time to launch a political campaign," he said. The nation was at war. The bands, balloons, and bunting could wait.

His decision amounted to a masterful political stroke. *The Washington Post*'s Mary McGrory said that "professional politicians of both parties were wowed by McCain's beau geste. . . . McCain has made himself the de facto Republican foreign policy spokesman, and is getting yards of publicity for a non-event." The kudos kept pouring in, as did even more demands for him to appear on news-oriented TV talk shows. On one day alone, Monday, April 5, he could be seen arguing his case on Fox News's *Crier Report*, CNN's *Larry King Live*, PBS's *Charlie Rose*, two programs on CNBC, and two more on MSNBC, according to the *Post*'s Dan Balz. Balz quoted one Republican strategist as labeling the conflict in Kosovo "All McCain, all the time." By week's end, syndicated columnist Mark Shields, on CNN's *Capital Gang*, said, "Let me just say in thirty-five years in Washington, I have never seen a debate dominated by an individual in the minority party as I've seen this one dominated by John McCain."

On Tuesday, April 13, McCain issued a brief statement that read in part:

"While now is not the time for the celebratory tour I had planned,

I am a candidate for President and I will formally kick off my campaign at a more appropriate time. As President I hope to restore to the White House the kind of leadership Americans expect in crises like this one and to reform our institutions of government to make us proud again. I look forward to a vigorous campaign and the opportunity to present my message to all Americans."

He was in it, and now the question was could he win it. His long, often painful, frequently comic odyssey had taken him from Annapolis to Hanoi to the halls of Congress. For most men that would be enough. But for McCain it was an unfinished odyssey and he seemed as curious as anyone else to find out how it would all turn out.

A NOTE ON RESEARCH METHODS

The reader is rightly wary of a book about one Naval Academy graduate written by a second. In particular, the reader reasonably wants to know the relationship between the principal and the author. The question of what agreements, if any, existed between principal and author is equally pertinent.

I graduated from Annapolis in June 1964, six years after John McCain. I met him in 1987, a few months after he was elected to the Senate. I was among a group of White House reporters who questioned him as he left a West Wing meeting with President Reagan. I interviewed him a month or so later for an article about James Webb and Oliver North entitled "The Secret War of Ollie and Jim" that ran in the March 1988 issue of *Esquire*.

During the course of researching and writing *The Nightingale's Song*, a period of seven years, I interviewed McCain at length at least twenty times, probably more, and shadowed him in Arizona in 1988, 1992, and again, on an unrelated assignment, in 1997. I did not offer to let him see my work prior to publication, and he did not ask.

Since publication of *The Nightingale's Song* in July 1995, I have followed McCain's career and interviewed him on three occasions on unrelated assignments.

Some final points. There are passages in the book in which thoughts or emotions are described. In each instance those descriptions are supported by direct statements by the individuals involved, almost exclusively in statements to me during interviews.

On a very few occasions I have relied on the recollections of individuals who spoke to me on the condition that they not be identified or who asked that a portion of their comments not be attributed to them by name.

As for quotations, they are used here only when at least one participant in a conversation provided them, in interviews with me, in their own writings, or, on a few occasions, in other published material. To the extent possible, the quotations were checked against the recollections of other participants.

NOTES

PROLOGUE

The quotes from Ronald Reagan about the Vietnam War are from *President Reagan: The Role of a Lifetime*, by Lou Cannon. Barbara Feldon told the tale of the nightingale on March 30, 1987, to a U.S. Labor Department conference on Work and Family.

CHAPTER 1. The Punk

The description of John McCain as a youth is based on interviews with him; his mother, Roberta McCain; and his brother, Joseph P. McCain. Accounts of McCain at Episcopal were provided by schoolmates Sandy Ainslie, Rives Richey, Angus McBryde, Malcolm Matheson, Bentley Orrick, and masters Riley Deeble, Allen Phillips, and Patrick Henry Callaway. The flavor of the institution was rendered by an alumnus, Ken Ringle, in "The School with a Southern Accent," which appeared in *The Washington Post* on November 11, 1989, on the occasion of Episcopal's 150th anniversary. Richard Pardee Williams's book about the school, *The High School: A History of the Episcopal High School in Virginia at Alexandria*, also was of assistance. The description of John S. "Slew" McCain is based on accounts in various publications, notably *Bull Halsey*, by E. B. Potter, and *Admiral Halsey's Story*, by William F. Halsey and J. Bryan III. John S. "Jack" McCain, Jr., was described in interviews by his wife, Roberta McCain; sons John and Joseph; Nicholas Brown; Herb Hetu; Isaac Kidd, Jr.; and others, as well as in numerous publications.

CHAPTER 2. IHTFP

The quote from Rear Admiral Habermeyer is from a December 1988 interview. The history of the Academy is drawn from Jack Sweetman's *The U.S. Naval Academy: An Illustrated History*. The description of plebe year is based on conversations with Fred Fagan and other Annapolis men, James Webb's *A Sense of Honor*, James Calvert's *The Naval Profession*, and David Poyer's *The Return of Philo T. McGiffin*, augmented by the personal experiences of the author. The letter from Ronald Benigo was written to the author in 1990. Also of assistance was *Reef Points, 1993–1994: The Annual Handbook of the Brigade of Midshipmen, 88th Edition.*

CHAPTER 3. Halos and Horns

McCain's account of his time at Annapolis was supplemented by interviews with Roberta McCain, Carol McCain, Frank Gamboa, Charles Larson, John Dittrick, Ron Fisher, William Hemingway, and Nils "Ron" Thunman.

CHAPTER 4. Fields of Fire

No source was more important to the writing of this chapter than *Chance and Circumstance: The Draft, the War and the Vietnam Generation*, by Lawrence M. Baskir and William A. Strauss. Equally valuable were *The Best and the Brightest*, by David Halberstam, and *Vietnam: A History*, by Stanley Karnow.

James Fallows's "What Did You Do in the Class War, Daddy?" which appeared in the October 1975 issue of the *Washington Monthly*, was one of the most perceptive and powerful articles written about the Vietnam era.

The comment about Vietnam veterans going to ground is from Harold G. Moore and Joseph L. Galloway, *We Were Soldiers Once . . . and Young: Ia Drang, the Battle That Changed the War in Vietnam.*

The anger reflected in this section came out in scores of interviews with Vietnam veterans. Paul Goodwin, Robert Bedingfield, and Milton Copulos are quoted directly.

CHAPTER 5. Fire at Sea

This chapter is based primarily on interviews with John McCain, Carol McCain, Charles Larson, and Ron Fisher.

McCain vividly recalled his experiences in the July 29, 1967, fire aboard the *Forrestal.* Fisher provided an extraordinary video of the tragedy, *Trial by Fire: A Carrier Fights for Its Life*, produced in 1973 by the Naval Photographic Center. The video, relying on manned and unmanned cameras, recorded the sights and sounds of the conflagration.

CHAPTER 6. The Crown Prince

Throughout discussions of his imprisonment, John McCain was a reluctant witness and a difficult interviewee, at least when discussing his own experiences. For the most part he confirmed incidents described by prisonmates or discussed in published accounts. He did tell funny prison stories and often recalled the heroism of others, never his own.

Those interviewed for this and other chapters on McCain's imprisonment were Carol McCain, Roberta McCain, Joseph McCain, George "Bud" Day and Doris Day, Isaac Kidd, Jr., William Lawrence, Charlie Plumb, Ned Shuman, James Stockdale, Orson Swindle, Konrad Trautman, Jack Van Loan, and James Warner.

Dealing at length with McCain in prison, and indispensable to recreating prison life, was *P.O.W.: A Definitive History of the American Prisoner-of-War Experience in Vietnam, 1964–1973*, by John G. Hubbell, in association with Andrew Jones and Kenneth Y. Tomlinson. See also John Dramesi, *Code of Honor;* Stephen A. Rowan, *They Wouldn't Let Us Die;* James and Sybil Stockdale, *In Love and War;* Jeremiah Denton, *When Hell Was in Session;* Ernest C. Brace, *A Code to Keep: The True Story of America's Longest-Held Civilian Prisoner of War in Vietnam;* and George E. Day, *Return with Honor.*

McCain told part of his tale in "Inside Story: How the POWs Fought Back," published in *U.S. News & World Report* on May 14, 1973.

Over the Beach: The Air War In Vietnam, by Zalin Grant, vividly recreated the lives of Navy pilots on Yankee Station.

CHAPTER 7. Do You Want to Go Home?

See Notes to Chapter 4.

McCain's refusal to accept early release is memorialized in a secret cable, now declassified, dated September 13, 1968. W. Averell Harriman, at the time chief U.S. negotiator to the Paris Peace Talks, relates a discussion with his North Vietnamese counterpart, Le Duc Tho: "At tea break Le Duc Tho mentioned that DRV had intended to release Admiral McCain's son as one of the three pilots freed recently, but he had refused."

CHAPTER 8. 'Tis the Season to Be Jolly

See Notes to Chapter 4.

CHAPTER 9. Long Tall Sally

See Notes to Chapter 4.

CHAPTER 10. Reentry

Interviewed for this chapter were John McCain, Carol McCain, Roberta McCain, Michael Deaver, Nancy Reynolds, Diane Lawrence (formerly Diane Rauch), William Lawrence, James Lake, Arnold Isaacs, Edwin "Ned" Shuman, and Carl Smith.

An Associated Press photograph of John McCain limping from a plane at Clark Air Base ran on page 1 of *The New York Times* on March 15, 1973.

The picture of McCain shaking hands with Richard Nixon was taken by United Press International. It ran in *The Washington Post* on May 25, 1973, and in other publications.

McCain's article "Inside Story: How the POWs Fought Back" appeared in the May 14, 1973, issue of *U.S. News & World Report.*

CHAPTER 11. Guerrilla Warfare

Primary sources for this chapter were John McCain, Cindy McCain, Carol McCain, William Cohen, James Holloway, William Bader, Albert "Pete" Lakeland, James Jones, James McGovern, and Clarence "Mark" Hill.

John Poindexter was Admiral Holloway's executive assistant in 1977 when the CNO tapped his classmate John McCain for the Senate liaison post, but Poindexter played no role in the selection.

CHAPTER 12. The Candidate from Hanoi

Those interviewed included John McCain, Cindy McCain, Carol McCain, J. Brian "Jay" Smith, John Kolbe, Sam Stanton, Michael Murphy, and Orson Swindle.

Jay Smith provided a videotape compilation of McCain's television ads. The First District race was covered closely by *The Arizona Republic* and the *Phoenix Gazette.* Articles from both papers, and others, were utilized as background for this chapter. Several key pieces are listed in the Bibliography. Kolbe, of the *Gazette*, first reported (May 20, 1982) Jim Mack's unsuccessful effort to elicit damaging personal information about McCain from ex-wife Carol.

CHAPTER 13. The Shadow of Vietnam

John McCain's remarks on Lebanon on the House floor are printed in the *Congressional Record* of September 28, 1983.

William Greider's "Profiles in Cowardice," about the House debate on Lebanon, was published in the November 24, 1983, issue of *Rolling Stone.*

The September 28 House vote on Lebanon was reported in *The New York Times* and elsewhere the following day.

Interviewees included McCain and Lisa Boepple, a McCain aide.

CHAPTER 14. The White Tornado

Interviewees included John McCain, Cindy McCain, J. Brian "Jay" Smith, Victoria "Torie" Clarke, John Kolbe, Wes Gullett, Sam Stanton, Michael Murphy, William Cohen, John Warner, and Thomas Ridge.

The *Washington Times* article "From Hanoi to the House" was written by George Archibald and appeared on February 3, 1983.

McCain's trip to Vietnam and the political benefits were well chronicled by the Arizona press. See especially "Coming Home: Political Bonanza Is Seen in McCain's Mission to Vietnam," by Joel Nilsson in *The Arizona Republic* of January 27, 1985.

"Honor, Duty and a War Called Vietnam" ran on CBS on April 10, 1985.

Once they got onto the story that the man who had been their publisher since 1980 had made up his war record, *The Arizona Republic* and the *Phoenix Gazette* covered the sad tale of Darrow "Duke" Tully vigorously and completely. Charles Kelley, based on his reporting and the reporting of other *Republic* staff members, wrote a gripping account of Tully's life entitled "A Hero That Never Was," published on January 26, 1986.

The 1986 U.S. Senate campaign in Arizona was covered closely by the state's major newspapers, including *The Arizona Republic*, the *Phoenix Gazette*, the *Arizona Daily Star* (Tucson), and the *Mesa Tribune.* Selected articles are listed in the Bibliography.

Phoenix Gazette political columnist John Kolbe wrote about McCain's temper on January 23, 1986. The article was entitled "Golden Boy McCain Has Unsettling Flaw—His Temper." Kolbe did so again on July 30, 1986, in an article entitled "Angry McCain Could Turn Senate Race into Contest After All."

Political columnist Pat Murphy of *The Arizona Republic* poked fun at Richard Kimball's campaign document in a February 20, 1986, article entitled "Mr. Kimball Tries to Go to Washington by Utilizing 'Progressivity.' "

McCain's growing national stature was noted during the 1986 Senate campaign by several syndicated columnists and national publications, including the following: Jack Germond and Jules Witcover in "A New Arizona Institution," *Phoenix Gazette*, April 7, 1986; George F. Will in "Hanoi to Phoenix to Washington," published February 20, 1986, in *The Washington Post* and elsewhere; and R. W. Apple, Jr., in "National Role Is Seen for Arizona Politician," *The New York Times*, November 2, 1986.

Richard Kimball attacked McCain for the political action committees contributing to his campaign in a July 18, 1986, press release entitled "Kimball: 'McCain Is Being Bought and Paid For.'"

The picture of McCain standing on a riser during the debate was taken by Suzanne Starr of *The Arizona Republic*. It ran with an October 18, 1986, article on the debate by Don Harris entitled "McCain, Kimball Clash on Arms, 'Contra' Aid." The cutline read: "John McCain, several inches shorter than Richard Kimball, stands on a box, making it easier for TV cameras to pan from one candidate to the other."

Anne Q. Hoy of *The Arizona Republic* provided a thorough and provocative postelection profile of McCain. The article, published on November 9, 1986, was entitled "Meteoric Climb: McCain's Rise to the Senate Caps Ambitious Career Path."

The election eve (November 3, 1986) article linking McCain to Charles Keating was entitled "McCain, Kolbe Tied to Lobby: Given Contributions; Aided Keating Firm in Battle over S&Ls." It was written by United Press International and the staff of *The Arizona Republic*.

In addition to their three natural children, Meghan, Jack, and Jimmy, the McCains have an adopted child, Bridget.

CHAPTER 15. Halos and Horns Redux

Interviewees included John Poindexter, John McCain, and Clarence "Mark" Hill.

CHAPTER 16. Bahama Mamas on the Beach

Interviewees included John and Cindy McCain.

Susan Rasky's article on McCain appeared in *The New York Times* on December 22, 1989.

Gavel-to-gavel coverage of the Keating Five hearings was provided by C-Span. All major newspapers and television networks covered the results of the Senate Ethics Committee investigation.

CHAPTER 17. The Road Back

Interviewees included John and Cindy McCain, Mark Salter, and several national political consultants, among them Eddie Mahe, David Keene, and James Lake.

John McCain, in his 1992 reelection race, again raised far more money than his opponents. According to the Federal Election Commission, he raised $3.3 million during the 1991–92 election cycle, compared to $288,000 for Claire Sargent and $90,000 for Evan Mecham.

The editorial cartoon of Cindy McCain shaking the child was by Benson. It ran in *The Arizona Republic* on August 23, 1994.

The author was present at the Naval Academy when McCain delivered the commencement address. The deaths of Midshipman Jeffrey Mascunana and Julie Ann Mace were reported in *The* (Annapolis) *Capital* on May 27, 1993.

McCain's crude joke was first reported by *The Washington Post* on June 12, 1998, in its "Reliable Source" column. The *Post* and *The Arizona Republic* reported the apology.

The U.S. Department of Veterans Affairs provided the number of living veterans.

The Arts and Entertainment Network told the McCain story as part of its *Biography* series. The show was entitled "John McCain: American Maverick."

McCain's letter to President Clinton regarding the president's appearance at the Vietnam Veterans Memorial was dated May 4, 1993. In it he said, "I have little doubt that my comrades who did not return with me to the country we loved so much would be as honored as I if you should decide to commemorate their service at the place where the nation publicly reveres their memory. I hope you will not be discouraged from doing so by the ill conceived and unjustified opposition of a few. I would be pleased to do whatever I can to support you in that effort."

Epilogue

Those interviewed included Mark Salter, McCain's chief of staff. In addition, McCain's activities relating to his presidential campaign and his involvement with the Kosovo issue were widely reported.

BIBLIOGRAPHY

BOOKS READ OR CONSULTED

Several of the books listed here deserve special mention for their pertinence, insight, or both. Jack Sweetman's *The U.S. Naval Academy: An Illustrated History* was a fine guide. The Vietnam War era is rendered superbly by David Halberstam in *The Best and the Brightest;* by Stanley Karnow in *Vietnam: A History;* by Neil Sheehan in *A Bright Shining Lie: John Paul Vann and America in Vietnam;* and by Lawrence M. Baskir and William A. Strauss in *Chance and Circumstance: The Draft, the War and the Vietnam Generation,* the last a truly invaluable resource. Out of print and difficult to find, John G. Hubbell's *P.O.W.: A Definitive History of the American Prisoner-of-War Experience* is a stunning chronicle.

Baskir, Lawrence M., and William A. Strauss. *Chance and Circumstance: The Draft, the War and the Vietnam Generation.* New York: Vintage Books, 1978.

Brace, Ernest C. *A Code to Keep: The True Story of America's Longest-Held Civilian Prisoner of War in Vietnam.* New York: St. Martin's, 1988.

Braestrup, Peter. *Big Story.* 2 vols. Boulder, Colo.: Westview Press, 1987.

Broughton, Jack. *Thud Ridge.* New York: Bantam Books, 1985.

Buell, Thomas B. *The Quiet Warrior: A Biography of Admiral Raymond A. Spruance.* Boston: Little, Brown, 1974.

Calvert, James. *The Naval Profession.* New York: McGraw-Hill, 1965.

Cannon, Lou. *Reagan.* New York: G. P. Putnam's Sons, 1982.

———. *President Reagan: The Role of a Lifetime.* New York: Simon & Schuster, 1991.

Cohen, William S. *Roll Call: One Year in the United States Senate.* New York: Simon & Schuster, 1981.

———. *One-Eyed Kings.* New York: Doubleday, 1991.

Day, George E. *Return with Honor.* Mesa, Ariz.: Champlin Museum Press, 1990.

Denton, Jeremiah A., Jr., with Ed Brandt. *When Hell Was in Session.* Clover, S.C.: Commission Press, 1976.

Frank, Benis M. *U.S. Marines in Lebanon, 1982–1984.* Washington, D.C.: History and Museums Division, Headquarters, U.S. Marine Corps, 1987.

Friedman, Thomas L. *From Beirut to Jerusalem.* New York: Farrar, Straus & Giroux, 1989.

Gaither, Ralph. *With God in a P.O.W. Camp.* Nashville: Broadman Press, 1973.

Grant, Zalin. *Over the Beach: The Air War in Vietnam.* New York: W. W. Norton, 1986.

Greene, Bob. *Homecoming: When the Soldiers Returned from Vietnam.* New York: G. P. Putnam's Sons, 1989.

Halberstam, David. *The Best and the Brightest.* New York: Random House, 1972.

Halsey, William F., and J. Bryan III. *Admiral Halsey's Story.* New York: Whittlesey House, 1947.

Hubbell, John G., in association with Andrew Jones and Kenneth Y. Tomlinson. *P.O.W.: A Definitive History of the American Prisoner-of-War Experience in Vietnam, 1964–1973.* New York: Reader's Digest Press, 1976.

Karnow, Stanley. *Vietnam: A History.* New York: Penguin Books, 1984.

Lovell, John P. *Neither Athens nor Sparta: The American Service Academies in Transition.* Bloomington: Indiana University Press, 1979.

Moore, Harold G., and Joseph L. Galloway. *We Were Soldiers Once . . . and Young: Ia Drang, the Battle That Changed the War in Vietnam.* New York: Random House, 1992.

Mulligan, James A. *The Hanoi Commitment.* Virginia Beach, Va.: RIF Marketing, 1981.

Myrer, Anton. *Once an Eagle.* New York: Holt, Rinehart & Winston, 1968.

Plumb, Charlie. *I'm No Hero: A POW Story as Told to Glen DeWerff.* Independence, Mo.: Independence Press, 1973.

Potter, E. B. *Bull Halsey.* Annapolis, Md.: Naval Institute Press, 1985.

Poyer, David. *The Return of Philo T. McGiffin.* New York: St. Martin's, 1983.

Reef Points, 1993–1994: The Annual Handbook of the Brigade of Midshipmen, 88th Edition. Annapolis, Md.: United States Naval Academy (no publication date).

Schulze, Richard C. *Leatherneck Square: A Professional Marine's Personal Perspective of the Vietnam Era.* Berkeley, CA: The Huckleberry Press, 1989.

Sheehan, Neil. *A Bright Shining Lie: John Paul Vann and America in Vietnam.* New York: Random House, 1988.

Smith, Hedrick. *The Power Game: How Washington Works.* New York: Random House, 1988.

Stockdale, Vice Admiral James B. *A Vietnam Experience: Ten Years of Reflections.* Stanford, Calif.: Hoover Institution, 1984.

Stockdale, Jim, and Sybil Stockdale. *In Love and War.* New York: Harper & Row, 1984.

Sweetman, Jack. *The U.S. Naval Academy: An Illustrated History.* Annapolis, Md.: Naval Institute Press, 1979.
Tower, John G. *Consequences: A Personal and Political Memoir.* Boston: Little, Brown, 1991.
Trewhitt, Henry L. *McNamara: His Ordeal in the Pentagon.* New York: Harper & Row, 1971.
Webb, James. *Fields of Fire.* New York: Prentice-Hall, 1978.
———. *A Sense of Honor.* New York: Prentice-Hall, 1981.
———. *A Country Such as This.* New York: Doubleday, 1983.
———. *Something to Die For.* New York: William Morrow, 1991.
Williams, Richard Pardee. *The High School: The History of the Episcopal High School in Virginia at Alexandria.* Boston: Vincent-Curtis, 1964.

ARTICLES AND DOCUMENTS

Agence France-Presse. "Hanoi Says McCain's Son Terms U.S. 'Isolated,'" *New York Times,* November 11, 1967.
Allen, Henry. "Vietnam: Hazy Images and Searing Memories—The Drama of the Absolutely Ordinary Soldier," *Washington Post,* November 11, 1992.
Alvarez, Everett, Jr. "Sound: A POW's Weapon," *U.S. Naval Institute Proceedings,* August 1976.
Andersen, Kurt, reported by Jay Branegan/Washington. "A Homecoming at Last," *Time,* November 22, 1982.
Apple, R. W., Jr. "Adm. McCain's Son, *Forrestal* Survivor, Is Missing in Raid," *New York Times,* October 28, 1967.
———. "National Role Is Seen for Arizona Politician," *New York Times,* November 2, 1986.
Archibald, George. "From Hanoi to the House," *Washington Times,* February 3, 1983.
Arizona Republic. "Those Key Races," September 5, 1982 (endorsement editorial).
———. "McCain Challenges Vietnam on POWs," February 24, 1985.
———. "U.S. Senate: John McCain Recommended," October 26, 1986 (endorsement editorial).
———. "McCain, Kolbe Tied to Lobby: Given Contributions; Aided Keating Firm in Battle over S&Ls," November 3, 1986.
Babington, Charles. "Vietnam War Looms Over Veterans Day," *Washington Post,* November 12, 1992.
Balz, Dan. "Bombing Campaign Gives McCain Added Prominence in GOP Field," *Washington Post,* April 7, 1999.

Beck, Melinda, with Mary Lord. "Refighting the Vietnam War," *Newsweek*, October 25, 1982.

Broder, David S. "Some Questions for the Secretary," *Washington Post*, December 23, 1984.

———. "McCain: Strong-Man Weinberger Finds Defense-Minded Arizonan Is Equally Tough Critic," *Arizona Republic*, January 3, 1985.

———. "Beaches and Peoples: A Matter of Time," *Washington Post*, July 19, 1987.

———. "Words vs. Deeds," *Washington Post*, April 14, 1999.

Broyles, William, Jr. "Remembering a War We Want to Forget," *Newsweek*, November 22, 1983.

———. "A Ritual for Saying Goodbye," *U.S. News & World Report*, November 10, 1986.

Buckley, Christopher. "Viet Guilt," *Esquire*, September 1983.

Burchell, Joe. "McCain, Kimball Start with Opposing Styles," *Arizona Daily Star* (Tucson), February 2, 1986.

———. "McCain Denies Letter's Charge He Is Insensitive to Senior Citizens," *Arizona Daily Star* (Tucson), June 21, 1986.

Cannella, David. "Kimball Seizes on Foe's Faux Pas, Will Chisel at 'Insensitive' McCain," *Arizona Republic*, July 13, 1986.

Cannon, Lou. "Of Arms and the Man," *Washington Post Book World*, December 8, 1991.

de Moraes, Lisa. "Tubby or Not Tubby? The Tinky Winky Stink Continues," *Washington Post*, February 15, 1999.

Des Moines Register. "McCain 1, Others 0," April 8, 1999.

Dowd, Maureen. "No Free War," *New York Times*, March 31, 1999.

Fallows, James. "What Did You Do in the Class War, Daddy?" *Washington Monthly*, October 1975.

Foreign Service of the United States of America. Telegram. W. Averell Harriman to Secretary of State, September 13, 1968.

Garrett, Major. "A Different Kind of Candidate," *U.S. News & World Report*, April 5, 1999.

Gerhart, Ann, and Annie Groer. "The Reliable Source," *Washington Post*, June 12, 1998.

———. "The Reliable Source," *Washington Post*, June 16, 1998.

Germond, Jack W., and Jules Witcover. "A New Arizona Institution," *Phoenix Gazette*, April 7, 1986.

———. "Moves in Gulf Becoming Risky," *Baltimore Evening Sun*, May 28, 1987.

———. "McCain's Shrewd Military Maneuver," *Baltimore Sun*, April 5, 1999.

Gibbs, Nancy. "The First Big Test," *Time*, April 12, 1999.

Glaser, Vera. "People to Watch: John McCain," *The Washingtonian*, April 1986.

Glasser, Susan B. "Bush's Dash for Cash," *Washington Post*, April 7, 1999.

Greider, William. "Profiles in Cowardice," *Rolling Stone*, November 24, 1983.

Griffin, Sean. "McCain Settles in at Senate, Hopes to Be There 'Long Time,'" *Phoenix Gazette*, April 20, 1987.

Grove, Lloyd. "At the Bosnia Crossroads— No: The Senator, Wary of the Perils of Failure," *Washington Post*, May 5, 1993.

Gugliotta, Guy, and Juliet Eilperin. "Clinton Urged to Plan Ground War, Returning Congress Faces Debate Over Future of Policy," *Washington Post*, April 10, 1999.

Harris, Don. "Former Prisoner of War Declares Candidacy for 1st District," *Arizona Republic*, March 25, 1982.

———. "GOP 1st District Quartet Singing Familiar Medley on Issues," *Arizona Republic*, June 13, 1982.

———. "Discord Sharpens Among Republicans as District 1 Contenders Trade Barbs," *Arizona Republic*, June 28, 1982.

———. "Newcomer Touts His Knowledge of Capitol Hill," *Arizona Republic*, July 11, 1982.

———. "GOP Primary in 1st District Termed Close," *Arizona Republic*, August 29, 1982.

———. "GOP Hopefuls Highlight Races for Congress," *Arizona Republic*, September 5, 1982.

———. "McCain Takes District 1 Primary," *Arizona Republic*, September 8, 1982.

———. "The Walking and Knocking Begins Again," *Arizona Republic*, September 9, 1982.

———. "McCain's Campaign Spending Leads in Congressional Races," *Arizona Republic*, October 21, 1982.

———. "Tully's Lies Rang True to Combat Flier McCain," *Arizona Republic*, January 4, 1986.

———. "Kimball Levels Conflict Charges Against McCain, Consultant," *Arizona Republic*, May 21, 1986.

———. "McCain, Kimball Clash on Arms, 'Contra' Aid," *Arizona Republic*, October 18, 1986.

———. "Kimball Says McCain Is Pushing U.S. Toward Latin America War," *Arizona Republic*, October 20, 1986.

———. "McCain, Kimball Spar in Second of 3 Senate-Race Debates," *Arizona Republic*, October 23, 1986.

———. "McCain Is Battling Label of 'Bought and Paid For,'" *Arizona Republic*, November 1, 1986.

———. "McCain Beats Kimball in Senate Race," *Arizona Republic*, November 5, 1986.

Hersh, Seymour M. "P.O.W.s Maintained Discipline but Had Some Quarrels," *New York Times*, February 23, 1973.

Hirsh, Michael, and John Barry. "How We Stumbled into War," *Newsweek*, April 12, 1999.

Hoy, Anne Q. "McCain Collects 13 Times Sum Raised by Kimball in Senate Bid," *Arizona Republic*, February 2, 1986.

———. "McCain Romping Ahead of Kimball in Raising, Spending Money," *Arizona Republic*, July 18, 1986.

———. "Meteoric Climb: McCain's Rise to the Senate Caps Ambitious Career Path," *Arizona Republic*, November 9, 1986.

Jennings, Max. "Kimball Peddling Foolishness: Demo Keeps McCain Misstep Before Voters," *Mesa Tribune*, July 13, 1986.

Johnson, Haynes, and David S. Broder. "Voting from a Vietnam Veteran's Perspective," *Washington Post*, January 13, 1991.

Kelley, Charles, with Carol Sowers, Jacquee G. Petchel, Art Thomason, and Earl Zarbin. "A Hero That Never Was: Ex-Publisher's 'Mitty-like' Fantasy a Life of Grief, Deceit," *Arizona Republic*, January 26, 1986.

Kimball, Richard, for U.S. Senate Committee. "Kimball: 'McCain Is Being Bought and Paid For,'" July 18, 1986 (press release from Kimball for U.S. Senate Committee).

Klassen, Teri. "McCain 'Seizure World' Crack Protested," *Arizona Republic*, July 9, 1986.

Kolbe, John. "Time, Circumstance Thin Ranks of Hopeful Rhodes Successors," *Phoenix Gazette*, February 15, 1982.

———. "John McCain, Surprise Leader in House Race, Target of Mudslinging," *Phoenix Gazette*, May 20, 1982.

———. "GOP Race for Rhodes' Seat Too Close to Call—Almost," *Phoenix Gazette*, August 26, 1982.

———. "Golden Boy McCain Has Unsettling Flaw—His Temper," *Phoenix Gazette*, January 23, 1986.

———. "Angry McCain Could Turn Senate Race into Contest After All," *Phoenix Gazette*, July 30, 1986.

———. "Traveling Burt and Johnny Show Not Politics as Usual," *Phoenix Gazette*, August 22, 1986.

———. "Enough! Senate Candidates Should Finish Kindergarten," *Phoenix Gazette*, October 1, 1986.

———. "Goldwater: A 'Prophet' with 'Real Ideas,'" *Phoenix Gazette*, December 3, 1986.

———. "McCain's Return to Grace Capped on Convention Dais," *Phoenix Gazette*, August 20, 1992.

Laake, Deborah. "A Hero's Image," *New Times*, May 28, 1986.

LaFraniere, Sharon, and Priscilla Painton. "President Leads Tribute to Vietnam Veterans: Ex-Soldiers Search for Familiar Faces," *Washington Post*, November 12, 1984.

Leonard, Susan. "Publisher Tully Quits; Made Up War Record," *Arizona Republic*, December 27, 1985.

Lewis, Michael. "Surrogates," *New Republic*, May 13, 1996.

———. "A Question of Honor," *The New York Times Magazine*, May 25, 1997.

Lopez, Larry (Associated Press). "McCain Remodeling Phoenix Home, Planning to Move from 1st District," *Arizona Republic*, October 29, 1986.

MacEachern, Doug. "Who Is John McCain Really? And What's He Up To in Congress?" *New Times*, January 18–24, 1984.

McCain, John S., III. "Inside Story: How the POWs Fought Back," *U.S. News & World Report*, May 14, 1973.

———. "Inside Vietnam: What a Former POW Found," *U.S. News & World Report*, March 11, 1985.

———. "Not in Vain: The Painful Lessons of the War Have to Be Faced," *Arizona Republic*, April 28, 1985.

———. "Where Is Their Alternative Policy?" *Washington Times*, March 25, 1987.

———. "Sailing into Harm's Way, Administration Overreacts in Plan to Reflag Tankers, McCain Says," *Arizona Republic*, June 21, 1987.

———. "McCain Statement on Kosovo," March 23, 1999.

———. "Statement by Senator John McCain on NATO Strategy for the Kosovo Crisis," March 29, 1999.

———. "Now That We're In, We Have to Win: The Cost of Failure Is Much Greater Than the Price of Victory," *Time*, April 12, 1999.

McGrory, Mary. "Where Front-Runners Stumble," *Washington Post*, March 4, 1999.

———. "Ahead of the Class," *Washington Post*, April 8, 1999.

Mesa Tribune. "McCain Bashing" (editorial), February 9, 1988.

Morrow, Lance. "1968," *Time*, January 11, 1988.

Murphy, Michael. "McCain Apologizes to Clinton for Joke; Jest Slurred Chelsea, Hillary, Reno," *Arizona Republic*, June 13, 1998.

Murphy, Pat. "Give 'Em Hell, John? McCain Whistles While He Works," *Arizona Republic*, February 4, 1986.

———. "Mr. Kimball Tries to Go to Washington by Utilizing 'Progressivity,'" *Arizona Republic*, February 20, 1986.

Newsweek. "The Price POWs Pay," April 12, 1999.

Nilsson, Joel. "Rhodes Will Leave House When Term Ends This Year," *Arizona Republic*, January 22, 1982.

———. "Cash Stirs Rancor in GOP Race," *Arizona Republic*, July 25, 1982.

———. "3 Perspectives on District 1 Race," *Arizona Republic*, October 11, 1982.

———. "Ex-POW McCain May Return to Hanoi," *Arizona Republic*, December 21, 1984.

———. "McCain, CBS News Crew Ready for Trip to Vietnam," *Arizona Republic*, January 18, 1985.

———. "McCain Barred by Vietnam, Heads Home," *Arizona Republic*, January 23, 1985.

———. "Return by McCain to State Follows Failure in Attempt to Enter Vietnam," *Arizona Republic*, January 24, 1985.

———. "Coming Home: Political Bonanza Is Seen in McCain's Mission to Vietnam," *Arizona Republic*, January 27, 1985.

———. "Kimball and His Campaign Move to the High Road," *Arizona Republic*, February 4, 1986.

Nyhan, David. "Relentless Reformer," *Boston Globe*, November 14, 1997.

Rasky, Susan. "Washington Talk; To Senator McCain, the Savings and Loan Affair Is Now a Personal Demon," *New York Times*, December 22, 1989.

Report of the DOD Commission on Beirut International Airport Terrorist Act, October 23, 1983. Dated December 20, 1983 (known as the Long Commission Report after the chairman, Admiral Robert L. J. Long, USN [Ret.]).

Ringle, Ken. "The School with a Southern Accent," *Washington Post*, November 11, 1989.

Robbins, William. "Ex-P.O.W.s Charge Hanoi with Torture," *New York Times*, September 3, 1969.

Schwartz, John. "Kimball Knocks on Doors, Raps Drug Use," *Arizona Republic*, September 7, 1986.

Shuey, P. J., and Angela Callahan. "Family Mourns 'Totally Dedicated' Mid," *The (Annapolis, Md.) Capital*, May 27, 1993.

Silverman, Amy. "Is John McCain a War Hero?" *Phoenix New Times*, March 25–31, 1999.

Smith, J. Brian. "Train Tour Traumas: The Anatomy of a Successful Media Event," *Campaigns & Elections*, July–August 1986.

Sowers, Carol. "Goldwater's Message Used Against McCain," *Arizona Republic*, September 7, 1982.

Sperling, Godfrey. "Presidential Prerequisite: Wit," *Christian Science Monitor*, March 30, 1999.

Stanley, Alessandra, and Bruce Van Voorst. "Healing Viet Nam's Wounds," *Time*, November 26, 1984.

Stanton, Sam. "McCain, 3 in GOP Tell Mecham to Quit," *Arizona Republic*, January 17, 1988.

Sterba, James P. "U.S. Planes Pick Up 108 Freed Prisoners from Hanoi," *New York Times*, March 14, 1973.
———. "P.O.W. Commander Among 108 Freed," *New York Times*, March 15, 1973.
Time. "1968: The Year That Shaped a Generation," January 11, 1988.
Torry, Saundra, and Nathan Abse. "Big Tobacco Spends Top Dollar to Lobby," *Washington Post*, April 9, 1999.
Wall Street Journal. "General Morris," April 7, 1999.
Washington Post. "McCain Delays Declaration of Candidacy," April 2, 1999.
———. "McCain Declares His Candidacy via News Release," April 14, 1999.
Washington Times. "An Inappropriate Award" (editorial), June 11, 1986.
Webb, James H. "The Invisible Vietnam Veteran," *Washington Post*, August 4, 1976.
———. "The Power of Remembering," *Washington Post*, May 25, 1981.
———. "Viet Vets Didn't Kill Babies and They Aren't Suicidal," *Washington Post*, April 6, 1986.
———. "The Military Is Not a Social Program," *New York Times*, August 18, 1993.
Weisman, Jonathan. "Ground War Plan an Option for NATO, White House Officials Say Blueprints Could Be Quickly Updated," *Baltimore Sun*, April 12, 1999.
Will, George F. "Hanoi to Phoenix to Washington," *Washington Post*, February 20, 1986.
Willey, Keven Ann. "Kimball Invades McCain Broadcast: Host Denies Debate Offered; Republican Declines Exchange," *Arizona Republic*, August 20, 1986.
Wynn, Bernie. "McCain Is Holding Edge in District 1 Campaign; Voter Turnout Will Determine Outcome," *Arizona Republic*, September 4, 1982.
———. "John McCain Showing Savvy Early in Game," *Arizona Republic*, November 28, 1982.

INTERVIEWS

# Denotes multiple interviews.
*Denotes U.S. Naval Academy graduate.

Lee S. "Sandy" Ainslie, Jr.
William B. Bader
*Col. William D. Bauer, USMC (Ret.)
*Cdr. Stephen E. Becker, USN (Ret.)
*Ronald Benigo
Lisa Boepple
*Cdr. Robert K. Caldwell, USN (Ret.)
Patrick Henry Callaway
*Vice Adm. James F. Calvert, USN (Ret.)
Jean Carl
Scott Celley
U.S. Sen. John H. Chafee
Victoria "Torie" Clarke
U:S. Sen. William S. Cohen
Milton Copulos
Charles Crane
The Hon. Lorne Craner
Col. George E. "Bud" Day, USAF (Ret.) and Doris Day
Michael K. Deaver
William Riley Deeble III
Amb. Robert S. Dillon
*Capt. John James Dittrick, Jr., USN (Ret.)
Capt. Kent W. Ewing, USN
*Col. Fred T. Fagan, Jr., USMC (Ret.)
Rear Adm. Jimmie B. Finkelstein, USN (Ret.)
*# Capt. James R. "Ron" Fisher, USN (Ret.)
*# Capt. Frank Gamboa, USN (Ret.)
Col. Paul B. Goodwin, USMC (Ret.)
Wes A. Gullett
*Rear Adm. Howard W. Habermeyer, Jr., USN (Ret.)
*Col. John W. "Bill" Hemingway, USMC (Ret.)
Capt. Herb Hetu, USN (Ret.)
*# Rear Adm. Clarence A. "Mark" Hill, Jr., USN (Ret.)
Arnold Isaacs
Lt. Gen. James L. Jones, USMC
David Keene
*Adm. Isaac C. Kidd, Jr., USN (Ret.)
John Kolbe
James Lake
Albert A. "Pete" Lakeland, Jr.
*Adm. Charles R. Larson, USN (Ret.)
Diane (Rauch) Lawrence
*Vice Adm. William P. Lawrence, USN (Ret.)
Angus McBryde
Carol McCain
Cindy McCain
*# U.S. Sen. John S. McCain III
Joseph P. McCain
Roberta McCain
*The Hon. James F. McGovern

William McGovern
Eddie Mahe
Gail and Malcolm Matheson III
Michael Murphy
Bentley Orrick
*Rear Adm. Kendell M. Pease, Jr., USN (Ret.)
*# Col. Fred C. Peck, USMC (Ret.)
Allen Carleton Phillips, Jr.
*Capt. Joseph Charles Plumb, Jr., USNRR
*# Rear Adm. John M. Poindexter, USN (Ret.)
Nancy Reynolds
F. Rives Richey
Gov. Tom Ridge
Lt. Col. Ralph Rosaker, USMC (Ret.)
Mark Salter
*Capt. Edwin A. "Ned" Shuman III, USN (Ret.)
The Hon. Robert B. Sims, also Capt. USN (Ret.)
Carl M. Smith
J. Brian "Jay" Smith
Sam Stanton
Vice Adm. James B. Stockdale, USN (Ret.)
Col. Orson G. Swindle, USMC (Ret.)
Cdr. Paul B. Thompson, USN
*Vice Adm. Nils R. "Ron" Thunman, USN (Ret.)
Col. Konrad Trautman, USAF (Ret.)
Col. Jack Van Loan, USAF (Ret.)
James H. Warner
U.S. Sen. John W. Warner
*# Capt. James H. Webb, Jr., USMC (Ret.)

Index

ABOUT THE AUTHOR

Robert Timberg is the author of the widely acclaimed 1995 book *The Nightingale's Song*, which focused on Annapolis graduates John McCain, James Webb, Oliver North, John Poindexter, and Robert McFarlane. The book explored the generational fault line between those who served in the armed forces during the Vietnam War era and those who used money, wit, and connections to avoid serving.

More recently, Timberg published *State of Grace: A Memoir of Twilight Time* (2004), a well-received tale of a football team playing on the sandlots of Brooklyn and Queens under the gathering cloud of Vietnam.

Timberg graduated from Stuyvesant High School in New York City in 1958 and spent a year at St. John's University before entering the U.S. Naval Academy in 1960. He graduated in 1964 and was commissioned a second lieutenant in the Marine Corps. He served with the First Marine Division in South Vietnam from March 1966 to February 1967.

Timberg was a newspaper reporter and editor for more than three decades. From 1973 to 1981 he worked for *The Baltimore Evening Sun*. In 1981 he joined the Washington bureau of *The Baltimore Sun*. From 1983 to 1988 he was the *Sun*'s White House correspondent. In 1986 he received the Aldo Beckman Award given annually by the White House Correspondents Association for excellence in covering the White House. He was deputy chief of the *Sun*'s Washington bureau from 1995 to 2005. He is currently editor in chief of *Proceedings*, the flagship magazine of the U.S. Naval Institute.

Timberg holds a master's degree in journalism from Stanford University. He was a Nieman Fellow at Harvard and a fellow at the Woodrow Wilson International Center for Scholars in Washington, D.C.

In addition to his books and newspaper work, Timberg has contributed articles to *Esquire*, *Washingtonian*, the *Washington Journalism Review*, and *Nieman Reports*.